EUROPEAN UNION LAW

Private Law Tutor Publishing
Foreword

Thank you for buying this book. The problem that I encountered when studying law is: knowing everything. There is so much to read and so little time to do it. If you skip some material, or a case you are none the wiser. So throughout my years teaching law I have devised a system and I am going to share this with you.

You may have encountered different methods or formulas to help when advising a client in a mock scenario. One of example is the *IRAC* method or another is *Celo*. These are well documented and you can read about these. I never used them, because I had a method in my head that worked. It was not until I started teaching that I spoke about it. I call my method the "**Fact Law Sandwich**". Let me explain. If you are asked to advise a party as to their legal rights this is how you present it:

FACTS
GENERAL PRINCIPLE
LAW
APPLY TO FACTS

In **Fact:** simply state what you have been told, this why you can never be accused of not considering the facts. In **General principle:** you simply state what the general rule of the relevant issue is. You express it as if you are speaking to a child who has no knowledge of law. In **Law**: you state "using the authority of.....and you go on to state which statute or case helps prove your point. Lastly in **Apply to Facts**: you apply the reasoning of the case to your factual scenario. Your advice will sound and look structured and professional. The reason it is called the "Fact Law Sandwich", is because the advice contains two outer layers of facts that sandwich the principle and law in the middle.

This book is written to provide the student with a good knowledge of the most important cases on their study. It is written in a way to facilitate the Fact Law Sandwich method. I provide the general principle, the name of the case with full citation, the facts, the Ratio (the thing the lecturers say you always need to use), and application i.e. how the case should be applied. No other book provides this information at your fingertips. I hope you enjoy using it.

European union Law
Private Law Tutor Publishing

Contents

Welcome/Introduction/Overview

This book provides you with basic information as a basis for you to form your own critical opinions on this area of law. Once you have mastered the basics, you will be inspired to question EU principles in your essays and apply them in mock client advisory scenarios. Again, for your convenience, we have also published a Q&A book providing you with examples of how to answer such questions and how to apply your knowledge as effectively as possible to help you get the best possible marks.

This aid is a fully-fledged source of basic information, which tries to give the student comprehensive understanding for this module. However, it is recommended that you compliment it with the further reading suggestions provided at the end of each topic, as well as read the cases themselves for more in-depth information. The book provides an analysis of the basic principles of modern European Union Law. The following is a summary of the book content:

- An introduction to the historical evolution of the integration of the European Union;
- The sources of EU Law;
- The relationship between EU Law and national Law;
- The internal principles of EU Law ;
- The main rights enshrined by EU Law;

The aim of this book is to:

- Provide an introduction to anyone studying or interested in studying Law to the key principles and concepts that exist in EU Law.
- To provide a framework to consider EU Law within the context of examinations.
- Provide a detailed learning resource in order for legal written examination skills to be developed.
- Facilitate the development of written and Independent Critical Thought skills.
- Promote the practice of problem solving skills.

- To establish a platform for students to gain a solid understanding of the basic principles and concepts of EU Law, this can then be expanded upon through confident independent learning.

Through this book, students will be able to demonstrate the ability to:
- Demonstrate an awareness of the core principles of EU Law.
- Critically assess challenging mock factual scenarios and be able to pick out legal issues in the various areas of EU Law.
- Apply their knowledge when writing a formal assessment.
- Present a reasoned argument and make a judgment on competing viewpoints.
- Make use of technical legalistic vocabulary in the appropriate manner.
- Be responsible for their learning process and work in an adaptable and flexible way.

Studying EU Law

EU law governs approximately 80% of the economic Law of its member-states. Therefore, it is vital that a student successfully pass this subject to become a lawyer. Even after Brexit, the UK will still count on the EU as one of its closer commercial partner. Hence, a good knowledge of EU Law remains needed for a British lawyer.

The primary method by which your understanding of the EU Law will develop is by understanding how to solve problem questions. You will also be given essay questions in your examinations. The methods by which these types of question should be approached are somewhat different.

Tackling Problems and Essay Questions

There are various ways of approaching problem questions and

essay questions. We have provided students with an in-depth analysis with suggested questions and answers at the end of each chapter.

Chapter 1 - The Treaties and the Historical Development of the EU

The General Ideology

Why and how did the EU come about? This question points precisely to the problem of *definition* and *identity* of the EU law and of Europe generally. *Functionalists* embraced a federalist concept based on two ideas in particular emerged as possible solutions to the wars that had so long plagued Europe:

(1) building cooperation among countries through the integration of one or more highly important economic function shared by all of them (functionalism); and

(2) directly establishing a European political federation (federalism). Both functionalist and federalist models, therefore, came into play at the earliest stages of discussion.

"The pooling of coal and steel production should immediately provide for the setting up of common foundations for economic development as a first step in the federation of Europe, and will change the destinies of those regions which have long been devoted to the manufacture of munitions of war, of which they have been the most constant victims." *Schuman Declaration, 9 May 1950.*

The European construction started just after WW2. It was initially based on an intention to bring the countries of the old continent together to avoid such atrocities from reoccurring. In Europe, millions of people died during the WW2 because neighbouring countries had been at war. Winston Churchill, speaking at Zurich University in September 1946, said:

"We must build a kind of United States of Europe… …freely joined

together for mutual convenience in a federal system. We must re-create the European Family in a regional structure called, it may be, the United States of Europe. Therefore I say to you: let Europe arise!"

This echoed the voice of the neo-federalists. Few years later, the declaration of the French Minister for Foreign Affairs Robert Schuman (1950) was a turning point in the European integration. It basically tells us that the political reconciliation of European countries needs to be pragmatic and should result on an economic cooperation. Consequently the European Coal and Steel Community (ECSC) was established the next year. The idea is to bind states to such a point that war becomes inconceivable. And it will be made by regulating the commerce of the main resources needed for a war: coal and steel. As Schuman put it "[t]he solidarity in production thus established will make it plain that any war between France and Germany becomes not merely unthinkable, but materially impossible." From then on, a progressing economic collaboration became the solution to maintain peace in Europe. But foreign countries also influenced the economic collaboration. In this respect, George Marshall, Secretary of State in the US, introduced the European Recovery Programme, aiming "to achieve a common programme of recovery". The Marshall Plan required European states to cooperate together to distribute the wealth and, even more importantly, to progressively remove trade barriers between themselves.

Nevertheless, in the aftermath of the Second World War, the ECSC is not the only international organization to be established to maintain peace. Slightly earlier, discussions started to rename the League of Nations by the United Nations (24th of October 1945). Closer in Europe, the Council of Europe was created in 1949, and it is very important to distinguish it from the European Union. This institution was created in response to Winston Churchill call for a united Europe with a European Assembly and a Court of Human Rights (Congress of Europe at The Hague, 1948). Indeed, the Council of Europe is a completely separated international organization with its own founding treaties and its

7

own institutions. The major difference with the EU is that it focuses only on the promotion of Human Rights and the maintenance of peace whereas the former has been further in the integration. While the EU is geographically centralized in Wester-Europe with its 28 member-states, the Council of Europe *rationae loci* is broader with 47 members-states. It includes Russia or Turkey for example. Moreover, these two institutions have two different Courts that should not be confused the Council of Europe has the European Court of Human Rights (ECtHR) while the Court of Justice of the European Union (CJEU) is the main judicial organ of the European Union.

Finally, there were other attempts by European countries to develop economic harmonisation. The Benelux nations (Netherlands, Belgium and Luxembourg) signed a customs convention to remove internal trade barriers on 5 September 1944 and resulted in trade barriers between the states being removed by 1956.

Why does the EU keep Expanding?

The European Union is *sui generis* organization that has unique features. It is very different from the traditional approach of international organizations. Some theories are discussed below.

Intergovernmental

Intergovernmentalism is an alternative theory of political integration, where power in international organizations is possessed by the member-states and decisions are made by unanimity. Independent appointees of the governments or elected representatives have solely advisory or implementational functions. Intergovernmentalism is used by most international organizations today. An alternative method of decision-making in international organizations is supranationalism.

Intergovernmentalism is also a theory on European integration which rejects the idea of neo-functionalism. The theory, initially proposed by Stanley Hoffmann and refined by Andrew Moravcsik suggests that governments control the level and speed of European integration. Any increase in power at supranational level, he argues, results from a direct decision by governments. He believed that integration, driven by national governments, was often based on the domestic political and economic issues of the day. The theory rejects the concept of the spill over effect that neo-functionalism proposes. He also rejects the idea that supranational organisations are on an equal level (in terms of political influence) as national governments.

Supranational

Supranationalism is a method of decision-making in political communities, wherein power is held by independent appointed officials or by representatives elected by the legislatures or people of the member states. Member-state governments still have power, but they must share this power with others. Because decisions are taken by majority votes, it is possible for a member-state to be forced by the other member-states to implement a decision. Unlike a federal state, member states fully retain their sovereignty and participate voluntarily, being subject to the supranational government only while remaining members.

Neo-Functionalist

Neo-functionalists argue that the supranational institutions of the European Union themselves have been a driving force behind European integration; reinterpreting agreed results from Intergovernmental Conferences in order to expand the mandate of EU legislation into new and more diverse areas. The theory of neo-functionalism is felt by some to be important as it may explain much of the thinking behind the early proponents of the European Union, such as Jean Monnet, who saw increased European integration as the most important precursor to a peaceful Europe. Neo-functionalism assumes a decline in importance of nationalism and the nation-state; it sees the executive power and interest groups within states to be pursuing a welfarist objective which is best satisfied by integration of EU states. The thinking behind the neo-functionalist theory can be best described by considering the three mechanisms which neo-functionalists see as key to driving the process of integration forwards. These are positive spill over, the transfer of domestic allegiances and technocratic automaticity:

- Positive spill over is the concept that integration between states in one economic sector will quickly create strong incentives for integration in further sectors; in order to fully capture the benefits of integration in the original sector.

- The mechanism of a transfer in domestic allegiances can be best understood by first noting that an important assumption within neo-functionalist thinking is of a pluralistic society within the relevant nation states. Neo-functionalists claim that, as the process of integration gathers pace, interest groups and associations within the pluralistic societies of the individual nation states will transfer their allegiance away from national institutions towards the supranational European institutions. They will do this because they will, in theory, come to realise that these newly formed institutions are a better conduit through which to pursue their material interests than the pre-existing national institutions.

- Finally, technocratic automaticity describes the way in which, as integration hastens, the supranational institutions set up to oversee that integration process will themselves take the lead in sponsoring further integration as they become more powerful and more autonomous of the member states.

An historical overview of the European Treaties:

1951   ECSC: EUROPEAN COAL AND STEEL
             COMMUNITY
             Treaty of Paris

1957   EEC: EUROPEAN ECONOMIC
COMMUNITY
             Treaty of Rome

1957	EURATOM: EUROPEAN ATOMIC ENERGY COMMUNITY Treaty of Rome
1965	MERGER TREATY Amalgamated institutions of the three Communities (in force 1967)
1973	FIRST TREATY OF ACCESSION UK, the Republic of Ireland, Denmark
1975	BUDGETARY TREATY Increased power of the Parliament
1979	SECOND TREATY OF ACCESSION Greece
1986	THIRD TREATY OF ACCESSION Spain, Portugal
1992	SINGLE INTERNAL MARKET In force 1 Jan 1993 – A result of the Single European Act 1986
1993	TREATY ON EUROPEAN UNION (TEU) (Maastricht) In force 1 Nov 1993
1994	FOURTH TREATY OF ACCESSION Austria, Finland, Sweden
1997	THE TREATY OF AMSTERDAM (ToA) In force 1 May 1999
2000	THE TREATY OF NICE In force 1 February 2003
2005	TREATY ESTABLISHING A CONSTITUTION FOR EUROPE

rejected by France and the Netherlands by
referendum

2005	FIFTH ACCESSION TREATY Ten new members

2005   FIFTH ACCESSION TREATY
        Ten new members

2007   Accession of Romania & Bulgaria

2007   THE TREATY OF LISBON
        Signed 13 December 2007
        Ratified by 24 Member States (at the time of
        writing)

The treaties establishing the European Communities

In the 1950s the creation of three European Communities
marked the birth of the European Union's predecessor. The
European Communities refer to the ESCS, the EEC and
EURATOM.

- The European Coal and Steel Community (ECSC):
  established by the Treaty of Paris (1951).

The ESCS owes its origins in the Schuman declaration. However,
if the declaration has been made by Robert Schuman, his main
collaborator on the "Schuman Plan", Jean Monnet (a French
economist and statesman) is usually forgotten. The idea, placing
economic cooperation as its core, included to remove these vital
wartime industries from the control of the national governments
to confer them to a supranational entity, in the hope of providing
a sounder foundation for peace and stability in Europe. The
pioneers thought that opening a common market between
European countries on the two wartime necessities would prevent
the rise of new wars between them. Another reason of this political
reconciliation lies on a wish to limit the development of
communism in Western Europe (very strong at the time in France
and Italy).

Initially, the pioneers only envisaged France and West Germany, but Schuman invited their close neighbours to join. As a result, France, West Germany, Italy and the three countries members of the Benelux signed the Paris Treaty and became the 6 founding members of the ESCS. The UK was invited for the negotiations but quickly left the negotiating table. This example shows that, from the beginning of the European construction, the UK was reluctant to participate.

To achieve its objective, the 6 founding members established several institutions. The High Authority, a sort of ancestor of the committee of ministers representing the member-states and taking the main decisions, was accompanied of an Assembly and a Court of Justice in charge of reviewing the legality of the acts of the High Authority. At that time, having such integrated institutions was a great progress in terms of development of international organizations.

The main concrete measure was achieved by 1954, which marked the removal of all trade barriers in coal and steel. The ESCS expired in 2002, after the ending of a 50 years term.

- The European Economic Community (EEC): created by the Treaty of Rome (1957).

The Treaty of Rome, officially the Treaty establishing the European Economic Community (TEEC), came into force on 1 January 1958. One of its instigators is the Belgium prime minister delivering a famous speech in Messina (1956). The idea was to focus on a greater harmonisation of the economy, above the mere areas of coal and steel. The 6 states agreed to integrate their economies, first by becoming a customs union to progressively move to a common market.

- The European Atomic energy community (EURATOM): established by Treaty signed in 1957.

This third Treaty dealt with cooperation in the domain of atomic energy. France strongly insisted for its conclusion. Even if EURATOM focused on an important but very specific industry, the EEC had a much broader scope.

If the three communities were provided with independent institutions to which different degrees of sovereign power was ceded by the Member States, it was agreed that the Assembly and the Court of Justice (initially established by the EEC) would be common to all three. However, each community had its own Commission and its own Council of Ministers. But this system changed for a greater centralisation with the conclusion of the Merger Treaty (1965) that provided for a single Commission and a single Council of Ministers to be shared by the communities.

More importantly in terms of Treaties deeper amendment of the European Communities; the Single European Act (SEA) was signed in 1986. The SEA increased the material scope of the EEC and laid the foundation for an internal market. In addition to this, it brought democratic and institutional changes to strengthen the accountability of the communities. The Assembly was renamed European Parliament as a symbolic progress towards integration. Finally, a Court of First Instance was established to relieve an overwhelmed Court of Justice.

The birth of the European Union

The European Union officially replaced the European Communities in 1993, date of the entry into force of the well-known Treaty of Maastricht (1992). The so-called Treaty on the European Union (TUE) sought to enlarge the scope of intergovernmental cooperation beyond the economic sphere. The intention of the Member States was clearly to find a common political agenda. For that purpose, they established the three pillars of the EU:

- **Pillar I** was constituted by the European Community; a single institution regrouping the former EEC, ESCS and Euratom.

- **Pillar II** established the Common foreign and security policy (CFSP); an intergovernmental collaboration of police and border services.

- **Pillar III** provided a framework for cooperation in justice or home affairs.

1948 **Brussels**	1951/52 **Paris**	1957/58 **Rome**	1965/67 **Brussels**	1986/87 **SEA**	1992/93 **Maastricht** (founded EU)	1997/99 **Amsterdam**	2001/03 **Nice**	2007/09 **Lisbon**

European Atomic Energy Community (EURATOM)

European Coal and Steel Community (ECSC)

European Economic Community (EEC)

↑European Communities↑

PILLARS

Justice & Home Affairs (JHA)

Police & Judicial co-operation in Criminal Matters (PJCC)

European Community (EC)

European Union (EU)

European Political Cooper

Common Foreign & Security Policy (CFSP)

16

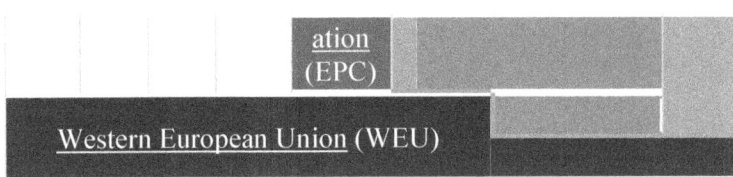

More importantly, the TUE created a monetary union between the Member States by the introduction of the euro as the common currency monitored by a European Central Bank (ECB). Nevertheless, it also marked the first concession for Member States to break the integration process with the "opt-out clauses". Indeed, the first ones to use it, The UK and Denmark, decided to keep their respective currencies while remaining in the EU. Finally, the Treaty of Maastricht also established a "social chapter" which dealt with workers' rights and other social issues. Once again, the UK managed to negotiate an opt-out exception.

The progressive amendments of the European Union

- The Treaty of Amsterdam (1997) resulted in two principal reforms. Firstly, it tried to make the existing structure of the Treaties more comprehensible. To that end, it completely renumbered the EC Treaty and the TEU. Secondly, the Treaty of Amsterdam reorganized the 1st and 3rd Pillars for a deeper cooperation in criminal matters.

- The main concern of the Treaty of Nice (2001) was to prepare the enlargement of the EU to more than ten members. The candidates were mainly from Eastern and Central Europe. This extension went ahead three years later.

- The Treaty of Lisbon (signed in 2007) entered into force in 2009. It is certainly the most important Treaty for the EU in terms of fundamental changes. The debate started with a declaration of the European Council (EU's institution) stating that along with an increasing integration and more sovereign powers attributed to the EU by its Member States; the organization needed to be more democratic, more transparent and more efficient. The Council even mentioned that it would have to come along with the adoption of a Treaty of a constitutional nature. Consequently, the Convention on the future of Europe, chaired by the former French president (Valéry Giscard d'Estaing), was established. The Convention was composed of members of national parliaments and governments but also representatives from the EU (Commission and Parliament). The meeting resulted on the draft of a Treaty Establishing a Constitution for Europe that was supposed to replace the existing Treaties. It was signed by the Member States in 2003 but the ratification process was never completed. Perhaps too ambitious at the time, the Constitutional Treaty was rejected in France and the Netherlands, and the project was later abandoned.

- Nevertheless, the Member States thought that there was still a pressing need of reform. In order to reassure the nationalists worried about the rise of a European State, the word Constitution has been removed and the existing Treaties were not replaced. Instead, the EC Treaty was renamed Treaty on the Functioning of the European Union (TFEU), and the Euratom incorporated in the Treaty of Lisbon. Finally, the Treaty of Lisbon merged the three pillars into a single structure, abolished the EC as a separate entity bust most importantly consolidated the distribution of the competences between the Member States and the EU in favour of the latter.

Accessions and evolution of the list of EU members

In order to become member of the EU, States have historically concluded accessions treaties between them and the EU. However membership is subjected to several conditions called *acquis communautaires* that States have generally to comply with, unless arrangements for a transition period are made. For example, a candidate State will have to present an economic, judicial and political system able to be integrated with those of the existing Member States.

However, if membership is usually enshrined by an accession Treaty, it is not always the case. For instance, East Germany automatically joined the EU after the reunification of Germany in 1990. Since the three initial communities of the 19950s were formed by France, West Germany, Italy, the Netherlands, Belgium and Luxembourg the following countries have also joined:

- o The United Kingdom, Ireland and Denmark in 1973; the EU was then composed of 9 Member States.

- o Greece in 1981; the EU was then composed of 10 Member States.

- o Spain and Portugal in 1986; the EU was then composed of 12 Member States.

- o Austria, Sweden and Finland in 1995; the EU was then composed of 15 Member States.

- o The Czech Republic, Slovakia, Slovenia, Poland, Lithuania, Latvia, Estonia, Hungary, Cyprus and Malta in 2004; the EU was then composed of 25 Member States.

- o Bulgaria and Romania in January 2007; the EU was then composed of 27 Member States.

- o Croatia in July 2013; The EU is now comprised of 28 Member States.

Nevertheless, in 2017, can we say that the EU is still comprised of 28 Member States, or does the recent Brexit change the counting?

Some territories have decided to withdraw from the European Communities in the past. This was the case of Algeria, in 1962, right after having gained independence. Algeria was part of the European Communities because it was at that time a French colony. The *rationae loci* of the Communities have always automatically integrated the overseas territories of the Members.

In addition to this, the other principal territory to withdraw was Greenland that is part of Denmark and therefore joined the Communities in 1973 when the latter got member. After having been granted significant autonomy to make its own choices, the Greenland People decided to not be part of the European Communities anymore in a referendum. They withdrew in 1985 after a negotiating process with the Member States. However, these few examples occurred in the era of the European Communities, is it that simple with Brexit?

Brexit

As we have seen it before, the relationship between the UK and the EU was special from the beginning. Throughout its membership, many politicians, the media or the wider public expressed scepticism or even hostility towards the EU. The first referendum on whether or not to stay a member was held in 1975. At this time, a majority of British citizens voted in favour to remain.

In 2013, the UK Prime Minister, David Cameron, promised another referendum on the EU issue if he was re-elected. After having been victorious in 2015, Cameron had to act in accordance to his commitment and started re-negotiating with the EU to achieve certain reforms. However, unsatisfied by the concessions made by the EU, the Prime Mister held a referendum on June 23rd last year. This time, a majority of 52% voted to leave. Even though the referendum was not legally binding in itself, it put political pressure on the UK executive to trigger article 50(2) of the TEU. It is the formal requirement that compels a Member State to officially inform the European Council of a wish to withdraw from the Treaties. This operation has been ordered by the new Prime Minister, Theresa May, in March 2017.

However, even though article 50 has been triggered by the UK, it remains a Member for now. Thus, the EU is still comprised of 28 Member States. Article 50 stipulates that the parties have to find an agreement for the withdrawal under negotiations that have to last at least 24 months, if no agreement is concluded before, and that can be extended by the parties.

The issue of the UK membership to the Council of Europe is not legally affected by Brexit. However, withdrawing from the Council of Europe is part of the Conservative political agenda. Actually, it was announced by Theresa May in 2016 while campaigning. Fortunately for the protection of Human Rights in the UK, the Conservative manifesto released few weeks ago, declared that they would be too busy with Brexit and would remain in the Council of Europe for the next legislature.

EU Law's major influence on UK Law after Brexit

Walker (Appellant) v Innospec Limited and others (Respondents) [2017] UKSC 47

Facts: John Walker, the appellant in these proceedings worked for the respondent, Innospec Ltd, from 1980 until his retirement in 2003. In 2006 Mr Walker asked Innospec to confirm that, in the event of his death, they would pay the spouse's pension, which the scheme provides for, to his civil partner. Innospec refused, because his service predated 5 December 2005, the date that civil partnerships were introduced in the UK, and any discriminatory treatment is therefore permitted under paragraph 18 of Schedule 9 to the Equality Act 2010. If Mr Walker was married to a woman (or indeed if he married a woman in the future) she would be entitled on his death to a "spouse's pension" of about £45,700 per annum. As things stand at present, Mr Walker's husband will be entitled to a pension of about £1,000 per annum (the statutory guaranteed minimum).

Preliminary question before the Court: Does paragraph 18 of Schedule 9 to the Equality Act 2010, permitting an employer to discriminate against employees based on their sexual orientation while attributing a survivor's pension, is compatible with EU Law?

Preliminary Ruling: According to the judgement gave by Lord Kerr, the UK provision is incompatible and EU Law should prevail: "paragraph 18 of Schedule 9 to the Equality Act 2010 is incompatible with EU law and must be dis-applied and (ii) Mr Walker's husband is entitled on his death to a spouse's pension, provided they remain married."

Application: This case underlines several major principles of EU Law in its relation with national Law such as supremacy or direct effect. In addition to this, the UK government just declared that after Brexit it would repeal the current national legislation on discrimination based on sexual activity to upgrade it to EU standards of protection. This demonstrates that even after Brexit, some parts of EU Law will still remain guidance for the UK courts.

Chapter 2: Constitutional Principles, Institutions and Sources of EU Law

Constitutional principles

The debate of the constitutionality of EU Law

The word Constitution is usually related to statehood. This is why the constitutionality of some areas of EU Law is so controversial. The EU remains an international organization, although not a traditional one. The question of constitutionality lays on the primary sources of EU Law only, in other words the founding Treaties. On this issue, two approaches are opposed:

- The internationalists are claiming that EU Law arose from Public International Law as a regular international organization. According to them, we cannot refer to Constitution of an international organization because this term belongs only to national legal system.

- The communautarists insist on the unique nature of the European legal system that has to be distinguished from traditional Public International Law. The EU would be closer to a State than an international organization. To them, some principles have a constitutional nature and would be at the top of the hierarchy of norms. The most radical branch of this movement claims for a greater integration towards a European State.

The founding Treaties were qualified as constitutional at the early stages of the European construction. For instance, the European Court of Justice in Costa v E.N.E.L. [1964] mentioned the Treaty EEC as being a constitutional charter of the communities. This issue reached its apogee in 2004 with the Treaty Establishing a Constitution for Europe (TECE). As said above, the nationalists were scared about the word Constitution therefore project was abandoned after two rejections by referendum in the Netherlands and France.

However, if the word Constitution was removed to allay the controversy, the Treaty of Lisbon kept the main content of the TECE. It consolidated the distribution of the competences between the Member States and the EU in favour of the latter. Also, it brings major reforms in the organization of the other sources that places it at a level of constitutional importance. In addition to this, the Treaty of Lisbon introduced symbolic measures of a statist nature such as flag and a common anthem.

In order to permit a comprehensive institutional analysis of EU law, the constitutional approach should be detached from its statist roots. Other international organizations dealt with constitutionalism without the rise of such controversies. For example, the founding treaty of the International Labour Organization (ILO 1919) is called "ILO Constitution". To conclude, the European legal system can definitely be analysed under a constitutional approach in terms of the function of primary sources in the EU legal system. Indeed, the founding treaties play a role that would play, in a national order, a Constitution.

Constitutional objectives and values of the EU

Article 2 TEU provides a range of values shared by the Member States:

"The Union is founded on the values of respect for human dignity, freedom, democracy, equality, the rule of law and respect for human rights, including the rights of persons belonging to minorities. These values are common to the Member States in a society in which pluralism, non-discrimination, tolerance, justice, solidarity and equality between women and men prevail"

The objectives of the EU are underlined in Article 3 TEU:

- To promote peace, its values and the well-being of its peoples.
- To offer its citizens an area of freedom, security and justice without internal frontiers.
- To establish an internal market.
- To establish an economic and monetary union whose currency is the euro. Note that the Euro zone is comprised of only 19 Member States.
- In its relations with the wider world, to uphold and promote its values and interests and contribute to the protection of its citizens.
- To pursue its objectives by appropriate means commensurate with the competences which are conferred upon it in the Treaties.

Competences

In order to pursue its objectives, the EU can only act within the competences it has been attributed by the Member States. This principle comes from article 5(2) TEU which provides:

"Under the principle of conferral, the Union shall act only within the limits of the competences conferred upon it by the Member

States in the Treaties to attain the objectives set out therein. Competences not conferred upon the Union in the Treaties remain with the Member States."

In other words, it means that in principle every matter that was not conferred to the EU remains competence of the Member States. Article 2 TFUE establishes three categories of competence, as listed below:

"1. When the Treaties confer on the Union exclusive competence in a specific area, only the Union may legislate and adopt legally binding acts, the Member States being able to do so themselves only if so empowered by the Union or for the implementation of Union acts.
2. When the Treaties confer on the Union a competence shared with the Member States in a specific area, the Union and the Member States may legislate and adopt legally binding acts in that area. The Member States shall exercise their competence to the extent that the Union has not exercised its competence. The Member States shall again exercise their competence to the extent that the Union has decided to cease exercising its competence.
[...]
5. In certain areas and under the conditions laid down in the Treaties, the Union shall have competence to carry out actions to support, coordinate or supplement the actions of the Member States, without thereby superseding their competence in these areas. Legally binding acts of the Union adopted on the basis of the provisions of the Treaties relating to these areas shall not entail harmonisation of Member States' laws or regulations."

The area of the competence will determine whether it is exclusive, shared or involves support. It is important to add that even if the Union is acting within an allocated competence, it has to do so in accordance with the specific powers it has been granted by the treaties. The Union has no legal authority to act without a treaty provision that confers a specific power to do so.

Exclusive	Shared	Support, coordinate or supplement
Article 3 TFEU:	**Article 4 TFEU:**	**Article 6 TFEU:**
• Customs union	• Areas not referred to in Article 3 and Article 6	• Protection and improvement of human health
• Establishing the competition rules for the internal market	• The principal areas are:	• Industry
• Monetary policy for the Member States whose currency is the euro	– Internal market	• Culture
	– Social policy for aspects defined within the TFEU	• Tourism
• The conservation of marine biological resources under the common fisheries policy	– Economic, social and territorial cohesion	• Education, vocational training, youth and sport
• Common commercial policy	– Agriculture and fisheries, excluding the conservation of marine biological resources	• Civil protection
	– Environment	• Administrative cooperation
	– Consumer protection	
	– Transport	
	– Trans-European networks	
	– Energy	
	– Area of freedom, security and justice	
	– Common safety concerns in public health matters for aspects defined within the TFEU	

Whenever the EU is not acting within the scope of an exclusive competence, its intervention has to compel with the principles of subsidiarity and proportionality. Consequently these principles only apply when the EU is dealing with a shared or supporting competence. The principle of subsidiarity is enshrined in the founding treaties by article 5(3) TEU:

"Under the principle of subsidiarity, in areas which do not fall within its exclusive competence, the Union shall act only if and in so far as the objectives of the proposed action cannot be sufficiently achieved by the Member States, either at central level or at regional and local level, but can rather, by reason of the scale or effects of the proposed action, be better achieved at Union level."

The principle was first established in the 1992 Treaty of Maastricht. It means that the Union should only act where its Member States could not achieve similar objectives as efficiently at the national level. The principle of proportionality, according to Article 5(4) TEU imposes that "the content and form of Union action shall not exceed what is necessary to achieve the objectives of the Treaties". These two principles are significantly preventing the EU of acting above the scope of its attributions in areas of shared or supporting competences. It is one of the safeguards of the Member States' sovereignty.

General principles: Initially, a protocol attached to the Treaty of Amsterdam provided that any legislative proposal presented by the Commission, had to be expressly justified on the basis of subsidiarity. However, it has had a limited impact on integration. This is illustrated by many cases where subsidiarity has been considered. For instance in the case United Kingdom v Council (Working Time Directive) presents a restrictive approach about the enforcement of the application of subsidiarity.

United Kingdom v Council (Working Time Directive) (Case C-84/94) [1996] ECR I-5755
Facts: The UK was contesting an EU directive invoking a

violation of the principle of subsidiarity because the institutions failed to demonstrate that the action would be more efficient at the Union level than at the national level.

Primarily ruling: The Court of Justice did not recognize a violation of the subsidiarity principle and stated that "once the Council felt the need to act, as evidenced by the preamble to the Directive, it was inevitable that they would wish to harmonise the law in this area".

Application: This approach to subsidiarity effectively gave the institutions a free hand and rendered subsidiarity all but non-justiciable.

Finally, the Lisbon Treaty introduced a better mechanism of scrutiny from the Member States that implies the intervention of national parliaments. Every national Parliament is informed of the EU legislative proposals and can submit some reasoned opinion as to why the proposal does not respect the subsidiarity requirement.

If a threshold of reasoned opinions from national parliaments is reached, a "yellow card" is raised forcing the Commission to reconsider its draft proposal.

- **The Institutions**

General ideology
The original concept and the general structure of the institutions of the EU were established in the ECSC Treaty. The major progress in terms of integration of international organizations was to create supranational institutions independent from their Member States.

Nonetheless, the EU institutions should not be confused from the institutions belonging to the Council of Europe. The Council of Europe has a separated Court (the ECtHR), an assembly (the PACE) and a Committee of ministers. As it stands, the EU is structured as it follows:

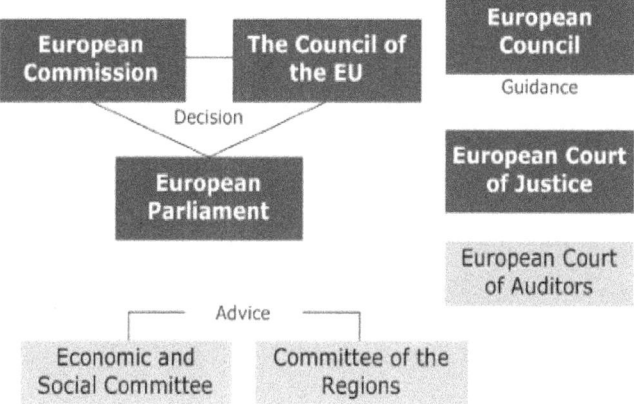

More precisely, article 13 TUE lists the 7 official institutions:

- The European Parliament
- The European Council
- The Council of the European Union ('the Council')
- The European Commission
- The Court of Justice of the European Union (including the General Court)
- The European Central Bank
- The Court of Auditors

The role of these institutions is attributed according to the division of tasks to achieve the objectives of the European Union. Rather than following a traditional separation of powers between the executive the legislative and the judiciary, they are designed to compromise the interests and the representation of the different actors of the EU. In this respect, the citizens are represented in the European Parliament; the national interests of the Member States are represented in the Council; and the overall interests of the Union are represented in the Commission.

The main institutions are: the Parliament, the Commission and the Council. Those three have a role the play in the law-making process. Thus, the legislative function is split between these institutions that have to work together. It is the same idea for the executive function, which is shared by the Commission, the Council and the European Council.

These institutions have to be distinguished from the EU bodies. They are: The Committee of Permanent Representatives (COREPER), the European External Action Service (EEAS), European Economic and Social Committee (EESC), the European Committee of the Regions (CoR), the European Investment Bank (EIB), the European Ombudsman, the European Data Protection Supervisor (EDPS).The institutions will be examined below in turn.

The European Parliament

Initially called "Assembly" by the EC Treaty, it was not a democratically elected body for a long time. Indeed, it was composed of appointed nominees from each Member States. Consequently, it had no legislative power and it could only play a consultative role in the law-making process.

However, this institution nowadays is called "European Parliament" (EP) is governed by Articles 123-234 TFEU. Since 1979, the institution's democratic features have been improved: members are elected every five years with a proportional representation. Article 14(2) TEU provides that: "The European Parliament shall be composed of representatives of the Union's citizens. They shall not exceed seven hundred and fifty in number, plus the President. Representation of citizens shall be degressively proportional, with a minimum threshold of six members per Member State. No Member State shall be allocated more than ninety-six seats."

The European Parliament is supposedly representing the interests of more than 500 million European citizens. The Parliament total MEPs is 751. The number of seats allocated to each Member States depends on their population. For instance, Germany and France are the most represented (96 and 74 seats), whereas the

Cyprus or Luxembourg have the minimum of seats (6).

Malta	6
Luxembourg	6
Cyprus	6
Estonia	6
Slovenia	6
Latvia	6
Lithuania	9
Ireland	11
Croatia	11
Finland	13
Slovakia	13
Denmark	13
Bulgaria	17
Austroa	17
Sweden	18
Hungary	18
Czech Rep.	18
Belgium	18
Portugal	18
Greece	18
Netherlands	26
Romania	33
Poland	54
Spain	60
Italy	77
UK	77
France	79
Germany	96

Officially based in Strasbourg, the European Parliament's committees sit in Brussels and its secretariat is divided between Brussels and Luxembourg. The efficiency of this division and the costs attached to the frequent travels of the MEPs are discussed. Nevertheless, if the dissenters want to relocate all the offices in Brussels, Strasbourg remains the official location for its symbolic feature: the Franco-German friendship.

The European Parliament sits one week per month (except in

August), for the plenary sessions. However, MEPs can also meet if punctual issues require discussions. Parliament elects its own president and various officials. The voting system lies on a simple majority basis. Throughout the European construction, the role of the Parliament has been enlarged and it came along with progress in terms of transparency and democratization of this institution. The Parliament currently undertakes a range of legislative, budgetary and supervisory functions.

Legislative function: Under article 294 TFEU, the Parliament has an important role in the ordinary legislative procedure, previously known as the co-decision. This procedure is by far the most common method for introducing legislation.

The ordinary legislative procedure main objective is to get the Parliament and the Council to agree on one text. The Commission initiates the proposal and the text then goes back and forth to the Parliament and the Council for two readings. During both reading, the text can be adopted, amended or dropped by both institutions. Ultimately, a text can only be adopted if both of them find a compromise. If they do not, a conciliation committee composed equally of representatives of both institutions is established. Thus, under this procedure, the European Parliament can make amendments and actively participate to the law-making process.

In addition to this, it has sort of veto power to prevent legislation of being adopted as long as the procedure subjects the adoption of a text to the agreement of both the Council and the Parliament. Under the co-operation procedure, introduced by the SEA, the Parliament has only a consultative role.

Supervisory function over the others institutions. This is particularly the case with the Commission. The Parliament has a say on each new Commission, it can decide to approve or to pass a motion of censure. The legal effect of a motion is the resignation of the entire Commission. Article 17 (7) also subjects the nomination of important officials, including the President of the Commission and other commissioners to the Parliament's approval. The EP can also submit questions to the Commission and discuss its general annual report. Finally, the Parliament can ask oral and written questions to the Council related to its work, but this comes through traditional democratic scrutiny between the institutions that are not as ambitious as the supervision of the Parliament over the Commission.

Budgetary function: Parliament is required to approve the annual budget of the European Union. The Treaty of Lisbon has attributed this function to Parliament. Under Article 314 (4) TFEU, Parliament can even amend parts the budget, whether compulsory or non-compulsory.

The Council of the European Union ('the Council')

While the TFEU (Article 237-243) merely refers to it as the Council, the institution was traditionally called "the Council of ministers". It was also referred to Council of the European Union following the TEU (Article 16). The Council is the main decision-making body within the EU, having both executive and legislative powers. The Council is based in Brussels. Its main role is to represent the executive of each Member States. The Council is normally composed of the national ministers, but on specific issues a Member States might permit a minister from a regional government to represent it. Ministers are subjected to the representation of the Member States; they are therefore politically accountable to their national governments. The composition of the Council is depending on the subject matter under consideration. For example if the Council deals with a transport concern, the national representative will be the transport minister.

Article 16 (1) TEU identifies the key functions of the Council:

Legislative function: the Council is the main co-legislator, in collaboration with the Parliament, under the ordinary legislative procedure. For marginal procedures, it was often said that "the Commission proposes and the Council disposes".

Budgetary function: the Council also shares with the Parliament the power to approve or amend the budget of the European Union.

Executive function: The Council has important responsibilities of developing the coordination and cooperation between Member States on different matters such as economic policies, common foreign and security policies and judicial systems.

Prior to the Lisbon Treaty, the Council had a rotating presidency. Each Member States was sending a representative to preside the Council for six months. Instead, there is now a system of team presidencies that are elected according to the areas covered by the agenda.

The Council has two main types of voting procedures (Article 205 TFEU): unanimity and qualified majority voting. It is important to bear in mind that Member States are usually representing their national interests. Therefore, simple majority, although recognized by the treaties as valid, is rarely used because it would imply some Member States to adopt decisions although they voted against them. Member States are reluctant because they would cede too much power to others in the decision-making process.

Unanimity is required for certain delicate issues such as common foreign and security policies or immigration. Conversely, every Member State enjoys a veto on these issues.
The Luxembourg Accords appears to still be valid as a "legal basis" for this practice. Actually, this possibility arose from political practice and the legal effect of this kind of declaration is controversial because it has not been formally consented by all the Member States.

However, in order to avoid institutional blockages before the EU enlargement in the 2000s, the Treaty of Nice reduced quite drastically the areas where unanimity is required. Under Article 16(3) TEU, the qualified majority voting (QMV), is used for every decisions except where the Treaties provide otherwise. The process was designed to prevent large States from abusing their power at the expense of smaller ones. Qualified majority voting (QMV) was redefined to introduce a combined threshold for votes to pass. However, the old weighted voting system introduced by the Treaty of Nice was replaced by the Treaty of Lisbon.

From 1 November 2014, under Article 16(4) TEU and Article 238(3) TFEU, decisions in the Council of the EU (Council of Ministers) requiring a 'qualified majority' are adopted by means of the new 'double majority'. The change lowers the threshold required for adoption by Council, and is intended to increase the speed and efficiency of Council decision-making and to make it more transparent and legitimate. The adoption of acts by the Council now requires the approval of 55% of Member States (16) (72% if the act has not been proposed by the Commission), which must represent at least 65% of the EU's population (currently approximately 328.6 million of a total 505.5 million).

The European Council

The European Council was not part of the initial founding Treaties. It was agreed on by a meeting of heads of States in 1974 and formally established in 1986 by the SEA. Nowadays it is governed by articles 235-236 TFEU and 15 TEU: *"The European Council shall provide the Union with the necessary impetus for its development and shall define the general political directions and priorities thereof. It shall not exercise legislative functions."*

It involves meetings of heads of States and their foreign ministers, twice a year, which are usually referred as "summits" (Article 15 (3)). Members of the European Council will mainly discuss issues such as common foreign policy, police and judicial cooperation or immigration. The former system of presidency used to rotate. The Lisbon Treaty amended this provision by implementing a 30 months term with an election at the qualified majority. This gives the European Council a stable and established voice on the international stage.

The European Commission

The Commission represents the overall interests of the Union. The provisions dealing with the Commission are Articles 244-250 TFEU. It actually works as an executive arm of the EU. The Commission's staff is composed of more than 35000 people. It tends to be the most supranational and independent institutions relating to the conception of the pioneers of the European construction. The Commission is today comprised of 20 Commissioners. A rotation system has been established to permit a fair representation of every Member State (Article 213 TUE). A new Commission is appointed every five years. Commissioners are nominated by their Member States but submitted to the approval of the European Parliament.

The particularity of this institution is its independence; Commissioners do not represent any State and have to take an oath "to be independent and neither to seek or to take instructions from their Member States" (Article 213 TUE). The Commission is headed by a president, nominated by the governments and approved by the European Parliament. Under article 250 TFUE, he is responsible for the internal organization of the Commission and its general political guidance. The Commission voting system relies on a simple majority basis. Its key responsibilities are:

- To **initiate the law-making process**. The Commission proposes drafts for legislation to the Council and the Parliament on any matters covered by the Treaties. However, the Commission proposals have to respect the subsidiarity principle.

- To **enforce EU Law**. In this respect, the Commission is referred as the "guardian" of the Treaties. Under Article 4(3) every Member State undertakes to achieve the objectives of the Treaties and the Commission as to make sure that they are doing so properly.

- The Commission's concern can relate to a breach of EU Law for example, and then it will launch an "infringement procedure". It the case of a failure to respond from the targeted Member State, then the Commission can refer the case to the CJEU.

- To **implement the policy and the EU budget**. It is the executive function of the Commission. For instance, the

Commission will have a role in the supervision of regional bodies expenditures compared to the money actually attributed by the budget.

- To **represent the EU internationally**. The Commission representatives are allowed to speak up for the Member States in the UN or the World Trade Organization, but more importantly they have the legal capacity to conclude international agreements on the behalf of the EU. It has been the case for the Cotonou agreement that has been concluded by the Commission for the EU and African nations.

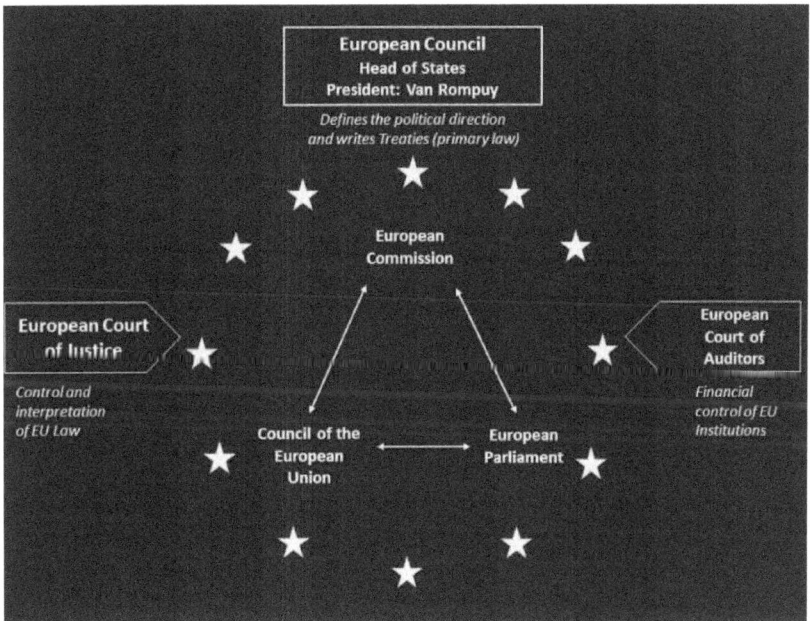

The Court of Justice of the European Union (including the General Court)

The CJEU is governed by its statute but also the TFEU (Articles 251-281). The Court is both composed of Judges (*juges rapporteurs*) and advocates general. Under Article 253 TUE, both of them are appointed under certain conditions. They should be persons whose independency is "beyond doubt", and present the highest knowledge of Law with corresponding positions in their Member States. In addition to this, all the members of the Court must swear an oath on impartiality. According to Article 19 TEU, they should be a Judge per Member State (28) and 9 advocates general. Both the judges and the advocates serve a six-year term. A president is elected by the Judges from among themselves for a three-year term.

Article 13 (2) TEU limits the Court Jurisdiction's to the areas expressly mentioned by the Treaties. The Courts seeks to achieve three objectives:
- Ensuring that the interpretation and application of law is observed;
- Resolving disputes between institutions, Member States and individuals;
- Protecting individual rights;

The Court hears five main types of action brought before it:

- References from Member States for a preliminary ruling on an interpretation of EU Law (Article 27 TFEU). Also known as indirect actions.
- Actions against Member States for failing to implement Treaty obligations (Article 258 TFUE). Also called direct action or "infringement proceedings".
- Actions against an institution for abuse of power (Article 263 TFEU)
- Actions against an institution for failure to act (Article 265 TFEU)
- Actions for damages against an institution that have been responsible of a loss suffered by an individual (Article 240 TFEU).

Traditionally, most issues were heard by the Court in plenary session. However, enlargement of the EU has made it materially difficult. The Nice treaty established a Grand Chamber of fewer

Judges that are still subjected to Article 17 TFEU: every Chamber shall be composed of an uneven number for a decision to be valid. Decisions of the Court are based on a simple majority in a mostly inquisitorial judgement. Contrary to the Common Law model, it is not possible for Judges to dissent individually in the Judgement. The role of the Advocate general is to propose a reasoned opinion for the Court. It is not binding the Judges but these opinions have a major influence on the decision.

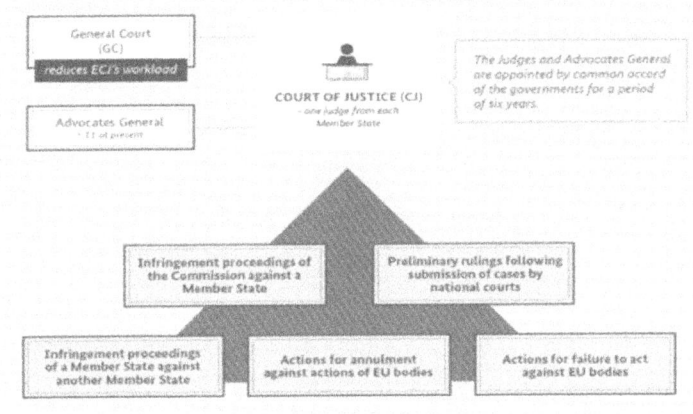

Court of Justice of the European Union (CJEU)

© Federal Ministry of Labour and Social Affair 2017

The General Court, previously called Court of First Instance (SEA 1986), was created to release the Court of Justice of its excesses of workload and to avoid the unreasonable delays that resulted from this. The Treaty of Nice enlarged the jurisdiction of the General Court (GC). The system of appointment of its members is the same than for the CJEU. The GC is competent to hear all actions under Articles 26,265,268,270 and 272 that are not already attributed to the CJEU.

Other major institutions and bodies

- The Committee of Permanent Representatives (COREPER): is a permanent body of representatives from all Member States that is governed by article 240 TFEU. It prepares the discussions of the Council and has a first look at the proposals of the Commission.

- The Court of Auditors, regulated by Articles 285–287 TFEU, controls and supervises the EU budget. It is composed of 28 members that check all the revenue and expenditure of the institutions.

- The Economic and Social Committee (ESC) falls under article 300 TFEU, and advices either the Council or the Commission on social and economic matters. Advice is given in the form of opinions. For example, before initiating a proposal, the Commission might request an opinion from the ESC.

- The Committee of the regions is an advisory body governed by articles 305-307 TFEU. Its function is to represent local and regional interests. Its concerns are public health, culture or other matters of social dimension. This body participates to a greater representation of Europe from all levels of public authorities.

- The European Central Bank (ECB) was necessary to produce and control the development of the single currency in the Euro Zone. Governed by article 282-284 TFEU, it is the only body allowed to issue Euro banknotes. Its main objective is to maintain price stability.

- The European Ombudsman (Articles 20, 24 and 228 TFEU) listens and investigates complaints of maladministration from EU citizens (abuse of power, discrimination, unnecessary delay). If the Ombudsman considers it necessary, it can refer the case to other institutions in order to take appropriate actions.

Sources of EU Law

Primary sources

The Treaties are the most significant source of EU Law. The founding Treaties are primary sources of EU Law because all subsequent law must fulfil their objectives. The founding Treaties are the EC Treaty and the TEU (now TFEU).

But other Treaties are also primary sources:

- All the accession Treaties
- The Merger Treaty 1965
- The SEA 1986
- The Amsterdam Treaty 1997
- The Treaty of Nice 2000

Moreover, primary sources are also composed of the Treaties concluded between the EU and third parties (Non-EU States or other international organization). Usually negotiated by the Commission, these treaties bind every Member States as a primary source of EU Law. For instance the *Lomé* Conventions are trade agreements between the EU and non-EU members. Nevertheless, the most important one is certainly the TFEU in terms of establishing the legal order. The TFEU is qualified as of a constitutional significance.

Secondary sources

"Secondary sources" is a generic term that refers to all the various types of law that the European institutions can make. Secondary sources such as directives and decisions are the concrete laws or provisions taken by the EU, but they are still subordinated to the primary law contained in the treaties. Secondary sources can only be used to achieve the objectives of the Treaties. This is an illustration of the existence of a hierarchy of norms within EU Law. Article 288 presents the four types of EU laws: Regulations, Decisions, Directives and Recommendations & Opinions (usually treated together). Another distinction is usually drawn up between binding and non-binding secondary sources, depending on the obligation or not for the Member States to respect and implement them.

Binding secondary legislation

- Regulations: Article 288 (2) TFEU provides that "A regulation shall have general application. It shall be binding in its entirety and directly applicable in all Member States." In other word, this type of measures applies generally to all Member States, it gives no choice to them as to whether or not to give them effect and finally that it does not need any incorporation in national legal systems to be enforceable.

- Directives are defined by paragraph 3 of Article 288 TFEU: "A directive shall be binding, as to the result to be achieved, upon each Member State to which it is addressed, but shall leave to the national authorities the choice of form and methods". Directives differ from Regulations that have to be absolutely uniform for every Member States. Directives rather set out some guidelines and then the Member States have a margin of appreciation to implement them nationally. These measures are usually used to ensure that the Member States progressively harmonize their laws by letting them the freedom to decide on how to do it.

  However, Member States are legally bound to implement the directive within a set deadline. They were obviously not designed to directly create rights for individuals, or to compel national Courts to give them effect regardless if they were implemented or not. Nevertheless, the CJEU had to acknowledge it in order to ensure that they would be enforced. In this respect, these measures are governed by the following principles: vertical direct effect, indirect effect and State liability. A more detailed explanation of these principles will be given in Chapter 5.

- Decisions: Article 288 (4) TFEU presents these measures as it follow: "A decision shall be binding in its entirety. A decision which specifies those to whom it is addressed shall be binding only on them." The main difference with regulations is that a decision is only binding the parties to whom it is addressed to. They can be either binding or not binding, depending on their content. Some decisions only lay down guidelines and do not create real obligations. All binding secondary legislation is published in the Official Journal of the European Union (L series), the Legislation Edition of the Official Journal. Citation is by reference to the provision's year of adoption and its number.

Non-binding secondary legislation

Recommendations and opinions are qualified by Article 288 (5) as having "no binding force". This provision allows the Commission to formulate recommendations and to deliver opinions. It does not mean that these measures are ineffective; it is a useful way to clarify the state of some areas of Law without having to introduce formal and weighted binding legislation. Even if these measures clearly cannot be enforced as Law, they can have a persuasive effect before the Courts. The ECJ went even further in the case **Grimaldi v Fonds Des Maladies Professionnelles** (Rec 1989,P 4407) (Sv89-287 Fi89-287) (Judgment): ECJ 13 Dec 1989, by affirming that national Courts should take recommandations and opinions into consideration when deciding cases. Since then, this rule has not really been enforced in practice.

Tertiary sources

- The case law of the CJEU is an undeniable source of EU Law. Indeed, the CJEU jurisprudence role has been, from time to time, to enlighten and clarify the broad terms used by the founding Treaties and to interpret, to some extent, secondary sources and their legal effect. Unlike the traditional Courts belonging to the Common Law, the CJEU is based on a continental legal system. Hence, there is no strict binding precedents as such, in other words the court is not bound by its past decisions. However, the Court generally did not depart from its past decisions without strong reasons and presented a significant consistency over the years throughout the decisions given. This shows the CJEU's eagerness to be legislatively active in the achievement of the objectives of the Union. It actually occurred via two different types of interventions. Firstly, the Court has ensured that the objectives of the Treaties would be realistically achievable by developing the principles of supremacy and direct effect of EU Law (see Chapters 3 & 4). These principles are at the core of every analysis of EU Law; they are the key rules regulating the relationship between EU Law and National Law. While the importance of the objectives of the EU and the primary sources are not discussed, they could not be enforced without the supremacy and the direct effect of EU Law that are crucial to the functioning of the EU. Secondly, the Court has defined the main rules that apply to specific areas of EU Law such as Competition Law, Anti-Discrimination Law or the "Four freedoms".

- The general principles of Law are recognized as an unwritten source of Law that has been developed by the CJEU. These principles were developed partly on the basis of the provisions of the founding Treaties. For example, Article 6(1) of the TEU, identifies the main principles of the Union: Liberty, democracy, the Rule of Law and fundamental freedoms. But also partly on national Law, because most of them were shared by the Member States before the rise European construction. The idea is to subject the interpretation of law to these general principles. The main general principles of European Union Law are:

  - The protection of fundamental human rights
  - Equality
  - Natural Justice
  - Legal certainty
  - Proportionality
  - Subsidiarity

The general principles of Law, and particularly the protection of fundamental rights, will be studied in Chapter 6.

Chapter 3: EU Law and National Law: Supremacy.

Supranationalism and the origins of supremacy

Supremacy is a legal principle involving that, in areas where EU Law is relevant to a case that presents a conflict of norms; EU Law should prevail over national Law. It is one of the key principles created by the ECJ that ensure the enforceability of the European legal order. Supremacy comes along with direct effect, indirect effect and State liability (topics covered in Chapter 4).

Supremacy is rooted in supranationalism. Supranationalism is a method of decision-making by a community of States, wherein officials are representing their Member States. Unlike federalism Member States remain sovereign because they decided voluntarily to be part of the organization and are free at any time to leave it. However, Member States are delegating some of their sovereign powers to the community. They might, for instance, be forced to implement a decision that they did not consent with, as far as

45

decisions are taken by majority votes.

The principle of supremacy is not written in the founding treaties, yet is considered to be a fundamental principle of the European Union. It is linked to the doctrine of autonomy, which implies that EU's institutions are independent from its Member States, and creates an external source of Law despite being created by the Member States themselves. Supremacy's main consequence on the EU legal order is to reinforce its autonomy. The importance of supremacy in the integration of the European construction was highlighted by Cruz at the time of the European Communities, which he claimed: "without supremacy community law ceases to be *communataire*".

The rise of the new European legal order

While supremacy is about the relationship between national Law and EU Law, it is necessary to present the different approaches of international Law within the different Member States. On this issue, European States have adopted two different conceptions: monism or dualism. The monistic conception, on the one hand, provides that international accords, which through ratification bind a country in international law, are considered to be part of the internal legal system without the need for specific measures to incorporate them. The principle of monism is well known in many EU countries, such as France for example, and has been accepted quite early by the Court of Justice.

The dualistic conception, on the other hand, implies that international accords do not become part of the internal legal system at the moment of ratification but only if and to the extent that they are specifically incorporated into national law. This approach is normally taken by the United Kingdom. In addition to this, the particular importance attributed to the sacred parliamentary sovereignty worsens the compliance with the principle of supremacy.

The development of EU Law created much more problem within dualist States. At first it appears to be conflicting with the main principles regulating the European legal order: supremacy, direct effect and indirect effect. Supremacy is also known as "primacy of EU law", from the French *primauté du droit de l'Union.* The reasons of its development by the Court are various. First of all, while the main objective of the Communities was to create a single Market, Law had to be harmonized through a uniform application of EU Law within the Member States.

In addition to this, the whole structure of Europe was already based on supranationalism which implies that the interests of the community prevail over national interests. Therefore, supremacy was a necessary component of uniformity and consistency across the Union. The recognition of EU supremacy has two major consequences on the competences of national institutions, often referred to as the doctrine of pre-emption:

- It places the CJEU above the national Courts in case of conflict of interpretation of EU Law.
- It prevents legislative bodies in the Member States from enacting legislation that might be incompatible with EU Law.

The European construction has been going on for more than 60 years and there is still a debate about supremacy. This is probably because it touches one of the most delicate areas of EU Law because it is related to sovereignty. The nationalists' biggest fear is to lose sovereignty to the benefits of the community. Unionists would rather qualify it as a mere transfer of sovereignty.

While nothing in the founding treaties was expressly mentioning EU supremacy, the closest the pioneers tackled this issue was this so-called "duty of loyalty" enshrined by Article 10 EC (now replaced by article 4(3) TUE) which stipulates: *"The Member States shall take any appropriate measure, general or particular, to ensure fulfilment of the obligations arising out of the Treaties or resulting from the acts of the institutions of the Union".*

The abandoned Treaty Establishing a Constitution for Europe (TECE) included a special provision on supremacy. Instead, declaration 17 of the Lisbon Treaty merely mentions the "primacy", making reference to the CJEU's case law. However, the recognition of EU supremacy is mostly due to an intense legislative activism of the ECJ, which has built the principle throughout a range of cases.

The Court, in its case law, before going into a detailed definition of supremacy, acknowledged the "specificity" of the EU legal order that has a "special and original nature" (**ECJ Costa v ENEL** (Case 6/64) [1964]). This is why supremacy is referred as the rise of a new legal order. The EU is a *sui generis* entity, it is unique and it differs from the traditional models of national or international law.

The famous case affirming the specificity of EU Law is **Van Gend en Loos.** Nevertheless, it mainly concerns the principle of direct effect of EU Law, another crucial pillar of EU Law enforceability, and will therefore be more fully discussed in the next Chapter.

General principle: The EU must be regarded as a unique legal order distinct from either national or international Law.

Van Gend en Loos v Nederlandse Administratie der Belastingen (Case 26/62) [1963] ECR 1
Facts: The case was related to the introduction of a Dutch law on taxes, relatively increasing the duty payable and resulting on a loss suffered by the claimant that which claimed an incompatibility with European Law. The importer was charged 8% tax on importation of chemicals from Germany, placing him at a disadvantage over domestic sellers.
Preliminary Ruling: *"The Community constitutes a new legal order in international law for whose benefits the states have limited their sovereign rights, albeit within limited fields".*
Application: The EEC Treaty that was at stake in the case was not an ordinary international Treaty because Members agreed to limit their sovereignty rights. **Van gend en Loos** does not give a complete definition of supremacy. However, by declaring that the Treaty had established a new legal order in which Member States had limited their sovereign rights, the judgment paved the way for the establishment of this principle of EU law.

General principle: National law cannot override EU law.

Flaminio Costa v ENEL (Case 6/64) [1964] ECR 585
Facts: ENEL was an electric company that has been put under state ownership by the Italian government. Costa, a shared owner of the company before its nationalisation, has suffered a loss attributable to the Italian Government. He argued before its national Courts that the Italian law nationalizing the industry was incompatible with EC monopoly laws. The case was referred to the ECJ. Throughout the procedure, the Italian government claimed that national law should prevail as it was enacted after the law ratifying the EC Treaty.
Preliminary question before the Court: Whether or not a national law, enacted after the law ratifying the founding treaties of the Communities, could contravene to its main objectives?
Preliminary Ruling: The answer of the Court is clearly negative; incompatible domestic provisions cannot override Community

law, regardless whether or not they were enacted after the ratification of the founding treaties.

The ECJ based its reasoning on the framework of **Van Gend en Loos** but extended it: *"By creating a Community of limited duration having (...) a transfer of powers from the states to the community, the member states (...) have thus created a body of law which binds both their nationals and themselves"*. Thus, according to the Court, the supremacy of EU law logically stems from the Member Stats' transfer of power that created an independent body of law. **Application:** This case defines and develops the principle of the supremacy of EU law justifying it by the "special and original" nature its legal order.

A clear conclusion can be made about the inputs of **Costa and Van Gend en Loos.**

The Member States have transfer certain of their sovereign powers to the Community in order to make law that would bind them and their individual. As a result Member States cannot introduce new national laws that would contradict EU Law.

General principle: No provision of national law, of any nature whatsoever, can override EU Law.

Internationale Handelsgesellschaft mbH v Einfuhr- und Vorratsstelle für Getreide und Futtermittel (1970) Case 11/70
Facts: A regulation required the introduction of export licences in respect of certain agricultural products falling under the Common Agricultural Policy (CAP). Another requirement of this regulation involved the transfer of a deposit that would be forfeited if no exportations were realized during the period of the licence, and this is how the applicant suffered a loss. The applicant claimed that this EU regulation was incompatible with the German Constitution for having contravened with the right to run a business freely. The unconstitutionality was acknowledged but the German Court was uncertain about the consequences of such a decision.

Preliminary question before the Court: The German Court used Article 177 to ask the ECJ whether or not national constitutional law prevails over EC law?

Preliminary Ruling: The Court simply replies: *"The validity of* *a Community measure or its effect within a member state cannot be affected by allegations that it runs counter to either fundamental rights, as formulated by the constitution of the state or the principles of a national constitutional structure".*

Application: Internationale Handelsgesellschaft enlarges the scope of the supremacy principle: no provisions of national law, of any nature whatsoever, can override EU Law. In the event of any conflict or inconsistency between any provisions of national law, regardless its nature, and EU law, the domestic courts have an absolute requirement to give effect to EU Law.

General principle: When national law conflicts with EU law, national law should immediately be set aside by national Courts.

Amministrazione delle Finanze v Simmenthal SpA (1978) Case 106/77

Facts: Simmenthal, a company importing beef into Italy from France, was required to pay a tax at the border, which clearly contradicts the EC provisions on freedom of good at the time.

Preliminary question before the Court: After acknowledging the incompatibility, the Italian Court referred the case to the ECJ to know if EU Law had to be applied directly of if it should wait for the traditional constitutional Court procedure to strike it down for incompatibility to higher norms?

Preliminary Ruling: The Court mentions in its Judgement that any EC provision *"renders automatically inapplicable every conflicting provision of current national law".*

Application: The effect of EU Law supremacy is immediate, there is no need to wait for national procedures to strike down the impugned law, and it is rendered automatically inapplicable.

General principle: All incompatible domestic law shall be repealed.

Case 167/73, Commission v France (Re French Merchant Seamen) [1974] ECR 359

Facts: A French statutory provision required that certain of crew on French registered merchant ships had to be French. This provision was violating the rules of freedoms of worker under article 45. The French government argued that its domestic Courts were no longer giving effect to this provision and that nothing in the Treaty required repeal.

Preliminary question before the Court: Do Member States have to repeal every out-dated incompatible law, even though their Courts are to giving them effect anymore?

Preliminary Ruling: The mere existence of such provision was creating uncertainty that was unacceptable in the pursuit of harmony.

Application: All previous domestic law that appears incompatible to EU Law, regardless whether or not it is still applied by domestic courts shall be repealed by Member States.

Finally, the supremacy of laws taken at the international level is not a revolution in itself. Actually, it is generally accepted by States in Public International Law (Treaties and Customs prevail over national law). However, the particularity of EU supremacy lies on two points. Firstly, this principle is effectively enforceable in practice. And this is quite rare in the international order that a Court has the courage and the resources to go against the States' will. Secondly, as it has been mentioned in the case previously presented, the Member States have transferred powers to the Union, so that they can be forced to implement decisions for which they were in disfavour. This is certainly why the supremacy issue is so controversial. Conversely, in Public International Law nothing, except for the exception of the *jus cogens*, no rules can be imposed on States if they did consent to them.

The impact of supremacy on UK Law

The UK compliance with supremacy was probably the most far-reaching of the EU. Partly because dualist states are generally not designed to integrate international orders implying any sort of supremacy. According to Dicey's traditional definition of Parliamentary sovereignty, it makes Parliament the supreme legal authority in the UK, which can create or end any law. Generally, the courts cannot overrule its legislation. Parliamentary sovereignty is the most important part of the UK constitution.

However, the CJEU case-law on supremacy requires national Courts to suspend operations, declare as invalid and dis-apply acts of Parliament. This approach is completely opposed to the UK conception of the role of Judges. The United Kingdom being a dualist system allowed EC law to get an automatic incorporation through the European Communities Act 1972(ECA). Section 2(1) of this act particularly conveyed how the UK limited its sovereign rights in favour of the EC. However section 2(4) limited the EU's sovereignty over domestic law by ensuring that all domestic enactments had effect only subject to directly applicable rules of community law. The ECA 1972 had two major consequences on the traditional UK system: overriding the usual presumption that any later enactment overruled prior law inconsistent with it and clearly terminates any effect of acts of Parliament purporting to contradict EU Law. UK judges took the following positions:

E Coomes (Holdings) Ltd v Shields [1978] IRLR 263 CA,
Facts: Miss Shields was employed as a counterhand in the appellants bookmakers' shop in Sussex Street, London, on an hourly rate of 92p, whereas her men colleagues were significantly paid better for the same job. UK law appeared to be incompatible with EU Law.
Question before the Court: In case of conflict between UK and EU Law, which provisions should prevail?
Ratio: Lord Denning stated that "By the 1972 Act, parliament enacted that we should abide by the principle as laid down by the European Court".

English judges have not always reacted in this manner and there has inevitably been a controversy that arose from the case **Mcarthys v Smith.**

Macarthys Ltd v Smith (No.2) [1980] EWCA Civ 7 (17 April 1980)
Facts: This case involved a claim about equal pay based on EC Law that appeared to be contradicting with the Westminster's Equal Pay Act 1970.
Question before the Court: In case of conflict between UK and

EU Law, which provisions should prevail?

Ratio: Lord Denning adopted a constructive approach that was contradicting EU supremacy, he says "*If the time should come when our Parliament deliberately passes an Act with the intention of repudiating the Treaty or any provision in it or intentionally of acting inconsistently with it and says so in express terms then I should have thought it would be the duty of our courts to follow the stature of our Parliament.*" Justice Cumming-Bruce in his dissenting judgement took position of EU supremacy.

Garland v British Rail Engineering Ltd. [1982] 2 WLR 918
Facts: There was a dispute between an employee and her company, another case relating to equal pay. The employee claiming discrimination alleged to be suffered by female employees who on retirement no longer continue to enjoy travel facilities for their spouses and dependent children although male employees continue to do so.
Question before the Court: Should the construction approach be applied when Parliament deliberately passes an Act with the intention to act inconsistently with EU Law?
Ration: Lord Denning's construction approach was applied in this case and EU Law has been set aside. This gave rise to a significant controversy as being incompatible with Van Gend en Loos (1963).

General principle: UK constructive approach is overruled and the supremacy of EU Law reaffirmed.

R (Factortame Ltd) v Secretary of State for Transport (Case C-213/89) 1990 ECR 1-2433
Facts: The case involved companies registered in the UK but mainly owned by Spanish nationals. The Merchant Shipping Act 1988 required a certain percentage of UK national ownership for the registration of a vessel. This provision expressly violated the "non-discrimination on nationality" principle of Article 12. The Divisional Court granted an interim relief suspending the operation of the impugned law. The House of Lords then made a reference to the ECJ arguing than nothing neither in the UK Constitution nor in EC Law permitted such interim.
Preliminary question before the Court: Does the incompatibility of an act of Parliament, enacted after accession to the Treaties and expressly introducing inconsistencies to EC Law, permits judges to suspend the legal effect of the domestic provision?
Preliminary Ruling: The Court firmly recalls that any act of Parliament, even enacted after the accession Treaties, that would be inconsistent with EU Law cannot override it.
In addition to this, national Courts being confronted to inconsistencies or incompatibilities with EU Law are required to do everything necessary to set aside the impugned law.

Application: The UK constructive approach is overruled and the supremacy of EU Law is affirmed. There is now an external body competent to make laws affecting the United Kingdom, which are applied by the English Courts irrespective of the wishes of Parliament.

This brought about academic debate on the concept of parliamentary sovereignty. Authors such as **Wade** stated that the fact of dis-applying an act of Parliament for an allegedly incompatibility with a superior source meant that "something drastic had happened to the traditional doctrine of parliamentary sovereignty". He claimed that this was revolutionary on the grounds that the Courts were no longer prepared to uphold absolute parliamentary sovereignty. Alternatively **Craig and De Burca** argued that sovereignty remained intact. Parliament itself voluntarily decided to set the limits of its sovereignty. The ECJ just used the competence it has been attributed by the Member States. On the other hand **McCormick** argued that in the modern world it was no longer realistic to speak in terms of absolute sovereignty due to the inter-dependence of economies.

However many English Lawyers, did not accept the European Court's view. They contended that European law overruled English domestic law only because parliament had chosen to make it so, and that parliament could change its mind at any time. A balance is thus preserved between the supremacy of EU law in matters of substantive law, and the proper supremacy of the UK parliament in establishing the legal framework within which EU law operates. The recent events that led the UK to trigger article 50 TFEU support this last argument. Brexit has shown that the UK Parliament voluntarily transferred some powers to the Union and was entitled to take them back at any time.

Another act is finally enacted in 2011, The European Union Act, by the coalition government that makes a number of statutory qualification about the future relationship between the EU and the UK. A very interesting provision related to the issue of supremacy can be found in section 18 of the act. The latter subjects the UK membership to the continuing will of Parliament. A simple act of

Parliament is all that is needed to exit from the EU.

The impact of supremacy on other Member States

In France, accepting EU supremacy did not raise such controversies. It can certainly be explained by the fact that it has a monist approach of international Law. At quite an early stage, the Court of *Cassation* in the case **Von Kempis v Geldof** (1976) 2 CMLR 462, acknowledged the recent CJEU case law in declaring that EU Law takes precedence over French legislation.

However, the UK is not the only country to presented difficulties with supremacy in their national jurisdiction. It was also the case in other European Union member states such as Germany and Poland. For example in Germany, the reluctance to accept supremacy was based on a fear of potential violation of Human Rights contained in the German Constitution.

Solange I judgment, German Constitutional Court (BVerfGE 37, 271) [1974] 2 CMLR 540
Facts: The case involved an A German import/export company for which an export deposit of DM17,026.47 was declared to be forfeited after the firm had only partially used an export licence gran-ted to it for 20,000tons of ground maize.
Preliminary Ruling: The German Constitutional Court complained about the legal uncertainty left by the lack of a codified catalogue of fundamental rights and held that the fundamental rights guaranteed under the West German constitution would prevail over EEC law for so long as this situation continued.

The German Constitutional Court finally abdicated in the case **Wunsche Hendelsgesellchaft (1987)** 3 CMLR 225 provided that the EU Law could guarantee as least an equivalent protection. On the issue of sovereignty, the German Constitutional Court always maintained a stable position: Germany remains the only sovereign. In the case **Brunner v The European Treaty** (1994) 1 CMLR 57, the Court states: "Germany is one of the 'Masters of the Treaties' … Germany thus preserves the quality of a sovereign state in its own right".

Chapter 4: EU Law and National Law: Direct Effect, Indirect Effect and State Liability

The concept of direct effect

General ideology

While supremacy defines the relationship between the EU and its Member-States, direct effect establishes the link between the EU and its citizens. It is the second pillar of the practical enforceability of EU Law. Direct effect enables individuals to immediately invoke a European provision before a national or European court. It ensures that EU citizens are able to enforce their rights before the domestic Courts.

Like supremacy, nothing in the founding treaties clearly mentions direct effect. It is a creation of the European Court of Justice. However, the principle of direct effect has to be distinguished from other close principles identified in the Treaties

Firstly the principle of general applicability merely refers to the idea that a particular measure applies equally in every Member States. Usually, in EU Law, if a provision does not specifically mentions that it is applying to particular Member States, it applies generally throughout the entire Union. In this way a Regulation is described as generally applicable.

Secondly, direct effect has to be distinguished from direct applicability identified by Article 288 TFEU. Direct applicability draws a line between EU secondary sources that have to be implemented in the Member States through domestic measures and those who do not. For instance, a regulation is directly applicable whereas a Directive effectively requires Member States to implement them internally.

The criteria of direct effect

The principle of direct effect has been considered for the first time in **Van Gend en Loos** the same case through which the Court developed the doctrine of supremacy. However, these two principles go hand in hand and are both complementary to ensure the effective enforceability of EU Law.

General principle: EU provisions, that satisfy the Van Gend en Loos criteria, create individual rights directly enforceable before national courts.

Van Gend en Loos v Nederlandse Administratie der Belastingen (Case 26/62) [1963] ECR 1
Facts: The case was related to the introduction of a Dutch law on taxes, relatively increasing the duty payable and resulting on a loss suffered by the claimant that which claimed an incompatibility with European Law. The importer was charged 8% tax on importation of chemicals from Germany, placing him at a disadvantage over domestic sellers. The so-called "standstill" Article 12 of the EC Treaty required that there should be no increases on existing duties. However, Article 12 contained no explicit mention to individual rights.
The Dutch Court, uncertain about the interpretation of this article, referred the case to the ECJ through an article 267 reference.
Preliminary question before the Court: The Dutch Court asked the ECJ if a provision of EU Law, not containing any explicit mention to it, could create rights for individuals which national courts were bound to protect.
Preliminary Ruling: The advocate general initially prepared a reasoned opinion, based on a pure literalist approach, arguing that Article 12 cannot be construed as to create individual rights. However, the Court preferred a purposive approach stating that since the Treaty was intended to affect individuals, it must clearly be capable of creating rights that would be enforceable by individuals before national Courts. The Court first recalls the function of the treaties: " *Independently of the legislation of the member states Community law… not only imposes obligations on individuals but is also intended to confer upon them rights which*

become part of their legal heritage", before adding : *"(Article 12) is ideally adapted to produce direct effect between member state and their subject."*

Application: This case is a pillar of EU Law's enforceability that can be invoked before national courts to ensure that the individual rights created by EU provisions are protected before them. **Van Gend en Loos** can also be mentioned to underline the specificity of the European legal order that relies on both its direct effect and supremacy.

However, the application of direct effect is subjected to several conditions that are usually referred to as the "**Van Gend en Loos** criteria". These conditions have been confirmed and developed by several cases (see for example **Rayners v Belgian State** (Case 2/74) 1974). Three main conditions are:

1. The provision must be sufficiently clear and precisely stated. In other words the wording of the text should not be too vague.
2. The provision must be unconditional or "non-dependant" in the sense that it des not require the intervention of another body neither from the Union nor from the Member States.

3. There must be in fact an identifiable right arising or emerging from this provision on which citizens can rely. However it does not mean that this right has to be expressly written in the text of the provision, it can be deduced from its context (this is what happened in **Van Gend en Loos**).

Even though these conditions appear to be quite flexible, not all EU provisions satisfy the "**Van Gend en Loos** criteria".

General principle: In order to acquire direct effect, the EU provision should create "unconditional obligations".

Guerrino Casati (Case 203-80), 1981 ECR 2595
Facts: The applicant exported some money, without the

authorisation required by Italian law, and was forced to pay a fine at the boarder between Italy and Austria. However, the old article 71 of the Treaty EC provided a general protection of competition "*member states shall endeavour to avoid introducing ... new exchange restrictions*".

Preliminary question before the Court: Did article 71 (now repealed), satisfy the **Van g-Gend en Loos** criteria and was therefore creating individual rights directly enforceable before national courts?

Preliminary Ruling: The Court held that the words "*shall endeavour*" were in fact insufficient to create unconditional obligations therefore the provision could not be directly effective.

Application: It is important to thoroughly verify that the provision satisfies all the conditions presented in **Van Gend en Loos**. This is particularly true for provisions that seem to present general objectives or obligations of conducts.

Furthermore, another distinction is important to the understanding of the direct effect principle. In this respect, the case **Defrenne v Sabena** identified two types of direct effect: vertical and horizontal.

General principle: National Courts have a duty to protect the EU rights of its citizens in both disputes opposing them with their Member States and disputes against other private persons.

Defrenne v. Sabena (Case 43/75), 1976 E.C.R. 455

Facts: The applicant brought an action before Belgian Courts for compensation for the loss she had incurred in terms of salary, allowance on termination of contract and pension in comparison with male members of the crew performing identical duties. She relied on article 157 that implies "equal pay for men and women for equal work". The particularity of this case was that the appellant was invoking the direct effect of a primary source of EU Law against her private employer. All the precedent cases dealt with individuals invoking direct effect of EU law against their Member State.

Preliminary question before the Court: Can individuals invoke directly before their national courts a provision of EU Law against their private employer?

Preliminary Ruling: The ECJ answered positively by recognizing the duty for national courts to protect the individual rights of European citizens emerging from EU law, even when they invoke them against an other private person.

"The prohibition of discrimination based on sex applies not only to bodies of a public nature, but also extends to all agreements which are intended to regulate paid labour collectively, as well as to contracts between individuals".

The Court, in its reasoning, explains that the reverse solution would equates to inconsistency by recognizing rights to individuals but denying them effective remedies.

Application: The Court identifies in **Defrenne v Sabena** two different types of direct effect: vertical direct effect and horizontal direct effect.

On the one hand, vertical direct effect entitles every citizen to enforce their individual rights created by EU law before their national courts, when facing in a trial their Member State's government, public bodies or every other emanation of the State. On the other hand, horizontal direct effect is related to the same right but is concerned instead with relationships between individuals. These "individuals" can include any private bodies including companies. However, horizontal direct effect does not apply to Directives, because of their particular nature (this will be explained in details later). Both vertical and horizontal direct effect is very important in terms of enforceability of the rights already conferred to European citizens. Without those principles, individuals would own some rights while being unable to enforce them.

Vertical Direct Effect (VDE)

State (D)

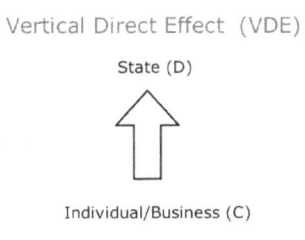

Individual/Business (C)

Horizontal Direct Effect (HDE)

Individual/Business (D)  Individual/Business (C)

Direct effect of primary EU Law

The concept of direct effect enshrined by **Van Gend en Loos,** involved in fact a Treaty article (Article 12 of EC Treaty at the time). Therefore, at first, direct effect was intended to apply to EU primary legislation and was later extended to other sources. In **Van Gend en Loos,** the provision was a "standstill" Article that prevented the Member States to act. The question arose to know whether the principle would also apply to provisions that require positive action from the Member States. Indeed, direct effect has been applied by extension to cover all the substantive Treaty articles by **Defrenne v Sabena** (see also **Van Duyn ECJ 1974** or **Van Binsbergen 1974**). Finally, a Treaty article will be both vertically and horizontally directly applicable before either national or European courts.

Direct effect and Regulations

Article 288 TFEU presents Regulations as both of "general application" and "directly applicable". As previously stated, directly applicable in the terminology of the treaties only means that there is no need of further implementations. If this does not automatically confer direct effect to every Regulation, it satisfies one of the **Van Gend en Loos** criterions that require the provision to be unconditional. In this respect, the main condition that is analysed by the Court for Regulation is whether or not the provision is stated in sufficiently clear and precise terms. In practice, Regulations generally have direct effect. Furthermore, if a regulation satisfies the direct effect criteria, it can be both used vertically and horizontally.

General principle: Regulations generally have direct effect as far as they are stated in sufficiently clear and precise terms.

Orsolina Leonesio v Ministero dell'agricoltura e foreste (Case 93-71) 1972 ECJ
Facts: A Regulation concerned the provision of subsidies for dairy farmers prepared to slaughter their dairy herds. The applicant had killed her cows, as directed by the Regulation, but was denied her subsidies.
Preliminary question before the Court: The question asked by the Italian Court is to know whether or not a Regulation has direct effect, and if so under which conditions.
Preliminary Ruling: The ECJ answers by acknowledging the direct effect of Regulations because they satisfy the **Van Gend en Loos** criterion. On this last point, it explains that while the condition of direct applicability is automatically satisfied by every Regulation, they still have to be stated in sufficiently clear and precise terms.
Application: If Regulations will generally have direct effect in practice, it is still important to verify that they are not too vague in their wording.

Direct effect and Decisions

A Decision is defined by article 288 TFEU as being "binding in its entirety on the party to whom it is addressed". These measures are usually addressed by the Commission to Member States that are in breach of EU Law. In this sense, many citizens suffer losses as a result of those breaches and have no possibility to enforce their rights. Therefore, it was important to provide them effective remedies.

General principle: Decisions have direct effect as far as they satisfy the Van Gend en Loos criteria.

Grad v Finanzamt Traustein (Case 9/70) 1970 ECR 825
Facts: A German Company was challenging a tax imposed on it. The company both argued for the direct effect of a Directive and a Decision that added its time limit.
Preliminary question before the Court: The question was to know whether or not a Decision could have a direct effect and if so under which conditions.
Preliminary Ruling: The Court firstly acknowledged the presumed direct effect of Decisions: *"The effectiveness of such a measure would be weakened if ... nationals ... could not ... invoke it ... and the national courts could not take it into consideration".*
Secondly, the Court recalls in its judgement that every provision should be subjected to the **Van Gend en Loos** criteria.
Application: In order to analyse the direct effect of a particular Decision, it has to fulfil the **Van Gend en Loos** conditions. If the direct effect is recognized it can be used both vertically and horizontally.

Finally, since recommendations and opinions are not binding forms of EU law, they cannot be directly effective (**Grimaldi v Fonds des Maladies Professionnelles** (Case C 322/88) [1989] ECR 4407).

The issue of enforceability of Directives

Direct effect and Directives

The particularity of Directives compared to other sources, as presented by article 288 TFEU, is to always require an implementation at the national level. In other words, the Directive fixes the objectives and the Member States are free to choose how they are going to achieve them. Ultimately, the major feature of Directives seems to be incompatible with the **Van Gend en Loos** criteria that clearly requires for the provision to be unconditional and not subjected to other interventions of institutions. Thus, one would think that Directives are not directly enforceable by individuals before their national courts. However, once again, the ECJ has been very active on this issue and came up with a different solution.

It is important to understand that the issue of direct effect Directives only concerns the unimplemented or improperly implemented Directives. Conversely, in the case of Directives properly implemented; there is no point to invoke the Directive anymore if the individual can directly invoke the domestic law implementing it.

General principle: A Directive, even though conditional by nature, can be directly effective as far as it satisfies the other conditions of the Van Gend en Loos criteria.

Van Duyn v Home Office 1974 (C-41/74) ECJ
Facts: This case concerned a Dutch scientologist offered work as a secretary at the Church of Scientology headquarters in London. She was refused entry into the UK. However, article 45 TFEU and Directive 64/221 protects the free movement of workers. The Directive was not implemented yet in the UK. Nevertheless, the applicant tried to enforce her rights before the UK national courts by invoking the direct effect of the Directive.
Preliminary question before the Court: The UK courts referred the case to the ECJ as to know whether or not a Directive, although conditional by nature, could have a direct effect?
Preliminary Ruling: The Court held that Directive can directly effective if it is sufficiently clear, precisely stated and if it grants an identifiable right upon which individuals can rely on. The Court justified its decision by explaining that the reverse solution would be incompatible with the binding effect of Directives: *"The useful effect of such a act would be weakened if individuals were prevented from relying on it before their national courts and if the latter were prevented from taking it into consideration"*.

Therefore, Members States owe their citizens obligations to implement the directives in order to effectively render enforceable the rights that they contain. In addition to this, the ECJ mentions in its judgement that the direct effect of Directives is only intended to be vertical.

Application: Directives should be analysed as having a direct effect if they respect the two other conditions of the **Van Gend en Loos** criteria, regardless their conditional nature. However, it should be noted that the other conditions must be verified thoroughly. This decision was not well received by certain national courts in France and Germany, which accused the Court of Justice of exceeding its jurisdiction and refused to give direct effect to directives.

General principle: A Directive can only be directly effective once the deadline for its implementation has passed. Furthermore, Member States are prevented from invoking their own failure to implement a Directive to avoid its direct effect.

Pubblico Ministero v Ratti (Case 148/78) [1979] ECR 1629
Facts: Ratti, an Italian company, packed its products in conformity with the requirements of an unimplemented Directive. The applicant was convicted for infringement to Italian law (which was stricter on the packaging). The deadline for the implementation had not passed yet.

Preliminary question before the Court: The Italian Court questioned the ECJ as to know whether or not an unimplemented Directive should be directly effective even though its implementation date had not passed yet.

Preliminary Ruling: On the main question, the Court replied that Directives only acquire direct effect once their implementation deadline has passed. Thus, as far as the implementation date for the Directive at stake was still running, the Directive had no direct effect. In addition to this, the Court stated on another interesting issue about the implementation:

"Consequently a member state which has not adopted the implementing measures required by the Directive in the prescribed periods may not rely, as against individuals, on its own failure to perform the obligations which the Directive entails."

This rule is based on the civil maxim: *"Nemo auditur propriam turpitudinem allegans"*. In other words: no one can be heard to invoke his own turpitude.

Application: Another condition to the **Van Gend en Loos** criteria is added by the ECJ: the deadline for the unimplemented directive has to be passed to be directly effective. The test for direct effect seems to be stricter.

General principle: Directives can have vertical direct effect but certainly no horizontal direct effect.

Marshall v Southampton and South West Area Health Authority (Teaching) (No 1) (Case 152/84) [1986] ECR 723

Facts: The case was about a woman that was dismissed at 62 based on a mandatory requirement. Her employer was the health service, an organ of the State. The applicant challenged UK law based on the argument that different requirement ages for men and women amounted to sex discrimination under Directive 76/207. The UK government replied that, although being an organ of the State, the health service was acting as an employer and not as a public authority therefore the Directive should not have direct effect.

Preliminary question before the Court: The UK government raised the issue as to whether or not Directive should have direct effect, when the public organ in a dispute with an individual, is acting as an employer and not in its initial public capacities?

Preliminary Ruling: The Court first held that a person could rely on a Directive against the State regardless of the capacity its body at this moment. But more importantly, this case limits the **Van Gend en Loos** principle by affirming that it only gives rise to vertical direct effect of a directive but certainly not horizontal direct effect. The following extract of the judgement illustrates this point: *"With regard to the argument that a directive may not be relied upon against an individual, it must be emphasised that the binding nature of a directive, exists only in relation to 'each Member State to which it is addressed'. It follows that a directive may not of itself impose obligations on an individual and that a provision of a directive may not be relied upon as such against such a person."*

Application: A Directive is directly effective in a dispute between an individual and an organ of the Member States but not in disputes between individual or private bodies.

This case was confirmed by **Dori v Recreb Sri** (Case C-91/92) [1994] ECR I-3325.

The main reason for this principle implying that a Directive cannot be directly effective in a dispute between privates lies on the responsibility of the implementation. Usually, the purpose of vertical direct effect of a Directive is to penalize the Member States for their failure and to compel them to properly implement it.

Indeed, the reverse solution would amount to "sanction" a private person for the failure to implement or the default in the implementation attributable to its Member State. However, private persons should not be held accountable for the breaches of the obligations belonging to their Member States.

Moreover, recognizing the horizontal direct effect of Directives would amount to affirm that they do not need implementation, in any situations, to be enforced before national Courts. There would be no difference between Directives and Regulations anymore, although Article 288 TFEU clearly points the distinction. The main principle enshrined by **Marshall v Southampton** seems to give rise to situations where individuals are not provided neither the possibility to enforce their rights nor the remedies to get reparation.

Fortunately, the European Court of Justice devised four ways to avoid these problems of enforcement: the expanding concept of emanation of the State, indirect effect, incidental horizontal direct effect and State liability. These points will now be examined in turn.

Emanation of the State: an expanding concept

While limiting the direct effect of Directives to disputes between individuals and Member states, the ECJ kept on expanding the concept of emanation of the State. Also known as "arms of the State"; a range of bodies was considered by the Court as belonging to the State and therefore triggering the direct effect of Directives.

General principle: An emanation of the State is a body that provides a public service, subjected to the control of the State or having special powers generally not available to private bodies.

Foster v British Gas plc (Case C-188/89) [1990] ECR I-3313
Facts: The applicant was dismissed for having passed the mandatory retirement age. It was fixed in the UK at 60 for female employees and 65 for male employees. She invoked her right to be protected against sex discrimination emerging from Directive 76/207.
At the time, her employer, British Gas Company, was owned by the UK.
Preliminary question before the Court: The House of Lords, in a reference to the ECJ under article 267, posed the question of whether a private company publicly owned was a body against which a Directive could be directly effective.
Preliminary Ruling: In its judgement, the Court developed a test to determine if a body can be classified as emanation of the State. This test is presented in paragraph 20: "*It follows from the foregoing that a body, whatever its legal form, which has been made responsible, pursuant to a measure adopted by the State, for providing a public service under the control of the State and has for that purpose special powers beyond those which result from the normal rules applicable in relations between individuals is included in any event among the bodies against which the provisions of a directive capable of having direct effect may be relied upon*".
Application: In a case opposing a dispute between a company and an individual claiming, the **Foster** test must be satisfied to classify the body as an emanation of the State and possibly trigger the direct effect of a Directive. This case opens up many possibilities for employment disputes where the line between public and private body is very thin.

Reiser Internationale Transporte GmbH v Autobahnen und Schnellstrassen Finanzierungs AG (Asfinag) (Case C-157/02) [2004] ECR I-1477

Facts: This case concerned an Austrian company, which had been incorporated as a private company but whose sole shareholder was the Austrian State. By delegation from the State under a contractual licence, the company was responsible for the construction, operation and maintenance of Austrian motorways. The government was frequently consulted over the company's activities and could impose objectives about traffic organisation.

Preliminary question before the Court: The question was to know whether or not Asfinag, an Austrian company, was an emanation of the State, according to the **Foster** test?

Preliminary Ruling: The Court classified the Austrian company as an emanation of the State, therefore subject to vertical direct effect of the directive. The Court explained that the company was engaged in a public service (the construction and operation of the motorways of the country), the company was under the control of the State (publicly owned and the existence of a contract permitting the government to impose objectives on the company's activities) and finally had special powers generally not available to private bodies (the State delegated the responsibilities to the company).

Application: This case is a mere application of the **Foster** test, reviewing the three conditions to classify a body as emanation of the State.

Indirect effect

The ECJ also introduced the principle of indirect effect, also known as "sympathetic interpretation" to consolidate the enforceability of EU Law. This process was first set up by the Court in the case **Von Colson**. It imposes a duty on national Courts to interpret national law in such a way to give full effect to EU Law, regardless whether the provision has direct effect or not. The indirect effect is a general principle that applies to every EU provisions, but it will be particularly useful in avoiding the problem of lack of horizontal direct effect of Directives.

General principle: National Courts have a duty to interpret national law in such a way to give full effect to EU Law (irrespective of whether or not it is directly effective).

Von Colson & Kamann v Land Nordrhein-Westfalen (Case 14/83) [1984] ECR 1891, combined with **Harz v Deutsche Tradax** (Case 79/83) [1984] ECR 1921

Facts: The case involved two female applying for work. The first one was applying to work for a State body, the prison service, whereas the second applied to work for a private company which activities were related to the same prison. Both had been rejected in favour of less well-qualified male applicants on the basis that there would be problems and risks in employing female workers in a male prison. The applicants argued that it amounted to sex discrimination prohibited by Directive 76/207. However, the Directive was improperly implemented in Germany. Nevertheless, because of the current state of law, the first applicant working for the public body could have benefited the direct effect of the Directive whereas the second had no remedies to enforce her rights.

Preliminary question before the Court: What can be done for individuals unable to enforce their EU rights domestically against their private employers?

Preliminary Ruling: The Court consolidated these problems of enforceability by devising the indirect effect of EU provisions. The Court based its judgement on the former Article 10 of the Treaty EC: *"Since the duty under article 10 to ensure fulfilment of an obligation was binding on all national courts ... it follows that ... courts are required to interpret their national law in the light of the wording and purpose of the Directive"*.

Application: The indirect effect of EU Law should always be analysed where an individual has no remedies to enforce its rights contained in a Directive, in a dispute against a private body for instance. In this case, the ECJ avoided the problem of horizontal direct effect of directive by providing an alternative that permits to bypass this issue.

However, **Von Colson** left quite ambiguous few points concerning the scope of indirect effect. It was not clear about how far national Court should go when applying it.

General principle: National Courts should, when dealing with

an unimplemented Directive in a horizontal dispute, read national law in the light of the Directive.

Marleasing SA v La Comercial Internacional de Alimentación SA (Case C-106/89) [1990] ECR I-4135

Facts: The applicant relied on the rules of constitution of companies set up by Directive 68/151 against another private company. However, Spain did not implement this directive about harmonisation of company Law.

The issue was about individual facing problems to enforce his rights contained in an unimplemented Directive because of the horizontal nature of the conflict.

Preliminary question before the Court: The Court was asked about the scope and the application of the indirect effect principle when dealing with unimplemented Directives.

Preliminary Ruling: Spanish courts had to read national Law as to give fully effect to the Directive on the harmonisation of company Law.

The ECJ affirmed the **Von Colson** principle and extended its definition by stating: *"In applying national law, whether the provisions concerned pre-date or post-date the directive, the national court asked to interpret national law is bound to do so in every way possible in the light of the text and the aims of the directive to achieve the results envisaged by it".*

Application: To some extent, while covering it under the heading of indirect effect, the Court enshrined in this particular case a sort of horizontal direct effect of Directives.

Incidental horizontal effect

The advocate general in the case **Faccini Dori v Recredb Srl** first claimed that Directives should be horizontally directly effective because they were not meant to create individuals rights and then hypocritically deny their enforcement. However the Court, who merely applied **Marschall** in this case, did not acknowledge his argument. Incidental direct effect of Directives is another solution devised by the ECJ to consolidate the lack of horizontal direct effect of Directives and to ensure enforceability. It is an exception to the rule enshrined by **Marschall**.

Instead of directly trying to enforce the rights of an individual by invoking a Directive in horizontal disputes, the direct effect of the Directive will rather be used to establish the illegal nature of any related national provision.

General principle: A Directive can be directly effective in a horizontal dispute to set aside a national law that did not implement it properly.

CIA Security v Signalson and Securitel (1996) C-194/94

Facts: Signalson, a Belgian company brought an action against CIA for unfair trading under Belgian Law. CIA security international is another private company. Therefore, the dispute is of a horizontal nature. The national provision at stake was implementing Directive 83/189. Signalson was not invoking the Directive but rather the national Belgian Law implementing it. However, CIA claimed that this Belgian Law should be set aside because it did not implement properly the Directive.

Preliminary question before the Court: Can a Directive be directly effective in a horizontal dispute to challenge the compatibility of a law implementing it?

Preliminary Ruling: The ECJ accepted the CIA's argument; a Directive can be directly effective, in a horizontal dispute, to disapply a national law that did not implement it properly.

The Court uses the term "incidental" because there were no EU rights being relied on; the Directive was merely being used to disapply national law.

Application: It is important to look at the correctness of the implementation by comparing the Directive and the national measure taken to implement it. If the Directive is not properly implemented, any individual, even in a horizontal dispute, could directly invoke it to set aside the impugned national provision.

General principle: A Directive can be directly effective in a horizontal dispute, as far as it does not involve rights on which individuals might rely.

Unilever Italia SpA v Central Food (2000) C-443/98
Facts: Italy adopted a law regulating olive oil market conflicting with Directive 83/189. The Directive was thus improperly implemented. Central Foods brought a claim against buyer Unilever (seller of oil), for refusing to pay because the labelling was not conform to Italian Law. Unilever argued that the labelling under Italian Law was incompatible with the labelling set up by the Directive. Therefore, national law should be set aside.
Preliminary question before the Court: The question asked to the ECJ by the Italian Court was to know whether or not, in a dispute opposing private persons, it was possible to invoke a Directive to disapply a national law incompatible with it?
Preliminary Ruling: The ECJ applied **CIA Security v Signalson** in this case by setting aside the Italian Law. More importantly, the Court added that this solution did not conflict with the traditional rules on horizontal direct effect of Directives since the Directive in this case did not involve rights on which individuals might rely.
Application: This case précises the scope of **CIA Security v Signalson** by limiting it to the Directives that do not involve individual rights. If the incidental direct effect of Directives is clearly affirmed, its ambit appears to be restricted.

State liability

The principle of State liability permits an individual to recover compensation for a loss suffered generated by a failure to fulfil EU Law obligations by his Member State. In other words, the State will have to repair the loss suffered by the individual because of its failure to comply with EU Law.

This fourth principle consolidating the weakness of Directives enforceability plays a crucial role in cases of individuals that lack remedies. State liability will be particularly useful for the individual when neither direct nor indirect or incidental effect apply to the Directive at stake. In these cases, State liability will be the last remedy available for the individual to enforce his rights.
General principle: Citizens, under certain conditions, should

be able to sue their Member States for non-implementation of a Directive (breach of EU Law obligations).

Francovich & Bonifaci v Italian Republic (Cases C-6/90 & C-9/90) [1991] ECR I-5357

Facts: The employers of Francovich and Bonifaci had become insolvent which resulted in them not being paid outstanding wages. Directive 80/987 appeared to cover just such a situation. It required each Member State to guarantee the payment of at least some of the lost wages. Italy did not implement the Directive after the set deadline.

Preliminary question before the Court: The Italian Court, by referring the case to the ECJ, raised the question of the liability of Member States towards their nationals, for having breached their EU Law obligations.

Preliminary Ruling: The ECJ found that Italy was in breach of its obligations and was liable to compensate the workers for the loss resulting from that breach.

The Court justifies this decision as it follows: "*It is a principle of Community law that the Member States are obliged to make good loss and damage caused to individuals by breaches of Community law for which they can be held responsible.*"

However, the Court then presents the three conditions to entail State liability:

• The Directive must confer individual rights
• The content of those rights must be identifiable in the wording of the measure
• There must be a causal link between the damage suffered by the individual and the failure to implement the Directive by the State.

Application: State liability should be envisaged by any individual seeking to enforce his EU rights when there is an inconsistency between EU Law and national Law. Nevertheless, the strict conditions of **Francovich** have to be satisfied.

General principle: A sufficiently serious (grave and manifest) breach of EU provisions conferring individual rights and presenting a causal link between the breach and the damage actually suffered, should give rise to State liability.

Brasserie du Pêcheur SA v Germany and R v Secretary of State for Transport ex p **Factortame Ltd (No 4) ('Factortame III')** (Cases C-46/93 & C-48/93) [1996] ECR I-1029)

Facts: Both cases involved obvious breaches of primary sources. The first one involved a German beer purity law that was incompatible with Article 34 at the time; the second was related to quotas on merchant ships that were infringing the right of establishment (Article 49). Both cases involved breaches with reference to the ECJ for clarification of the scope of State liability.

Preliminary question before the Court: Does State liability applies in a case of breach of primary EU legislation? If so, under which conditions?

Preliminary Ruling: The Court confirmed the breaches of EU Law obligations in both cases and declared both Germany and the UK accountable to compensate the applicants. The Court, when mentioning "State" refers to every acts and omissions of all the organs of the State. In addition to this, the ECJ redefined the conditions of **Francovich:**

- The rule of EU Law infringed must be intended to confer right to individuals
- The breach must be sufficiently serious and **grave and manifest;** and
- There must be a causal link between the damage suffered by the individual and the failure to implement the Directive by the State.

Application: The Court extended the State liability to every breach of EU Law, not only Directives, and widened the definition of States that can be linked to the principle of emanation of State.

The main uncertainties about this new test lied on the second criterion of the seriousness of the breach.

General principle: The seriousness of the breach, as a condition for State liability, cannot be satisfied when the Directive itself is not sufficiently clear, precise and unequivocal.

R v HM Treasury, ex p British Telecommunications plc (Case

C-392/93) [1996] ECR I-1631

Facts: BT sought damages for losses it suffered following from the manner in which the UK implemented Directive 90/351, dealing with procurement procedures in the telecommunications sector. The UK claimed that the Directive itself was not clear which could lead to confusion. The interpretation made by the UK through its implementation measures was shared by several Member States. In addition to this, there was no case law about this Directive that could have directed the Member States.

Preliminary question before the Court: Can State liability is triggered when there is an ambiguity about the interpretation of the Directive itself?

Preliminary Ruling: The ECJ did not find the UK liable for breach of its EU Law obligations. In its judgement, the Court recognizes that the Directive itself is imprecisely worded and that the meaning given to it by the UK government was indeed possible.

Application: Usually, the condition about the seriousness of the breach implies a significant inconsistency between the Directive and the state of national Law. Indeed, the classification as sufficiently serious breach will vary depending on the nature of the act and the amount of discretion available to the Member States.

General principle: A failure to implement a Directive by the due date is in itself a serious breach entailing State liability.

Dillenkofer v Germany (Joined Cases C-178-9 & 188-190/94) [1996] ECR I-4845

Facts: This case was about a failure of Germany to implement the package holiday and package tours Directive 90/314 for a year and a half after the deadline. This had resulted in holidaymakers not being able to benefit from rights in the Directive designed to ensure that the money they paid for a package holiday would be refunded if the package organiser became insolvent. Thus, the two first conditions about the right and causality being satisfied, the question lied on the seriousness of the breach.

Preliminary question before the Court: Is the mere inaction from a Member States, one year and a half after the end of the deadline for implementation of a Directive, enough in itself to be considered as a serious breach?

Preliminary Ruling: The ECJ held that a failure to implement a Directive by its due date is, in itself, a serious breach entailing State liability.

Application: When verifying the conditions of **Brasserie du Pêcheur,** it is important to check if the due date of implementation of the Directive has already passed. In such a case, the State is more likely to be found liable for breach of EU Law obligations.

Chapter 5: Administrative Law of the EU

How could an individual challenge a law passed by EU institutions? What are the different procedures? This is one of the main practical questions raised by EU Law. There are two ways of invoking EU laws: firstly through domestic Courts system and secondly by means of direct action for annulment before the CJEU.

Judicial enforcement at the national level

When a European citizen strives to enforce an EU provision that confers him individual rights before a national Court, the domestic judge has two options. If the judge considers that the provision is or is not directly effective, she or he can decide to apply or to not apply it. However, this decision is subjected to the judicial review of the Court of Justice. If the Judge is not sure about the effect of the provision or its interpretation, she or he can then refer the case to the Court of Justice under Article 267 TFEU. However, these procedures only ensure that EU Law is merely applied within the Member States, they will not avail the claimant who seeks to challenge an act of EU Law itself.

Preliminary reference procedure: Article 267

Article 267 TFEU defines the regular preliminary reference as it follows:

"The Court of Justice of the European Union shall have jurisdiction to give preliminary rulings concerning:
(a) The interpretation of the Treaties;
(b) The validity and interpretation of acts of the institutions, bodies, offices or agencies of the Union;
Where such a question is raised before any court or tribunal of a Member State, that court or tribunal may, if it considers that a decision on the question is necessary to enable it to give judgment, request the Court to give a ruling thereon."

In other words, whenever a case has an EU law element, a national court may ask the CJ to give a preliminary decision on the matter before that national court delivers its final judgement. As a matter of fact, the national Court (and not the parties) decides which specific issues should be referred to the CJ. However, the preliminary reference is not a final decision from a higher Court that will bind the lower Court in a sort of hierarchical system. Indeed, the Treaty makes the CJ and national Courts equal partners; their relation is characterized by cooperation. This is why the preliminary reference is not a traditional appeal where the higher Court can replace the decision of the lower Court by its own. Actually, after a preliminary reference the domestic Court is free to follow or not to depart from the CJEU's ruling. The reference procedure promotes uniformity of interpretation throughout the Union, and allows the Court of Justice to develop a consistent European legal order.

Why do we have preliminary rulings?

Article 267 is one of the most important procedural provisions of the Treaty. It facilitates dialogue between national courts and the European Court of Justice and provides the meeting point between national and Community law. It serves three main functions:

(i)   It ensures uniform application of Community law by providing ruling on the interpretation of Community law;

(ii)   It ensures unity of the Community legal order and the coherence of the system of judicial remedies established by the Treaty, by entrusting to the Court of Justice the power to rule on the validity of Community acts that is disputed in national proceedings; and

(iii)   It facilitates an access to Justice by making clear that Community law is to be applied not only by the European Court of Justice but first at national courts level, thus enabling citizens to enforce their Community rights in national jurisdictions.

The preliminary reference system has led, in effect, to a transfer of powers at three levels, namely: (a) from governments of the Member States to the institutions of the Community; (b) from the executive and the legislative to the judiciary and; (c) from higher national courts to lower national courts.

Combining the mechanism of preliminary references with the doctrines of primacy and direct effect enables individuals and companies to assert Community rights in national courts. Thus individuals may use Community law both as a "shield" (to defend themselves from action by national authorities which infringes Community rights) and as a "sword" (to challenge national measures on the grounds of incompatibility with Community laws). Consequently, the preliminary ruling procedure provides an opportunity for individuals and, indeed, national courts to question governmental actions.

Requirement for sending up a Question

According to Article 267, the Court of Justice can only give preliminary rulings concerning the interpretation or the validity of EU Law. Since the validity of the Treaties is not questionable as they represent the constituent documents of the EU, only their interpretation can be at stake. Conversely, it cannot rule on matters of facts nor of national Law. For this reason, the questions referred to the Court are generally phrased in general terms.

In addition to this, jurisdiction must arise from actual dispute. The ECJ will not accept jurisdiction in disputes contrived to settle hypothetical points of law, see **Foglia v. Novello** (1 & 2) [1980]. Which domestic institutions have the power to refer under Article 267? The wording of the Treaty allows *"any court or tribunal of a Member State"* to make a preliminary reference. However, the Treaty does not clearly define what constitutes a "court or tribunal".

General principle: A Court or tribunal is established by law, independent, permanent, subjected to the rule of law and has an inter-party procedure based on a compulsory jurisdiction.

Garofalo v Ministero della Sanita (Cases C-69 to 79/96) [1997] ECR I-5603

Facts: This case was about specific training in general medical practice.

Preliminary question before the Court: What are the main features of a "court or tribunal" under Article 267?

Preliminary Ruling: The Court of Justice replied that to be recognised as a "court or tribunal" under Article 267; the body concerned should be established by law; permanent; its jurisdiction should be compulsory; its procedure should be inter-party; it should apply the rule of law; and it should be independent.

Application: This case was major for the interpretation of Article 267 and its clarification. If the nature of a domestic institution is uncertain as to belonging or not to the qualification of Court or tribunal, this test should be applied. The test merely illustrates the traditional conception of Courts and tribunals shared by the Member States.

Discretionary ground to refer

Finally, Article 267 makes a distinction between power and obligation to refer. On the one hand, under the second paragraph, the domestic Court has generally discretion as to whether or not make a referral to the Court of Justice. The text formulates: "*it considers that a decision on the question is necessary to enable it to give judgement*". It is also called permissive Jurisdiction.

General principle: National Courts may refer the question even where the CJEU has already ruled on a similar point as the court is not bound by precedent and may depart from previous decisions.

Cases 28-30/62 *Da Costa en Schaake NV v. Nederlande Belastingadministratie* [1963] ECR 31, [1963] CMLR 224

Facts: Da Costa, a Dutch company, imported some products from Germany and was taxed at the boarder. This taxation contravened with EU Law.

Preliminary question before the Court: Can a national Court make an Article 267 preliminary reference on a question already answered by the CJEU?

Preliminary Ruling: In Costs en Shaake, the court calculated that if a matter had been previously decided and clarified there was no need for duplication of effort. However, it is not hard to envisage where a previously decided case may need correction, thus using it as guidance would be a false economy.

Application: When a question has already be answered, the Court of Justice may decide to apply its same previous ruling, unless it wants to change its position on the issue. Nevertheless, nothing precludes domestic Courts to make new preliminary references on a question that has already be treated by the Court. For instance, they will do it if they consider that a previous CJ's decision is ill founded. The Court can depart from its precedent rulings in recognition of new facts which may cast doubt on previous rulings; ECJ is very willing to admit errors.

Furthermore, the right of a lower court to refer is not fettered by the decisions of a higher court. Even in cases where a higher court has ruled on a matter and referred it back to the lower court, the latter may still make an Article 267 referral: Cases 146/73 and 166/73 *Rheinmulen-Düsseldorf* v. *Einfuhr- und Vorratsstelle für Getreide und Futtermittel* [1974] ECR 139,33, [1974] 1 CMLR 523

Mandatory ground to refer

However, on the other hand, the third paragraph of Article 267 transforms the power to refer into an obligation when there is no national remedy available under national law against the potential decision of the domestic Court. It is also called mandatory jurisdiction. This obligation concerns the highest appeal court in the land, which decisions are not subjected to appeals, for instance the UK Supreme Court or *Conseil d'Etat* in France.

General principle: The obligation to refer is waived when (i) the question is not relevant to the case at stake, (ii) the question has previously been answered, (iii) the answer is so obvious that it belongs to *acte clair*.

Srl CILFIT v Ministry of Health (Case 283/81) [1982] ECR 3415

Facts: Since the adoption of the Italian Law n° 30 of January'68, textile firms had paid by way of fixed health inspection levy a certain amount of wool, until the application of law n°1239 of December'70. The last mentioned law amended the levy, but textile firms had been required to pay a sum of the levy. Tribunal di Roma dismissed the plaintiffs' appeal in October'76. They argued that Law n° 1968 was inapplicable because Regulation (EEC) n° 827/68 was adopted.

Preliminary question before the Court: When is it an obligation for national Courts to make a reference for preliminary ruling to the CJEU?

Preliminary Ruling: The Court first recalls that it is generally for the national court to decide whether a question of EU law needs answering necessarily in order for it to provide a judgment. However, Courts and Tribunals against whose decisions there is no judicial remedy under national law to refer to the court every question of interpretation raised before them are bound to make a preliminary reference under Article 267(3).

Nevertheless, the Court of Justice added that here will be no obligation to refer if:

- The question it not relevant to the outcome of the national case
- The question, or a materially similar question, has previously been answered by the Court of Justice of the European Union.
- The answer is so obvious as to leave no scope for any reasonable doubt over the answer. This last possibility is the *acte clair* doctrine, mentioned for the first time in this case. The Court explained it as it follows: "*the correct application of Community law may be so obvious as to leave no scope for any reasonable doubt as to the manner in which the question raised is to be resolved*".

Effect of preliminary rulings

Once the preliminary reference is made, the Court of Justice gives its decision. Then, that decision is handed down to the national

Court which is not bound to apply the CJEU's position. However, if it does apply the decision of the CJ, it is bound by that ruling, according to the case **Milch-Fett und Eierkontor** (Case 29/68) [1969] ECR 165. A CJ's decision on a preliminary reference is applicable to all the national Courts of the Member States until any new preliminary reference is made. Thus the EU has opted for the simplest method of enforcement of the decisions of its Court of Justice. Rather than creating a federalist system with different levels of Courts, the founding Treaties ensure that the decisions of the CJEU are enforced domestically. This system relies on the main principles of EU Law enforceability enshrined by the Court of Justice: supremacy and direct effect. It ensures that general compliance with EU rules is facilitated and enhanced.

Enforcement at the EU level

Liability of national governments: Articles 258 and 259 TFEU

The principle of liability (see Chapter 4), provides individual with a remedy against governments of Member States for breach of EU Law. However, these actions are not only reserved to individuals suffering from the breach; State liability can also be initiated at the European level by the Commission (Article 258) or by other Member States (Article 259).

Article 258 TFEU:

"If the Commission considers that a Member State has failed to fulfil an obligation under the Treaties, it shall deliver a reasoned opinion on the matter after giving the State concerned the opportunity to submit its observations.
If the State concerned does not comply with the opinion within the period laid down by the Commission, the latter may bring the matter before the Court of Justice of the European Union."

Article 259 TFEU:

"A Member State which considers that another Member State has failed to fulfil an obligation under the Treaties may bring the

matter before the Court of Justice of the European Union.

Before a Member State brings an action against another Member State for an alleged infringement of an obligation under the Treaties, it shall bring the matter before the Commission.

The Commission shall deliver a reasoned opinion after each of the States concerned has been given the opportunity to submit its own case and its observations on the other party's case both orally and in writing.

If the Commission has not delivered an opinion within three months of the date on which the matter was brought before it, the absence of such opinion shall not prevent the matter from being brought before the Court."

The Commission, also known as the "Watchdog of the treaties", is the final mediator representing the Union before the case goes to the Court. In practice, before launching the formal procedure, the Commission holds a range of investigations on factual and legal matters. Then the Commission usually directs informal negotiations with the Member State presumed to have breached EU Law. The Commission will always try, at first, to find amicable resolution of violations. Therefore, when a case of breach of EU Law reaches the point of a reasoned opinion, it is usually that the State presumed to be in breach is not prepared to rectify the situation.

- The Commission's intervention: reasoned opinions

A reasoned opinion of the Commission is formally records a violation committed by a Member State. If the case goes to the Court, this will help the preparation of the hearing. Partly by designating the issues raised before the Court and partly by helping the Member State to construct its argument. This reasoned opinion is thoroughly prepared as it will have a crucial important in the further legal proceedings. Indeed, the issues answered by the Court depend on the reasoned opinion. Therefore, the Commission will not be entitled to raise new allegations later before the Court, see **Commission v Italy** (Case 166/82) [1984] ECR 459. In its opinion, the Commission sets a time limit for the

State to end the violation. This time has to be passed before the Commission can refer the case to the Court.

General principle: The time limit to end the violation should be reasonable.

Commission v Belgium (Case 293/85) [1988] ECR 305)
Facts: A violation of EU Law from the Belgian State resulted on a discriminatory rule in the sector of education that differentiated between European according to their nationalities.
The Commission, in a notification to Belgium, set a time limit of eight days.
Preliminary Ruling: The Court declared that the time limit set by the Commission has to be reasonable. Indeed, within eight days, it is very difficult for the Member State to proceed to the necessary modifications for the compliance with EU Law. Generally, reforming an act of Parliament takes at least several weeks. The Court resumed its decision as it follows: "*where the time-limits set are unreasonable, the commission cannot prevent its application from being declared inadmissible by asserting that the time-limits laid down were not absolute and that consequently replies given after their expiry would have been accepted*".
Application: This decision implies that the time limit set by the Commission should not be too short. We can presume from the reasoning of the Court that it has to be of at least few months.
In addition to this, by using the term "reasonable" the Court also prevents the Commission to set too long time limits. For instance, a time limit of two years in a reasoned opinion would be likely to be declared unreasonable.

- The judicial involvement of the CJEU in enforcement actions

Under this procedure, the Court has full competence to consider the issues raised by the Commission. Unlike the preliminary reference, the Court of Justice delivers a judgement that applies to the facts in enforcement actions.

General principle: The Commission can only bring cases of

Member States that did not end the breach within the time limit. If the Member State complies after the time limit but before the judgement of the Court, the Court is still competent.

Commission v Italy (Pork Imports) (Case 7/61) [1961] ECR 317

Facts: Italy suspended the import of Pork from certain other Member States. These measures were in breach of competition Law. After a reasoned opinion delivered by the Commission, Italy did not terminate the breach within the time limit. However, it finally followed the Commission's opinion by terminating the breach just before the judgement of the Court.

Preliminary Ruling: The Court is competent to rule on the breach of EU Law committed by Italy, as far as the Member State did not comply with the reasoned opinion within the time limit, regardless whether or not it has terminated the breach since then.

"In the case of an action under the second paragraph of article 169 of the eec treaty, it is for the court to say whether the failure has occurred, without having to examine whether, subsequent to the bringing of the action, the state in question took the measures necessary to bring the infringement to an end".

Application: The Court is strengthening the requirement of compliance with the reasoned opinions of the Commission within the time limit. It prevents Member States to wait for years before taking measure to comply with EU Law.

If the Court, in its judgement, finds the Member State to be in breach with EU Law, this latter has to take every necessary measure to comply with it. Under article 279 TFEU, the Court can issue an interim measure. An interim measure is close in nature to English interlocutory injunctions. Interim measures are usually ordered to ensure that none of the interests of the parties to the litigation are harmed. These interim measures will have similar effects to the expected judgment on the merits.

General principle: The Court can order an interim measure only if there is an urgent need to avoid irreparable damages.

Commission v Germany (Road Tax) (Case C-195/90 R), [1990] ECR I-3351

Facts: The case involved a breach of EU Law resulting of the imposition of road tax. In its reasoned opinion, the Commission asked the Court to take an interim measure to stop the loss suffered by thousands of vehicles illegally taxed.

Preliminary Ruling: Before issuing such a measure, the Court will consider three factors. First, it will consider the likelihood of the main proceeding being successful – no order will be made if the claim in the main action is manifestly unfounded. Secondly, it must be shown that the need for the order is urgent. Thirdly, the Commission will normally be required to demonstrate that irreparable damage to the EU's interests will occur if the order is not given.

The Court explained the process as it follows:

"The urgency of an application for interim measures, as referred to in Article 83(2) of the Rules of Procedure, must be assessed in relation to the necessity for an order granting relief in order to prevent serious and irreparable damage by the immediate application of the measure which is the subject of the main proceedings. In principle, pecuniary damage is not to be regarded as irreparable".

Once the judgement of the Court is delivered, if the breach is still lasting, the Commission step back in the procedure. It will give a second reasoned opinion recording the non-compliance with the CJEU's judgement.

According to article 260 TFEU, the Commission may then advise the Court on a pecuniary penalty for breach of EU Law. This provision has been introduced in 2002 to secure the practical enforceability of EU Law. It is usually quite efficient. As a matter of fact, these penalties are calculated by day of non-compliance (they can be fixed at 10,000 euros a day for instance).

- Defences

A defense, available to the Member State that is in breach, permits to escape liability by justifying the wrongful act by a lawful excuse.

General principle: Administrative or practical difficulties are not usually accepted as a valid defense to a breach of EU Law.

Commission v Belgium (Case C-42/89) 1990
Facts: This defence was used by the Belgian Government as an excuse for not complying with a Community Directive on the quality of drinking water. The Belgian Government pleaded that the complexity of construction works at the water station in a Belgian town meant that the authorities needed a longer time to comply with the European norm. Four years after the time line of compliance set by the Commission, Belgium had not taken any measure to comply with it.
Preliminary Ruling: The pleading of administrative or practical difficulties are not recognized as a valid defense. The Court held: *"Member State may not plead practical or administrative difficulties in order to justify non-compliance with the obligations and time-limits laid down in Community directives. The same holds true of financial difficulties, which it is for the Member States to overcome by adopting appropriate measures"*.
Application: The Court has overridden the practical argument raised by the Member States to escape liability after having breached EU Law.

General principle: Force majeure is a valid defense justifying a breach of EU Law if the Member State can prove the occurrence of an extraordinary event that was beyond its control.

Commission v Italy (Case 101/84) 1985
Facts: The Italian government failed to compile statistical returns according to Community Directive 78/546. Therefore, Italy was in breach of EU law. However, the Italian government had a very strong excuse: the Italian Data Processing Centre had suffered a bomb attack in 1978 and its vehicle register had been destroyed.
Preliminary Ruling: The Court accepted the argument, confirming in its judgement that *"A member state which has encountered momentarily insurmountable difficulties may plead*

force majeure to justify its failure to comply with its obligations imposed by a community directive".

Application: Force Majeure is an accepted but rarely used defence under EU law. It refers to an extraordinary event or circumstance beyond the control of a Member State, such as a war, strike, riot, crime, or an event described by the legal term "act of God" (such as flooding, earthquake, or volcanic eruption), which prevents that Member State from fulfilling their obligations under EU law.

Actions for Annulment and Judicial Review of EU Law: Article 263TFEU

The Court of Justice is also competent regarding the claims challenging acts of the EU itself. Most of the decisions, which we have examined, were brought before the Court under the Article 267 preliminary ruling procedure. As we have seen, this enables the Court to become involved in private disputes. However, the Court also has an important public law function, which can be equated with the judicial review process in English Law under which the High Court can review the legitimacy of actions taken by the State or agencies of the State. Similarly, the ECJ is empowered, under the Treaties, to review the legitimacy of the actions of the EC institutions.

Challenges of EU acts might come before the Court through two different procedures. A challenge can be made indirectly when a national Court asks the Court of Justice to give a preliminary ruling about the validity of a particular provision. In this case, a regular preliminary reference is made under article 267. Nevertheless, a challenge can be brought directly before the Court, without having to wait for a specific case related to the impugned act, via the procedure identified by Article 263. This is what we are going to focus on for the next sections.

- Reviewable acts

Article 263 TFEU stipulates that:

"The Court of Justice of the European Union shall review the legality of legislative acts, of acts of the Council, of the Commission and of the European Central Bank, other than recommendations and opinions, and of acts of the European Parliament and of the European Council intended to produce legal effects vis-à-vis third parties. It shall also review the legality of acts of bodies, offices or agencies of the Union intended to produce legal effects vis-à-vis third parties."

Article 263 clearly covers all binding legislative acts but expressly excludes non-binding Recommendations and Opinions. However, certain acts fall into a grey area in that, although they are not legislative, they still have legal consequences. Such acts may still be subject to review in certain circumstances.

General principle: The Court can only review acts having a binding effect or acts that bring any distinct change in the legal position of the applicant.

International Business Machines Corporation v. Commission [1981] ECR 2639

Facts: The Commission sent a letter to IBM that it was bringing proceedings for abusing a dominant position, under EU competition law, inviting it to put a case. IBM sought to challenge the letter in judicial review proceedings, and the question was whether the letter was a reviewable act.

Preliminary Ruling: The Court held that *"... any measure the legal effects of which are binding on, and capable of affecting the legal interests of, the applicant by bringing about distinct change to his legal position is an act or decision which may be subject to an action under Article 173 [263 TFEU] for a declaration that it is void ... measures of purely preparatory character may not themselves be subject to application."*

A mere letter from the Commission without any legal effect, which main purpose was to inform the applicant, could not be reviewed under article 263.

Application: The court upheld that the key test in this situation was to know whether or not the act or decision has brought about any distinct change "in the legal position of the applicant".

Additionally, it is important to remind that the proceedings to challenge an act shall be instituted within two months after the act has been published. This is a traditional requirement in administrative Law that ensures a threshold for legal certainty. In this respect, Article 263 (6) provides:

"The proceedings provided for in this Article shall be instituted within two months of the publication of the measure, or of its notification to the plaintiff, or, in the absence thereof, of the day on which it came to the knowledge of the latter, as the case may be".

- Standing to contest legality of EU Acts

In judicial review proceedings, one of the most difficult issues concerns *locus standi*; does an individual have a sufficient interest in the matter to deserve standing to bring proceedings? Article 263 TFEU grants standing to so-called "privileged" applicants. This allows actions to contest the legality of EU acts to be brought by a Member State, the European Parliament, the Council or the Commission. The Article also grants standing to "non-privileged" applicants. In practice, "non-privileged" applicants are natural or legal persons. They can be companies, individuals, a third State, a regional government of a Member State etc.

(i) Standing: Privileged Applicants

According to Article 263(2) the Member States, the Council and the Commission or the European Parliament have automatic standing. It means that they never have to prove an interest to have standing.
The main evolution in the hierarchy of applicants came from the European Parliament. At first, it was denied access to challenge EU acts, then it became a semi-prvileged applicant with the Maastricht Treaty in 1992 before passing to privileged applicants in 2001 when the Nice Treaty was signed. However, this upgrade in the Parliament status came along with the progressive recognition of its crucial role in the legislative process.

The term 'Member States' only encompasses national governments; thus a regional or local authority does not have automatic standing, see Comunidad Autonoma de Cantabra v. Council of the EU [1999] 3 CMLR 656.

Standing: Semi-privileged Applicants

Semi-privileged applicants are EU institutions or bodies that are privileged compared to ordinary applicants but still have to prove an interest to have standing. These applicants have to prove that they are acting to protect their prerogatives. They are for example the European Central Bank or the Court of Auditors.

Standing: Non-privileged Applicants

The standing rights of other private individuals or other legal persons such as companies under Article 263(4) have given rise to the greatest difficulties. Ultimately, the addressee of a decision has standing; his interest in the matter is obvious. However, applicants, other than the addressee, might acquire standing in the following situations.

(i) The act contested is not specifically addressed to the applicant but nevertheless is of direct and individual concern to them

Article 263(4) also refers to the fact that other persons may have standing where the decision is of "direct and individual" concern to them. Firstly, the applicant must show that the act is of direct concern to them.

General principle: The act itself, and not its implementation by the addressee, should directly affect the applicant in its legal position.

NV International Fruit Company v Commission (Case 41-44/70) [1971] ECR 411
Facts: This case involved International Fruit Company, a private company that applied to the Produktschap voor Groenten en Fruit, the Netherlands Agency hereinafter referred to as 'the PGF', for

import certificates for eating apples from third countries. The PGF replied that on the basis of Regulations Nos 459/70, 565/70 and 686/70 'the application must be rejected'.

In proceedings brought on 5 August 1970 (Joined Cases 41 to 44/70) those firms made applications to the Court for the annulment of the Community measures which formed the basis of the rejection by the PGF.

If the applicants were not the addressees of the act contested, they were affected by it.

Preliminary question before the Court: Under which conditions, a non-privileged applicant, which is not the specific addressee of the act, can claim for a judicial review under EU Law?

Preliminary Ruling: In its judgement, the Court developed the first criterion requiring that the applicant must show that the act is of direct concern to them. The Court of Justice interpreted as it follows: the act must affect the legal position of the applicant and must do so directly without leaving the addressee any discretion as to how it is to be implemented.

Application: In other words, any implementation of the act by the addressee must be purely automatic so that it is the EU act itself rather than the implementation of the act by the addressee which can be said to have affected the applicant's legal position.

Secondly, the act must be of individual concern to the applicant. In the leading case of Plaumann, the ECJ formulated a so called "closed category test" for determining whether a person, other than the addressee of a decision, should be afforded *locus standi* in the matter.

General principle: The applicant must prove that the act affected him as much as a person directly addressed would have been affected.

Plaumann & Co v. Commission [1963] ECR 95
Facts: Clementines were imported from non-EU countries on which there was a common customs tariff, (CCT), this was set at 13%. The German government sought permission to suspend this

customs duty form the Commission. This permission to suspend CCT on clementines was refused, and addressed to the German Government. This matter was of great importance to clemintine importers; they had the problem of challenging the Commission because the decision was not addressed to them. They argued that they were closely affected by the decision, hence they deserved standing.

Preliminary question before the Court: Under Article 263(4) how can an applicant, that is not the addressee of a contested act, be "individually concerned" by this act?

Preliminary Ruling: The Court held that the applicant has to be very closely connected to the decision and should be distinguished from the general public in the same way that the addressee is. The following paragraph illustrates this solution: *"...to establish individual concern the applicant must show that the measure affects him by reason of certain attributes peculiar to him or by reason of circumstances that differentiate him from all other persons just as in the case of the persons directly addressed"*.

In the particular situation of the company Plaumann, the Court considered that the "closed category test" was not satisfied. The company was not part of a closed group as far as anybody could join the trade.

Application: The Court has made it very difficult to satisfy this criterion. Basically, the applicant has to prove that he was affected by the act as a *de facto* addressee.

General principle: The test devised in Plaumann has been notoriously difficult to satisfy, except in exceptional situations. Therefore, many criticisims arose as to present a large number of EU acts as practically immune. A recent application of these two criteria shows how restrictive both the direct concern and the individual concern requirements can be.

Inuit v European Parliament and Council (Case T-18/10) [2011] ECR II-5599 and the appeal in Grand Chamber Inuit v European Parliament and Council (Case C-583/11P) [2013] ECR I-0000

Facts: Members of the Inuit community who were involved in the hunting and trapping of seals and certain organisations which represented their interests had sought to bring an action for the annulment of Regulation 1007/2009 which, with some narrow exceptions, banned seal products from being placed on the European internal market.

Preliminary question before the Court: Can a provision, applying equally to every traders of an open market, affect directly and individually some actors in this market?

Preliminary Ruling: The Court of justice held that the ban was expressed in a general manner and capable of applying equally to any trader who is covered by the Regulation. There was nothing to distinguish these four applicants from any other trader who places seal products on the market. The Court explained its judgement by mentioning that nothing distinguished the applicants from the general public as a directly addressed person would have been.

Application: In this recent case, the Court strictly applies the restrictive approach presented earlier in **International Fruit Company** and **Plaumann**.

Thus, an applicant, other than the addressee, wishing to subject an EU act to judicial review, has to show exceptional circumstances of close connection with the act contested as if he would if we was directly addressed by the act.

(ii) The act contested is decisions "in the form of a regulation" which is direct concern to the applicant and does not entail implementing measures

In order to improve the access of non-privileged applicant to judicial review, the Treaty of Lisbon, under Article 263(4) TFEU, intrduced another category of act that seems to be easier to challenge. It only applies to EU binding measures that do not need implementation: Regulations and Decisions. Regulation and decisions are both secondary types of legislation. The basic distinction is that Regulations are generally applicable, whereas Decisions are addressed to specific parties. These types of acts are also known as decisions "in the form of a regulation".

General principle: Under article 263(4), the only criterion for a non-privileged applicant to challenge a regulatory act is to prove that he was directly concerned.

Microban International Ltd v Commission (Case T-262/10) [2011]
Facts: Microban was a manufacturer of additive antibacterial affected by a ban of the Commission from being used in certain materials.

Microban was directly affected by the regulatory measure as far as it changed its legal position, rendering impossible for this company to sell its main product in Europe.

However, Microban could not show that it had been individually affected by the measure, as there was many other manufacturers in the market, it failed to prove that it belonged to a closed category particularly affected by the decision.

Preliminary question before the Court: Is it sufficient, under article 263(4), for a non-privileged applicant to show that he was directly affected by a regulatory act to acquire standing to challenge it?

Preliminary Ruling: The challenge was upheld by the General Court to be admissible and Microban was able to obtain an annulment of the Commission's ban. The admissibility of a challenge to such regulatory acts is only subject to the direct concern requirement, no need to satisfy the individual concern requirement.

Application: At first, the test in this category of acts appears to be way more flexible than in **Inuit**. If the act has a regulatory nature (a Regulation or a Decision), it is important to always advice the applicant to try to challenge the act under Article 263 (4).

However, the Court distinguished regulatory acts from legislative acts.

General principle: Decisions "in the form of a regulation" under Article 263(4) do not encompass acts that have been adopted using the ordinary legislative procedure.

Grand Chamber Inuit v European Parliament and Council (Case C-583/11P) [2013] ECR I-0000

Facts: It will be recalled that this case involved an action for annulment of Regulation 1007/2009 which prohibited seal products from being placed on the European internal market. The Regulation challenged had been adopted via the ordinary legislative procedure before; *inter alia,* the European Parliament. The General Court, in a decision of 2011, held that a regulatory act had to be distinguished from a legislative act.

Preliminary question before the Court: Can a Regulation, adopted via the ordinary legislative procedure, be classified as a "regulatory act" under Article 263(4)?

Preliminary Ruling: The Court upheld the decision adopted by the General Court. An act which adopted by using the ordinary legislative procedure in the European Parliament is a legislative act and not a regulatory act. The court of Justice justified this solution as it follows: *"The new standing rule was meant to maintain a restrictive approach in relation to actions by individuals against legislative acts".*

Application: It is important to verify that the challenged Regulation or Decision was not adopted under the ordinary legislative procedure otherwise it will be classified as a legislative act. This decision reduces significantly the ambit of acts that can be challenged under Article 263 (4).

- Plea for illegality: an additional form of challenge in an annulment action

Article 277 TFEU provides that:

"Notwithstanding the expiry of the period laid down in Article 263, sixth paragraph, any party may, in proceedings in which an act of general application adopted by an institution, body, office or agency of the Union is at issue, plead the grounds specified in Article 263, second paragraph, in order to invoke before the Court of Justice of the European Union the inapplicability of that act."

In other words, an act can still be challenged after the 2 months deadline following its publication, on a case by case basis. This implies that one of the parties, where an act is at stake in a particular case, invokes the inaplicability of the latter, regardless to the date of publication of this act. Article 277 does not provide for an independent cause of action, it is an additional form of challenge of acts under an annulment action (Article 263). However, plea for illegality is restricted by two limits. Firstly, it cannot be used where the parties already challenged it elswhere before a Court and secondly it also cannot be used where the parties have had the opportunity to challenge the act but did not take up that opportunity.

- **The grounds of review**

Once a person has established standing in a matter, she or he must establish the ground upon which the measure can be challenged. Four specific grounds are set out in Article 263:

- Lack of Competence;
- Infringement of an Essential Procedural requirement;
- Infringement of the Treaty or any rule of law relating to its application; and
  - Misuse of power.

Note that there may be a substantial overlap between the different grounds and it is usual to plead most, or all of them, in the alternative.

(i) Lack of competence

EU Instituions have to exercice the powers allocated to them by the treaties, and cannot assume new ones. Therefore, every measure taken by an institution has to be based on a provision of the treaties allowing it. Otherwise, the institution is acting *ultra vires*; beyond the scope of its prerogatives. In practice, it is very difficult to challenge EU acts on this ground due to the broad and purposive manner in which the Treaties are interpreted by the Court of Justice. This approach is based on the Unionist doctrine of the implied powers. In this respect, the TFEU itself contains provisions that can be interpreted very widely to extend the competences of the institutions. Article 352(1) provides that:

"If action by the Union should prove necessary, within the framework of the policies defined in the Treaties, to attain one of the objectives set out in the Treaties, and the Treaties have not provided the necessary powers, the Council, acting unanimously on a proposal from the Commission and after obtaining the consent of the European Parliament, shall adopt the appropriate measures. Where the measures in question are adopted by the Council in accordance with a special legislative procedure, it shall also act unanimously on a proposal from the Commission and after obtaining the consent of the European Parliament".

This provision allows the Council to basically create new powers for the institutions in order to meet the Treaty objectives. One of the few cases successfully in which lack of competence challenge was successful is **France v Commission** (Case C-327/91).

General principle: An act is void for lack of competence if it was obviously taken by the wrong EU institution.

France v Commission (Case C-327/91)
Facts: The Commission had concluded an agreement with the United States to lessen the possibility of conflict on the application of competition rules. If the founding treaties say that the Commission can negotiate and represent the European Union internationally under Article 260 TFEU, the Treaty also provides that such agreement have to be formally concluded by the Council.
Preliminary question before the Court: The question was to know whether or not an act of the Commission taken under the prerogatives of the Council, could be challenged for lack of competence?
Preliminary Ruling: The Court held that the action in annulment was admissible for lack of competence: *"In order for an action to be admissible under the first paragraph of Article 173 of the Treaty, the contested act must be an act of an institution which produces legal effects. Since it is apparent from the actual*

wording of an agreement concluded by the Commission with a non-member country that that agreement is intended to produce legal effects, the act whereby the Commission sought to conclude the agreement must be susceptible to an action for annulment". The CJEU then explained why the Commission was lacking competence to adopt the decision: *"Even though the Commission has the power, pursuant to Article 89 of the Treaty and Regulations Nos 17 and 4064/89, to take individual decisions applying the rules of competition, that does not give it the power to conclude an international agreement with a non-member country in that field. That internal power is not such as to alter the division of powers between the Community institutions with regard to the conclusion of international agreements, which is determined by Article 228 of the Treaty".*

Application: Even though the approach on the ground of lack of competence for challenging acts appears to be very restricted, the Court might acknowledge some very obvious situations of institutions acting *ultra vires*.

A challenge for lack of competence is more commonly used in the particular situation of an EU institution having a valid legal basis to adopt a decision but actually acting upon another one (see **Commission v Council (Re Titanium Dioxide Waste)** (Case C-300/89)).

(ii) Infringement of an essential procedural requirement

In this matter, EU Law has been strongly inspired by the Law of its Member States. Infringement of an essential procedural requirement is a very popular ground for judicial review. Its equivalent in English Law would be *procedural ultra vires*. It comprises breaches of formal requirements contained in the Treaty and informal rules of fairness that are required by the general principles of EU Law as discussed below.

Right to be heard

The right to be heard implies that the addressee of a decision has a right to present an argument before the decision is taken. It usually also includes the right to have notice of the nature of the case and reasonable time to respond to it. It is a fundamental right enshrined by Article 41 of the Charter of Fundamental Rights of the European Union. It is a bare minimum of fairness that applies regardless of whether it is specified in a Treaty article, regulation, directive or decision.

Duty to consult

Under the principle of cooperation of the institutions and their scrutiny, several procedures imply the consultation of an institution before the adoption of a decision by another one.

General principle: Where a measure provides for consultation, failure to do so will amount to an infringement of an essential procedural requirement.

Roquette Freres SA v. Council [1980] ECR 3333
Facts: The applicant complained the European Parliament had not been consulted on a regulation, in accordance with the procedure laid down in the Treaty, thus a breach of procedural requirement. The council argued that it had in fact asked the parliament for its opinion; however it had been late in responding.
Preliminary Ruling: The CJEU upheld that the decision was void for breach of the duty to consult. According to the Court, the consultation requirement, was a fundamental democratic principle, thus it was not a mere formality but rather a crucial function and a ground for voiding the regulation.

However, the infringement will only be acknowledged if the duty is expressly mentioned in a Treaty article or in any EU norm (see **Atlanta** (Case C-104/97)). In this sense, the Court would not accept an institutional customs as a valid duty to consult for example.

Duty to give reasons

Article 296 TFEU presents the most important procedural requirement. It involves that secondary legislation must state the reasons why the decision is adopted.

General principle: Where from the nature and the context of a decision stems an obligation to give reasons, failure to do so will amount to an infringement of an essential procedural requirement.

Eugenio Branco Ld v Commission (Case T-85/94) 1998
Facts: This case dealt with Commission decisions withdrawing approval or partial support of projects financed by the European Social Fund. The Commission did not provide any reasons for having adopted this decision. Besides the obligation imposed by Article 296 TFEU, there was also a breach of Article 6(1), Regulation 2950/83 which stated that before deciding to suspend reduce or withdraw financial aid, the Commission had to give the relevant Member State the opportunity to comment.
Preliminary question before the Court: In which situations decisions have to be jointly notified with their reasons to be valid?
Preliminary Ruling: The Court held that the extent of the obligation to give reasons will depend on the nature and context of the measure at stake. The CJEU then reminded the importance of this duty: *"According to a consistent line of case law, the purpose of the obligation to state reasons on which an individual decision is based is to entitle the Community judicature to review the legality of the decision and to provide the person concerned with sufficient information to make it possible to ascertain whether the decision is well founded or whether it is vitiated by a defect which may permit its legality to be contested. The extent of that obligation depends on the nature of the measure in question and on the context in which it was adopted".*
Application: The test to identify whether or not the institution adopting the decision has a duty to give reasons depends on broad concepts that leave a certain uncertainty about their application.

(iii) Infringement of the Treaty or any rule relating to its application

The broad nature of the terminology of this ground allowed the Court of Justice to develop it extensively with a margin of interpretation. It is an area with an abundance of case law that progressively recognized Human Rights, the principle of proportionality or the principle of legal certainty as valid grounds.

Fundamental rights

If a decision is adopted while breaching the fundamental rights of EU citizens, gathered in the European Charter for Fundamental Rights, it will obviously be void for infringement of the Treaty, as far as the Charter is considered as being part of the treaties having a constitutional significance.

However Member State legal systems and international law recognise that protection of fundamental rights may not be absolute at all times. Therefore, it would give rise to certain exceptions.

Proportionality

Article 5 of the TEU provides that the Union shall only act within the powers conferred on it by the Treaty and actions shall not go beyond what is necessary to achieve the objectives of the Treaty. It is referred to as the principle of proportionality. This ground can be used to challenge an act of the European institutions.

General principle: The proportionality of a measure has to be assessed by taking into consideration its necessity, suitability and reasonableness.

Germany v European Parliament and Council (Case C-233/94)
Facts: The case involved a Directive about deposit-guarantee schemes. Germany brought an action under Article 173 of the EC Treaty for annulment of Directive 94/19/EC of the European Parliament and of the Council of 30 May 1994. Germany argued that the decision was void for breaching the proportionality principle, the Union allegedly acted beyond its powers allocated by the treaties.
Preliminary Ruling: The Court devised a test to establish whether a measure is proportionate based on three questions: (a)

was the measure suitable to achieve the desired end; (b) was it necessary to achieve the desired end; and (c) whether the measure imposed a burden on the individual that was excessive in relation to the objective to be achieved.

Application: In practice, the Court will usually assess if the measure is appropriate to its legitimate aim. The test presented only serves as flexible guideline.

Legal certainty

The principle of Legal Certainty comes as a part of the EU commitment to the Rule of Law. For example, one of its implementation is the prohibition of retrospectivity: no rule should apply retrospectively to a situation that occurred prior to the date on which any given rule was promulgated. Another aspect of legal certainty is legitimate expectations. It is closely connected to the notion of "good faith".

General principle: Any individual who was given precise assurances by the Administration of the Union is entitled to challenge a subsequent decision under a breach of legitimate expectations.

Efisol SA v Commission of the European Communities 1996 (Case T- 336/94)

Facts: The case involved a Regulation on environmental law that was suddenly repealed. The applicant claimed that the decision was void for having created legitimate expectations.

Preliminary Ruling: The court upheld that *"any individual who is in a situation in which it is apparent that the Community administration, by giving him precise assurances, has led him to entertain justifiable expectations.* However, the Court of Justice limited this solution as it follows: *"A legitimate expectation cannot arise from conduct on the part of a Community institution which is inconsistent with Community rules".*

Application: If the test appears to be very broad considering the wording of the Court, it is however restricted in practice. The assurances given by the Administration have to be express and very clear. Consequently, the Administration will rarely give such precise statement. It permits to avoid the floodgate phenomenon.

Equality and non-discrimination

Any decision of the EU institutions promoting inequality or discrimination can be judicially reviewed. Equality and non-discrimination are part of the most important values of the Union. These principles can be found in several articles of the TFEU (Article 18 on the principle of non-discrimination, 40 and 110 specifically on discrimination in consummation and taxation and 157 on equal pay between men and women). However, these principles are also mentioned by several sources of secondary legislation, see for instance the following Directives:

- Gender and Services Directive (GSD), Council Directive 2004
- Employment Equality Directive (EED), Council Directive 2000
- Racial Equality Directive (RED), Council Directive 2000
- Recast Equal Treatment Directive (Recast ETD), Directive 2006

Misuse of power

The fourth ground for an action in annulment under article 263 comes from French administrative Law. Misuse of power means that a measure has been adopted for a purpose other than those for which it was intended. However, the conditions devised by the Court are quite difficult to satisfy. In this respect, only few cases have successfully proven misuse of power.

General principle: The applicant has to show "objective, relevant and consistent indications of misuse of power".

An application of this test can be found in the case **Gutmann v Commission** (Cases 18 and 35/65).

- Actions for failure to act: Article 265

The EU acts can be challenged before the Court of justice they the institution are exceeding their powers under 263. In addition to this, the Court can also review the omissions of the institutions. This relates to the failures of the institutions to carry out the duties imposed on them by the Treaty or some other provision having legal effect. Article 265 TFEU regulates the actions for failure to act:

"Should the European Parliament, the European Council, the Council, the Commission or the European Central Bank, in infringement of the Treaties, fail to act, the Member States and the other institutions of the Union may bring an action before the Court of Justice of the European Union to have the infringement established. This Article shall apply, under the same conditions, to bodies, offices and agencies of the Union which fail to act.
The action shall be admissible only if the institution, body, office or agency concerned has first been called upon to act. If, within two months of being so called upon, the institution, body, office or agency concerned has not defined its position, the action may be brought within a further period of two months.
Any natural or legal person may, under the conditions laid down in the preceding paragraphs, complain to the Court that an institution, body, office or agency of the Union has failed to address to that person any act other than a recommendation or an opinion".

General principle: The omission of an institution to adopt a decision on a matter on which it should constitutes a failure to act.

Ladbroke Racing (Deutschland) GmbH v Commission (Case T-74/92) 13 May 1993
Facts: Some of the provisions within the Treaty contain a clear obligation for the institutions to act, as for instance Article 105 TFEU does in relation to breaches of Articles 101 and 102.
Ladbroke had complained to the Commission about the denial of access for the televising of horse racing, alleging breach of Articles 101 and 102 by the German and French companies in the horse racing and communications business. After deciding to investigate the complaint in 1990, by 1992, the Commission had

still not defined its position. The applicant argued that the fact that he did not get any reply to his request on a complaint constituted a failure to act from the Commission

Preliminary question before the Court: Is a lack of decision enough to constitute a failure to act under article 265?

Preliminary Ruling: The Court of justice held that the Commission should have formulated its position on the alleged breach of Article 102, dismissed the complaint in a formal letter to the complainant, or made the reasoned decision not to pursue the complaint on the ground of the lack of Union interest. Lack of any decision constituted a ground for an Article 265 TFEU procedure.

Application: In practice, the action on failure to act is an important procedure that ensures that the European institutions are, at least, considering the requests of their citizens that they legally have to consider.

Chapter 6: Fundamental Rights and Other General Principles of EU Law

General ideology

The general principles of EU Law are used by the Court of Justice to interpret the Treaties and the secondary legislation. They are rooted in the common legal traditions of the Member States. EU Law did not create anything new; this traditional principle can be found in the national legal systems of the majority of the Member States. Subjecting interpretation of law to general principles originally comes from the "civil" or "Roman" legal tradition. There was originally nothing in the founding Treaties about the general principles of EU Law. It is finally article 6(1) TEU, as amended by the Amsterdam Treaty that first mentioned these principles. For example, article 6 TEU identifies the Rule of Law or Human Rights as the main general principles of EU Law.

However, the Court of Justice has also developed a certain number of general principles through its constant case law. In doing so, the Court fulfilled its obligation under article 220 TFEU which obliges it to interpret provisions so as to ensure that EU law is observed by the Member States. These principles will usually serve as an aid to interpretation of other sources of EU Law or as a ground to challenge Union actions.

The main general principles of EU Law are:

- The protection of fundamental rights
- Equality
- Natural justice
- Proportionality
- Legal certainty and legitimate expectation

Since the protection of fundamental rights is by far the most important principle, we will examine it separately in a first section. Then, in a second section, the other general principles will be analysed by turn.

Fundamental rights

Initially, there was no mention of Human Rights in the EC Treaty. This can be explained by the merely economic nature of the Communities at the time. Once again, the Court of Justice had to build up a legal framework. The Luxembourg Court progressively developed a fundamental rights jurisprudence both inspired by the common constitutional tradition of the Member States and by international Human Rights agreements. The European Union's protection of Human Rights has been developed so far that it is nowadays referred to as the specific term of "fundamental rights". This terminology has emerged because fundamental rights go beyond the traditional civil and political rights which are most commonly associated with conceptions of "Human Rights". Fundamental rights include civil and political rights but also socio-economic rights, environmental rights and rights to good administration. Recently, these rights have been officially enshrined in a bill of rights called Charter of Fundamental Rights.

The slow recognition and the progressive recognition as general principle of Law

(i) The Court firstly refused to receive arguments invoking fundamental rights

The Court of Justice was initially rejecting all the argument that mentioned fundamental rights, in absence of provision of the Treaties.

General principle: The Court cannot apply the fundamental rights as protected by the national constitutions of Member States. In addition to this, nothing in Community Law was equivalent at the time of the European Communities.

Stork v High Authority (Case 1/58) [1959] ECR 17; and
Geitling v High Authority (Joined Cases 36-38/59 and 40/50) [1960] ECR 423

Facts: The case concerned several decisions by the High Authority of the European Coal and Steel Community on the selling and condition of coal in the Ruhr region of West Germany. The applicants were challenging those decisions as to be contrary to fundamental rights, protected by almost all constitutions of the Member States and particularly by the West German Constitution. The applicants particularly claimed that the decisions violated their private property rights.

Preliminary question before the Court: The question raised before the Court was to know whether or not it could rely on fundamental rights to review an EU act?

Preliminary Ruling: The Court rejected the applicants' argument holding that the High Authority was only required to apply the law of the European Coal and Steel Community. In addition to this the Court was not empowered as to consider whether Community decisions infringed fundamental rights provisions of the West German Constitution. The CJ held that it could *"neither interpret nor apply provisions from national constitutions"*. More importantly, the Luxembourg Court denied the existence of any general principle or provisions of Community Law that would be equivalent.

Application: The Court recalled its inability to directly apply national constitutions and denied the existence of any protection of fundamental rights in Community Law. This jurisprudential shyness of the Court can be explained by its limited prerogative at the time and the mainly economic nature of the of the Union's predecessor.

(ii) The Court of Justice progressively recognised fundamental rights as general principles of law

The Highest national Courts have significantly influenced the Court of Justice on this evolution jurisprudence. They have exercised a pressure on the Luxembourg Court to provide a greater protection for fundamental rights in the EU. All of this started with the adoption of the EU supremacy principle in **Costa v. E.N.E.L.** It leads to crucial issues in terms of conflict of norms. Even though Community law at the time did not provide with any protection of fundamental rights, in case of an infringement with those rights by a Community provision, Member States were not allowed to set aside the impugned provision to apply their internal constitutions. National Courts, and particularly in Germany, started to present resistance. Therefore, the Court of Justice changed its approach in **Stauder.**

General principle: Fundamental rights are part of the general principles of EU Law.

Stauder v City of Ulm (Case 29/69) [1969] ECR 329
Facts: The Court had to interpret a Commission decision stimulating the sale of surplus of butter, which was incompatible with the West German Constitution protecting fundamental right (right to dignity).
Preliminary question before the Court: The question raised by the German Court was to know whether or not fundamental rights were part of the general principles of EU Law?
Preliminary Ruling: The Court of Justice held that fundamental rights were part of the general principles of EU law. The Court concluded its judgment as it follows: "the provision at issue contains nothing capable of prejudicing the fundamental human rights enshrined in the general principles of community law and protected by the Court".
Application: The Court, by enshrining fundamental rights as a general principle of EU Law, subjects the interpretation of EU Law to the compliance of these rights.

General principle: Fundamental rights, inspired by the common traditions of the Member States, have to be respected by the Union while accomplishing its objectives.

Internationale Handelsgesellschaft v Einfuhr und Vorratstelle für Getreide und Futtermittel (Case 11/70) [1970] ECR 1125
Facts: A regulation required the introduction of export licences in respect of certain agricultural products falling under the Common Agricultural Policy (CAP). Another requirement of this regulation involved the transfer of a deposit that would be forfeited if no exportations were realized during the period of the licence, and this is how the applicant suffered a loss. The applicant claimed

that this EU regulation was incompatible with the German Constitution for having contravened with the right to run a business freely.

Preliminary question before the Court: The question, after having recognized fundamental rights as general principles of EU Law, was to define them and precise the scope of their protection.

Preliminary Ruling: The Court stated: *"The protection of such rights, while inspired by the constitutional traditions common to the Member States, must be insured within the framework of the structures and the objectives of the European Community"*.

Application: It is another German reference to the CJEU, in **Internationale Handelsgesellschaft,** that forced the Court to engage more in details with the issue of fundamental rights. The Court of Justice went into a deeper definition of fundamental rights and unveiled the scope of their protection.

Even if this evolution was a huge progress in the Court of Justice's jurisprudence, it failed to satisfy the German Courts. In its so-called **Solange I** judgment (BVerfGE 37, 271) [1974] 2 CMLR 540, the German Constitutional Court complained about the legal uncertainty left by the lack of a codified catalogue of fundamental rights and held that the fundamental rights guarantees under the West German Constitution would prevail over EEC law for so long as this situation continued.

General principle: The fundamental rights recognized by EU Law are not only inspired by the constitutional traditions common to the Member States but also by international treaties protecting Human Rights.

Internationale Handelsgesellschaft. In Nold v Commission (Case 4/73) [1974] ECR 491

Facts: This case was about a Commission decision on thresholds for coal wholesalers to be able to buy directly from joint selling agencies in the Ruhr region of West Germany. One of the arguments raised by Germany was that, in addition to contravene with the West German Constitution, this decision was also incompatible with one of the main international Treaty on Human Rights, ratified by the majority of the EU Member States: the

European Convention on Human Rights.

Preliminary question before the Court: The question was to know whether or not international treaties could supply guidelines for the definition of fundamental rights that the EU should follow while protecting them.

Preliminary Ruling: The Court of Justice held that:

"As the Court has already stated, fundamental rights form an integral part of the general principles of law, the observance of which it ensures. In safeguarding these rights, the Court is bound to draw inspiration from constitutional traditions common to the Member States, and it cannot therefore uphold measures which are incompatible with fundamental rights recognized and protected by the Constitutions of those States. Similarly, international treaties for the protection of human rights on which the Member States have collaborated or of which they are signatories, can supply guidelines which should be followed within the framework of Community law".

Application: The Court of Justice, in this case, defined mire deeply the content of fundamental rights. Both the national traditions and the main international treaties on Human Rights can supply guidelines to define their content. However, the Court avoided to expressly mentioning the EConvHR.

Following these developments in the Court of Justice's jurisprudence, the German constitutional Court finally abdicated in the case **Re Wünsche Handelsgesellschaft** (2 BvR 197/83) [1987] 3 CMLR 225, better known as **Solange II**. The national Court acknowledged that the recent progress made by the Court of Justice in the protection of Human Rights. The German Judges concluded that as far as the protection is substantially (at least) similar to the protection provided by the West German constitution, they would accept a complete supremacy of EU Law. Concerning the relationship between EU Law and ordinary public international Law, the Court of Justice, in **Kadi**, has been very ambitious in reaffirming the specificity of the EU legal order.

General principle: International agreements, including UN measures, cannot have the effect of prejudicing to fundamental rights that are considered as "constitutional

principles of the Union".

Kadi and Al Barakaat International Foundation v Council and Commission (2008) C-402/05

Facts: EU legislated to implement a series of United Nations Security Council (UNSC) Resolutions which were adopted in the wake of the 11 Sept 2001 attacks, requiring all states to freeze the financial resources of any person or entity controlled by the Taliban or associated with Osama bin Laden or the Al-Qaeda network. A list of persons was communicated to all the UN members. These measures were taken under chapter VII, the only binding resolution that the UN can make. The EU was not part of the UN. Art. 103 UN Charter states that UN obligations prevail over all other treaty obligations. There was no review mechanism at the UN level. The applicant was listed to be associated with bin Laden or Al-Qaeda, but no hearing opportunity was given. His bank accounts in Switzerland were frozen. He argued that the EU legislation should be annulled as it violates, *inter alia,* his fundamental property rights and his right to a fair hearing. Considering the procedure, the General Court in 2005 held that: *"the EU must respect the UN Charter and UN law has supremacy. There was no review on grounds of general principles of EU law; otherwise it would constitute indirect review of UN Resolution".*

Preliminary question before the Court: Which source of international Law should prevail in case of conflict between EU Law and UN Law?

Preliminary Ruling: The Court started to recall that the EU legal order was based on the Rule of Law and that international agreements could not affect the autonomy of the Union. Fundamental rights form an integral part of the general principles of EU law: respect for human rights is a condition of the lawfulness of EU act. Measures incompatible with respect for human rights are not acceptable in the Community. Hence, The Court held by concluding that obligations imposed by an international agreement cannot have the effect of prejudicing the constitutional principles of the founding treaties, which include the principle that all Union acts must respect fundamental rights. Therefore, the contested EU regulation had to be annulled.

Application: The EU was expressly refusing to comply with the

UN Charter, certainly the most important International Treaty in terms of its universal application, and particularly on its most binding part: Chapter VII.

This case was received as a real storm by the traditional academics of public international law. **De Burca** claimed that *"If courts outside the European Union are inclined towards judicial borrowing, then the ECJ's ruling in **Kadi** seems to offer encouragement to them to assert their local understandings of human rights and their particular constitutional priorities over international norms, and in particular over Chapter VII resolutions of the Security Council".*

Goldsmith and Posner have concluded that: *"European countries must disregard the U.N. Charter -- the most fundamental treaty in our modern international legal system -- when it conflicts with European constitutional order. There is a simple explanation for all this. Europeans hold their values and interests dear, just as Americans do, and will not subordinate them to the requirements of international law".*

The adoption of the Charter

The Charter of Fundamental Rights for the European Union owes its origin to the European Council meeting at Cologne in 1999. It was decided that a catalogue of fundamental rights should be drawn up to provide more visible means of enforcement for EU citizens. The Charter was drafted by a Convention comprising representatives from the Governments and Parliaments of the Member States, the European Parliament and the Commission. It was signed by all the then 15 Member States at Biarritz in 2000 and solemnly proclaimed in Nice few months later. The Charter is based on six values (also used to divide its structure in six Titles):

- Title I: Dignity
- Title II: Freedoms
- Title III: Equality
- Title IV: Solidarity
- Title V: Citizen's rights

- Title VI: Justice

The Charter is quite innovative compared to other traditional charters or constitutions protecting Human Rights. Where traditional charters generally merely deal with civil and political rights, the European Charter goes further by recognizing socio-economic rights and even a right to a high level of environmental protection. But this can be explained by its late adoption that permitted to include the recent development of Human Rights Law. For example, in terms of prohibition of discrimination the European Convention on Human Rights does not include "sexual orientation" in its protected grounds, whereas the Charter does.

Article 52 presents the scope and interpretation of the Charter:
"1. Any limitation on the exercise of the rights and freedoms recognised by this Charter must be provided for by law and respect the essence of those rights and freedoms.

4. In so far as this Charter recognises fundamental rights as they result from the constitutional traditions common to the Member States, those rights shall be interpreted in harmony with those traditions.

5. The provisions of this Charter which contain principles may be implemented by legislative and executive acts taken by institutions, bodies, offices and agencies of the Union, and by acts of Member States when they are implementing Union law, in the exercise of their respective powers. They shall be judicially cognisable only in the interpretation of such acts and in the ruling on their legality."

The main provision of this article that needs to be reminded lies in paragraph 5. It significantly reduces the scope of the Charter. Indeed, the Charter only applies to Member States *"when they are implementing Union law"*. In practice, many cases involve applicants that cannot enforce their rights under the Charter because their Member States are acting under national competences. This is one of the reasons why the EU Charter is still weaker than the ECtHR, which applies almost unconditionally.

Initially, the legal status of the Charter was quite weak. Since it had been solemnly proclaimed in Nice, it was only a declaration that had no binding legal effect. The whole process had been designed to ensure that the Charter provided an authoritative statement of fundamental rights within the EU without taking on the attributes of a legally binding instrument.

The adoption of the draft Constitution for Europe, signed in 2004, would have granted it binding force. However, this project was abandoned after several failures in the ratification process. Nevertheless, the Treaty of Lisbon changed the legal status of the Charter to a legally binding provision. Since December 2009, article 6(1) TUE provides *"[t]he Union recognises the rights, freedoms and principles set out in the Charter of Fundamental Rights of the European Union [...], which shall have the same legal value as the Treaties"*.

Relationship with the European Convention on Human Rights

The ECHR and the judgments of the European Court of Human Rights have always been important influences on the Court of Justice's understanding of fundamental rights of EU law. In the early 1970's, the German government already invoked the major importance of the ECtHR in **Internationale Handelsgesellschaft. In Nold v Commission.** However, the Court of Justice avoided the main question by encompassing the Convention in the general term of "international treaties". The Court of Justice, under a strong pressure from the Member States, finally tackled the issue of the relationship between EU Law and the ECtHR.

General principle: Fundamental rights in EU Law are partly derived from the EConvHR.

Rutili v Minister for the Interior (Case 36/75) [1975] ECR 1219
Facts: An Italian national was working in France and his freedom of movement was restricted, because of his political and trade union activities. He argued about his freedom of expression under Article 10 ECHR.
Preliminary question before the Court: To what extent the EConvHR can impact on EU fundamental rights?
Preliminary Ruling: The Court held that certain rights in the Convention are also specifically manifested in EU law itself. It applied for example the famous test for derogations to Human Rights contained in the EConvHR: the derogation has to be *"necessary for the protection of interests in a democratic society".*
Application: This case stressed out the prime importance attached by the EU fundamental rights as derived in particular from the constitutions of the Member States and from the ECHR.

The Court went even further in **Johnston v RUC** (Case 222/84) [1986] ECR 1651 by holding that *"the principles on which that Convention is based must be taken into consideration in Community law"*. The strong ties between the EU fundamental rights and the EConvHR have officially been recognized by the Charter itself. Article 52 (3) stipulates:
"3. In so far as this Charter contains rights which correspond to

rights guaranteed by the Convention for the Protection of Human Rights and Fundamental Freedoms, the meaning and scope of those rights shall be the same as those laid down by the said Convention. This provision shall not prevent Union law providing more extensive protection".

In other words, the rights in the Charter that corresponding to the same rights within the EConvHR should be interpreted as having the same meaning and scope. In order to be perfectly clear on this question, the Charter even contains a table that sets out Articles of the Charter where both the meaning and the scope are the same as the corresponding Articles of the EConvHR.

Finally, the question of the accession of the EU to the EConvHR arose at the end of the XXth century. The EU, being entirely recognized as an international organization, has a legal personality permitting to be party to a Treaty, under the provisions of public international Law. This accession would have two main advantages for the EU. Firstly, it would simplify the understanding of the relationship between the EU and the Council of Europe on Human Rights since all the EU Members have ratified the EConvHR. Secondly, this would improve the protection of fundamental rights within the EU, as far as the EConvHR is widely recognized as being the best system of protection of Human Rights in the world.

Moreover, the Council of Europe was particularly insisting on this accession because of financial issues. Usually described as a "poor" institution, the Council was looking for new contributions. If the EConvHR was initially reserved to States, the Council of Europe expressly adopted protocol 14 to allow the accession of the EU. However, in 1996, just few years before the adoption of the Charter, the CJEU refused the accession in an opinion 2/94. It justified its reasoning by stating that the *"initial objectives of the EU was not to protect Human Rights"*. Nevertheless, the adoption of the Charter reopened the controversy. The Court of Justice was obviously not able to justify its decision by the lack of interest of the Union on Human Rights anymore.

It delivered another negative Opinion on 18 December 2014. This time, the Court insisted that *"accession did not take into account the particular characteristics of the EU by undermining the autonomy and supremacy of EU law"*. The main reason of this refusal lied on a provision of the draft Treaty that empowered the ECourtHR to review acts of the common foreign and security policy (CFSP) in the light of their respect with Human Rights. The EU Member States would never subject this very delicate matter implying defense and security measures, to a compliance with fundamental rights. These two consecutive refusals from the Court of Justice consequently closed the debate of the accession, at least for the few coming decades.

The application of Fundamental Rights in the Union

The consistent Jurisprudence of the Court of Justice on fundamental rights was crucial to ensure that the EU legal order was generally complying with them. The institutions have to strictly comply with fundamental rights. As stated earlier, the main restriction to the CJEU review on the Members States acts lies on Article 52 (3) if the Charter. In this respect, the case **Demirel v Stadt Schwäbisch Gmünd** (Case 12/86) [1987] ECR 3719 confirmed that Member States are not compelled to comply with the Charter when they are acting domestically in situations that fall outside EU Law. However, the CJEU's case law is compatible with Article 52 of the Charter, when Member States are implementing EU Law, they should do it while respecting fundamental rights because they are acting as "agents of the Union".

General principle: When implementing an EU provision, Member States should comply with fundamental rights, even if it implies to take further steps which were not required by the EU act.

Wachauf v Federal Republic of Germany (Case 5/88) [1989] ECR 2609
Facts: A German tenant farmer, upon the expiry of his tenancy, requested compensation for discontinuance of milk production for

sale. German law, implementing an EU regulation, required him to obtain the lessor's written consent, which was withdrawn by the lessor. The applicant could not get the compensation and sued Germany for violating his property right.

Preliminary question before the Court: To what extent do Member States have to comply with fundamental rights while implementing EU Law?

Preliminary Ruling: Member States are bound, when implementing EU law, by all of the same general principles and fundamental rights that bind the EU in its actions. Hence, the MS should endeavour to provide compensation for the applicant even if the EU regulation did not specifically required it.

Application: While implementing EU Law, Member States have a positive obligation to take the necessary steps to an effective compliance with fundamental rights.

Nevertheless, the concept of implementing EU law is ambiguous and depends on the interpretation given to it by the Court of Justice. This margin of appreciation gave rise to two exceptions of the Article 52 (3) principle.

General principle: Derogation to freedom to provide services, regardless whether or not the Member State is implementing EU Law can only be justified if compatible with fundamental rights.

Elliniki Radiophonia Tiléorassi AE (ERT) v Dimotiki Etairia Pliroforissis (DEP) (Case C-260/89) [1991] ECR I-2925
Facts: A state broadcasting monopoly in Greece was challenged under Article 46 (provision about freedom to provide services) for preventing other broadcasters from showing TV programmes. Greece argued a derogation in order to protect the national language under freedom of expression. Greece was clearly not implementing EU Law at the time, as its prerogative fell in the scope of exclusive national competences.

Preliminary question before the Court: Can derogation to freedom to provide services be justified by the necessary compliance to fundamental rights?

Preliminary Ruling: The Court held that a derogation to freedom provide services can only be justified if it is compatible with fundamental rights.

General principle: Member States have to comply with fundamental rights when their actions can be shown to have effect on the Union policies or interests.

Åklagaren v Fransson (Case C-617/10) [2013] ECR I-0000

Facts: A Swedish fisherman was convicted for tax evasion after having given false information about his tax return. In addition to the criminal prosecution, he has been ordered by the government to pay a penalty. The applicant invoked his right not to be tried or punished several times, under Article 50 of the Charter. The tax evasion in question included a failure to declare VAT which is partially governed by Directive 2006/112/EC on the common system of VAT. However, under the Directive, when red with Article 4(3) TFEU, Member States are under an obligation to take all measures to collect VAT and prevent tax evasion.

Preliminary question before the Court: The question was to know whether or not a Member State could be compelled to comply with fundamental rights when it was not directly implementing EU Law?

Preliminary Ruling: The Court held that Sweden had to act in accordance with fundamental rights, even if it was not directly implementing EU Law, when such actions would impact on EU policies or interests. Indeed, it was the Union financial interests that were at stake on the issue of tax evasion.

Application: This represents a wide interpretation of the notion of "implementation of EU law". It creates controversy because Sweden was clearly not implementing EU Law, and this decision appears to be expressly contrary to Article 52 (3) of the Charter.

The UK and the Charter

During the negotiation process before the Lisbon treaty, the UK and Poland obtained concessions from the Union secured under Protocol n°30. But the issue is to know whether or not the Charter of fundamental rights applies to them. Article 1 of the protocol provides that:

"1. The Charter does not extend the ability of the Court of Justice of the European Union, or any court or tribunal of Poland or of the United Kingdom, to find that the laws, regulations or administrative provisions, practices or action of Poland or of the United Kingdom are inconsistent with the fundamental rights, freedoms and principles that it reaffirms.
2. In particular, and for the avoidance of doubt, nothing in Title IV of the Charter creates justiciable rights applicable to Poland or the United Kingdom except in so far as Poland or the United Kingdom has provided for such rights in its national law".

However, UK governments kept on stating that it did not create an effective opt-out but merely clarified the effect of the Charter in the UK. They insisted on the fact that Article 1 (1) of the protocol was not expressly saying, at least in unequivocal terms, that the Charter did not apply at all to the UK and Poland.

General principle: Protocol 30 does not provide the UK and Poland with an opt-out from the application of the Charter.

NS v Secretary of State for the Home Department (Case C-411/10) [2011] ECR I-13905
Facts: This case concerned immigration Law and particularly the treatment of asylum applications under Regulation No 343/2003.
Preliminary question before the Court: The question concerned the interpretation of Protocol 30, was it creating an opt-out for the UK and Poland? Does the Charter apply to them?
Preliminary Ruling: The Court of justice confirmed the UK approach: the protocol was not an opt-out. It held that the protocol *"does not call into question the applicability of the Charter in the United Kingdom".* According to the Court, Article 1 (1) merely: *"explains Article 51 of the Charter with regard to the scope of thereof and does not intend to exempt the Republic of Poland or the United Kingdom from the obligation to comply with the provisions of the Charter or to prevent a court of one of those Member States from ensuring compliance with those provisions".*
Application: This case affirms that the Charter applies to both the UK and Poland. Therefore, individuals are entitled to enforce their

rights contained Charter before the courts of those Members States.

Other general principles of EU Law

Equality

The concept of equal treatment or non-discrimination is one of the funding principles of the TEU. According to Baroness Hale, anti-discrimination law aims to ensure that *"each person is treated as an individual and not assumed to be like other member of its "group""*. Initially, the TEU only prohibited discrimination based on: nationality (Article 18), equal pay for men and women (Article 157) and distinction made between producers and consumers under the CAP (Article 40). However, the protection has been extended to the traditional "protected characteristics" such as: sex, disability, age, race or ethnic origin, sexual orientation, religion and belief. It is interesting to note that the "sexual orientation" ground is very innovative, even the EConvHR does not contain it in its text (even though it has been recognized by the Strasbourg Court case law). Protected characteristics are the grounds upon which it is prohibited to discriminate against an individual. The main directives in EU Law on equality are the following ones:

- Gender and Services Directive (GSD), Council Directive 2004
- Employment Equality Directive (EED), Council Directive 2000
- Racial Equality Directive (RED), Council Directive 2000
- Recast Equal Treatment Directive (Recast ETD), Directive 2006

The Court of Justice has been proactive in combating discrimination and advancing equality on two main issues: equal pay for women and LGBTI rights.

General principle: Sex discrimination leading to unequal pay can only be accepted if it is based on objective justification.

Bilka-Kaufhaus GmbH v Weber von Hartz (1986) C-170/84

Facts: This case involved a female part-time worker, which had been working 15 years for the same company, unable to get a pension because of a facially neutral rule requiring to have 15 years' experience and to be a full time worker. The applicant claimed for indirect discrimination, since women were more working part-time than men, they were at a significant disadvantage.

Preliminary question before the Court: The question raised was to know whether or not it would be possible to provide a valid justification for unequal pay.

Preliminary Ruling: The Court of Justice held that sex discrimination leading to unequal pay should only be accepted if it is based on objective justification.

Application: The test for the objective justification can involve factors such as necessity and proportionality.

General principle: Discrimination based on gender reassignment is recognized by the CJEU as sex discrimination.

P. v. S. & CORNWALL CJEU C-13/94 ECR I-2143 1996:

Facts: P., the applicant in the main proceedings, used to work as a manager in an educational establishment, a period during which P. dressed and behaved as a woman, followed by surgery that gave to the applicant the physical attributes of a woman. The County Council, the employer, maintained that the reason for her dismissal was a mere redundancy plan. However, the applicant argued it was because of a recent gender reassignment. The United Kingdom and the Commission submitted that to dismiss a person because he or she is a transsexual or because he or she has undergone a gender- reassignment operation does not constitute sex discrimination for the purposes of the directive.

Preliminary question before the Court: Does the prohibition of sex discrimination encompasses a protection from discrimination based on gender reassignment?

Preliminary Ruling: Article 5(1) of the Gender and Services Directive (GSD), Council Directive 2004 precludes dismissal of a transsexual for a reason related to a gender reassignment. Discrimination based on gender reassignment is recognized by the

CJEU as sex discrimination.

Application: This is a huge progress in the protection of the transsexual minority that should not suffer disadvantage in treatment for having reassigned their gender.

Natural justice

This general principle is also referred to as "fairness". It lies on three distinct strands:
- The right to a fair and unbiased hearing
- The right to be heard before the making of a potentially adverse decision is made
- The right to a reasoned decision

This right is mentioned by many express provisions of EU Law. For example, Directive 2004/38 implies a fair hearing accompanied with a right to appeal the decision. In addition to this, Member States also have to respect the natural justice principle when making decisions on recognition of qualifications for establishment under Directives 89/48 or 92/51.

General principle: The right to a fair hearing implies that conditions applied to individuals have to be made known beforehand.

Transocean Marine Paint Association v Commission (Case 17/74) [1974] ECR 1063
Facts: The Commission addressed a decision to the applicant, failing to specify a condition in the decision that was later applied against them. The applicant brought an action in annulment for violation to general principles of EU Law.
Preliminary question before the Court: Can the EU institutions apply conditions against individuals although they were not expressly specified to them?
Preliminary Ruling: The Court accepted the applicant's argument that the unfair part of this decision should be annulled. The Court held that the applicants were denied access to a fair hearing.

Application: The European institutions, when making decisions addressed to individuals, have to comply with a duty of fairness that is rooted in the judicial principle of fair trial.

General principle: The European institutions have a duty to give reasons and should provide individuals with an opportunity to be heard.

Union nationale des entraîneurs et cadres techniques professionnels du football (Unectef) v Georges Heylens and others (case 222/86) 1987
Facts: A Belgian football trainer, with a Belgian diploma was refused the right to practice his trade in France without having been given any reasons. However, Member States have to respect the natural justice principle when making decisions on recognition of qualifications for establishment under Directives 89/48 or 92/51.
Preliminary question before the Court: Does the principle of natural justice imply a duty to give reasons?
Preliminary Ruling: The Court upheld a breach of process, stating: *"in a question of securing the effective protection of a fundamental right by the treaty on Community workers, they must be able to defend that right under the best possible conditions and have a possibility of deciding, with a full knowledge of the relevant facts, whether there is any point in applying to the courts"*. The Court added that the institutions had a duty to give reasons when making of a potentially adverse decision.
Application: In this case, the Court clarified the scope of the principle of natural justice; it implies a duty to give reasons for the institutions and a right to be heard by a Court.

Proportionality

The principle of proportionality, according to Article 5(4) TEU imposes that "the content and form of Union action shall not exceed what is necessary to achieve the objectives of the Treaties". In other words, nothing should be done than is more than what is necessary to achieve the end of a measure. The principle of proportionality is regularly used to determine whether or not legislation goes beyond what is necessary to achieve the objectives of the Treaties behind it. It has to be respected by both the actions of the Union in passing legislation and the actions of Member States in interpreting and implementing that legislation.

General principle: An EU measure should not create disproportionate offenses to individual that are not necessary to achieve its end.

Case 181/84 **R v Intervention Board for Agricultural Produce, Ex p. Man (Sugar)** [1986]
Facts: A sugar trader did not apply for a licence on time. As a result a Bank forfeited securities in accordance with Regulation 1880/83. This resulted on a loss of £1670 to the trader that contested the necessity of such a measure to achieve its end. He argued that the Regulation was disproportionate considering the offense he was suffering.
Preliminary question before the Court: Was the EU measure necessary to achieve its end?
Preliminary Ruling: The Court held that the offense suffered by the claimant was disproportionate to the mere sound management of the market that the measure was seeking to achieve. The forfeiture procedure under the Regulation was disproportionate and should not be applied.
Application: The principle of proportionality can be used to verify that the actual consequences of a measure do not depart from its initial purpose.

General principle: A penalty domestically provided by implementation, for infringement of an EU measure must be proportionate to the objectives of this measure.

Italy v Watson and Belmann (Case 118/75) (1975) ECR 1185
Facts: An English woman had settled in Italy without the necessary working permit. At the time, an EU Directive required registered working permits for the establishment in another Member State. The penalty was provided by the Italian implementation of the Directive. Under Italian immigration Law, it was deportation.

Preliminary question before the Court: Was the deportation proportionate to the objective of the Directive.

Preliminary Ruling: The Court held that the dramatic consequence of deportation was disproportionate to the Directive's objective. The Directive merely intended to regulate and record immigration flows.

Application: This case tells us that proportionality can also be used to control the reasonableness of sanctions for infringement to EU Law. All decisions that appear to be too heavy or abusive, should be questioned under this approach.

Legal certainty and legitimate expectation

The principle of legal certainty comes as a part of the EU commitment to the Rule of Law. It is another general principle of Law that is familiar to most legal systems. The main idea is that the law should be certain and predictable for everyone. For example, one of its implementation is the prohibition of retrospectivity: no rule should apply retrospectively to a situation that occurred prior to the date on which any given rule was promulgated. Another aspect of legal certainty is legitimate expectations. It is closely connected to the notion of "good faith". The first case recognizing legal certainty as a general principle of EU Law is **Officer van Justitie v Klophinguis Nijmengen** (cases 28 to 30/62) 1963. Legal certainty is also a basis for EU secondary sources such as the Acquired Rights Directive 77/187. EU Law should respect acquired rights and not withdraw them later, this is related to the legitimate expectations principles that can be summed up as it follows: *"precise assurances relied on in good faith should be honoured".*

General principle: EU Law should not fundamentally change a situation legitimately expected under a prior private agreement.

J. Mulder v. Minister of Agriculture and Fisheries 28 April 1988 (Case 120/86) ECE 2321

Facts: A private agreement required a diary farmer to not supply milk for a period in return to a payment. An EU Regulation implemented quotas on milk suppliers that did not provide provisions for the farmers parties to these types of private agreement, which resulted for them on a prohibition to sell milk after the term of the contract.

Preliminary question before the Court: The question was to know whether or not an EU provision could change a situation legitimately expected previously under a private agreement?

Preliminary Ruling: The Court of Justice held that the Regulation should not have legal effect for the applicant that must be entitled to resume supplying milk after the end of the agreement.

Application: The scope of this ruling appears to be very broad, does it mean that private agreements can be used to eschew the application of EU Law under the legitimate expectation principle?

However, this solution has been restricted in 1996 by the case **R v Minister of Agriculture.**

General principle: Legitimate expectations cannot be relied on where the Union is acting in furtherance of its objectives after a change of circumstances.

R v Minister of Agriculture, Fisheries and Food, ex parte Anastasiou (Pissouri) Limited and others Case C-5/94, ILEC 011 (CJEU 1996)

Facts: The UK ministry introduced a system of fishing licences in order to protect its waters that were endangered. Many fishing companies were affected by this decision, preventing them to supply the amount of fish previously agreed in several agreements. They contested this decision for incompatibility to the legitimate expectations principle.

Preliminary question before the Court: Can a change of circumstances give rise to measures contradicting prior legitimate expectations arising from a private agreement?

Preliminary Ruling: The Court held that the legitimate expectations argument must be rejected since arrangements have to be made in case of changes of circumstances.

In its judgement, the Court of Justice stated: *"The principles of legal certainty and the protection of legitimate expectations are fundamental to European Community law. Yet these principles are merely general maxims derived from the notion that the Community is based on the rule of law and can be applied to individual cases only if expressed in enforceable rules ... other principles ... run counter legal certainty and ... the right balance need to be struck"*.

Application: This case provides the Union institutions and their Member States a safeguard in case of change of circumstances that would otherwise prevent them to act in furtherance of the objectives of the Treaties.

Chapter 7: Free Movement of Goods I: Articles 28–30, 110 TFEU

General ideology

Article 26(2) TFEU provides that: *"The internal market shall comprise an area without internal frontiers in which the free movement of goods, persons, services and capital is ensured in accordance with the provisions of this Treaty".*

The four freedoms articulated in this provision are thus regarded as the essential characteristics of the internal market. The first of these freedoms, free movement of goods (FMOG), is one of the cornerstones of the European Union and is the subject of the two following chapters. Two introductory notions are crucial to understand free movement of goods. First of all, the Court of Justice had to define the notion of "good" because it can be interpreted broadly.

General principle: Goods are valuable products capable of forming the subject of commercial transactions.

Commission v Italy (the 'Italian Art' case) (Case 7/68) [1968] ECR 423
Facts: The Italian Law of 1939 on the protection of articles of artistic or historical interest contains several provisions relating to the exportation of such articles. In particular, it provides according to circumstances an absolute export prohibition (Article 35), the need for a licence (Article 36), and the imposition on exportation of a progressive tax on the value of the article, ranging by successive stages from 8 to 30 per cent. (Article 37). These provisions are obviously non compatible with the EU Law and free movement of goods. Therefore, the Commission asked Italy to remove the tax. The latter refused and the case was referred to the Court.
Preliminary question before the Court: The question was to know whether or not articles of artistic or historical interest are "goods" under the FMOG definition?

Preliminary Ruling: The Court confirmed that art articles are considered "goods" under the FMOG: *"The rules of the common market apply to articles possessing artistic or historic value subject only to the exceptions expressly provided by the treaty"*. More importantly, the Court of Justice delivered a definition of the meaning of "goods" under Article 26. Goods are: *"products that can be valued in money and which are capable, as such, of forming the subject of commercial transactions"*

Application: The Luxembourg Court in this case brings greater clarity over the meaning of the Treaties when they refer to the FMOG.

This definition appears to be very broad, the majority of products will be considered as goods. Secondly, it is important to recall why the FMOG have been introduced to fully understand this area of EU Law. Free movement of goods contributes to achieve the first and overriding objective of the Union: establishing a common market by removing barriers to trade. This objective was necessary to the achievement of a customs union, which economists regard as an essential step for the integration of markets. A customs union is an agreement between Member Sates to abide by two principles: a free trade area, where goods pass between the countries without the imposition of restrictions such as customs duties; and a system for the charging of a common customs tariff on goods coming into the free trade area from other countries. The first principle is regarded as the internal aspect of a customs union; the second is its external aspect. For example, honey should move freely between Germany and Spain, this is the internal aspect of the single market. In other words, no trade barriers should be applied to the circulation of this good between these countries. However, honey coming from Peru should be subjected to a same tariff regardless if it is exported to Germany or Denmark. This is the external aspect of the single market, and it ensures that the non-EU producers exporting honey have no specific advantage to export to one of these countries in terms of trade barriers. These two necessary notions of the single market are enshrined by article 28(2) TFEU:

"The Union shall comprise a customs union which shall cover all

trade in goods and which shall involve the prohibition between
Member States of customs duties on imports and exports and of
all charges having equivalent effect, and the adoption of a
common customs tariff in their relations with third countries".

This general article sets out the framework but many other Treaty
provisions enter into the details of free movement of goods.
However, the most interesting part of free movement of goods lies
on its internal aspect. The question is to know how Member States
should behave towards goods coming from the Union entering
their territories. The TFEU contains three main provisions dealing
with the internal aspect of the customs union. Their main objective
is to remove obstacles to the free movement of goods across the
Member States:

- Article 30 TFEU: the prohibition of customs duties and
  charges having equivalent effect;
- Article 110 TFEU: the prohibition of discriminatory
  taxation;
- Articles 34, 35 and 36 TFEU: the prohibition of
  quantitative restrictions and all measures having
  equivalent effect (Articles 34 and 35), and permissible
  derogations from this prohibition (Article 36).

In this chapter, we will focus on the analysis of article 30 and 110
TFEU, whereas next chapter will be treating Articles 34, 35, 36
TFEU. This distinction is made because the first Articles concern
barriers to trade of a pecuniary nature, whereas Articles 34 to 36
deal with non-pecuniary or "hidden" barriers. Article 30 concerns
tariffs for goods having crossed the border and entering a Member
State territory. Article 110 regulates charges that are levied as a
system of internal taxation within the state.

**Article 30 TFEU: customs duties and charges having
equivalent effect**

Article 30 TFEU provides:
*"Customs duties on imports and exports and charges having
equivalent effect shall be prohibited between Member States. This
prohibition shall also apply to customs duties of a fiscal nature".*

This provision has direct effect according to the famous **Van Gend en Loos** decision of the Court of Justice. As a matter of fact, it was the first EU provision declared as having direct effect. In practice, it means that individuals or companies can invoke the prohibitions of custom duties and charges directly before their national courts. As stated above, Article 30 concerns the trade barriers introduced for goods having crossed the boarders. They are the most direct and obvious infringement to free movement of goods.

Customs duties

Custom duties are express fees that have to be directly paid at the border indicating the tariff for the importation of a good into a State. This fare has to be charged solely because the good crossed the border. These measures result on placing significant barriers on the importation of foreign goods that is contrary to free trade. The intention of the State placing the barrier is not important. The prohibition of custom duties will apply regardless whether the State aims to make benefits or to limit its entrance on the market.

Charges having equivalent effect

Charges having equivalent effect (CEEs) than custom duties are also prohibited by Article 30, even if they are formulated otherwise, they give rise to the same consequences. The reverse solution would allow Member States to avoid the prohibition of custom duties by hiding them under the heading of charges or other appellations. The case **Sociaal fonds** (discussed below) delivered a definition of charges having equivalent effect than custom duties, they are: *"Any pecuniary charge, however small and whatever its designation and mode of application, which is imposed unilaterally on domestic or foreign goods when they cross a frontier, and which is not a customs duty in the strict sense, constitutes a charge having equivalent effect within the meaning of articles 9 and 12 of the treaty, even if it is not imposed for the benefit of the state, is not discriminatory or protective in effect or if the product on which the charge is imposed is not in competition with any domestic product"*. The Court of Justice designed their meaning and scope in the famous case **Statistical Levy.**

General principle: The charge need not be levied at the border so long as it is levied by reason of crossing the border.

Commission v Italy (the 'Statistical Levy' case) (Case 24/68) [1969] ECR 193

Facts: Italy imposed a levy on all imports and exports for the purpose of collecting statistical material. The Italian government argued that this measure would have been of benefits to traders in the sense that the study would have allowed them to trade more efficiently. The traders were disadvantaged comparing to trade in other country that did not have this levy, and it appears to contradict the FMOG. Therefore the case was referred to the CJEU.

Preliminary question before the Court: Is it possible to impose an internal levy, not directly at the border, on every imports and exports for having crossed the border?

Preliminary Ruling: The Court of Justice regarded the levy as a CEE that was prohibited by Article 30. It underlines the paragraph previously mentioned in **Sociaal fonds**: *"Any pecuniary charge, however small and whatever its designation and mode of application, which is imposed unilaterally on domestic or foreign goods by reason of the fact that they cross a frontier and which is not a customs duty in the strict sense constitutes a charge having equivalent effect even if it is not imposed for the benefit of the State, is not discriminatory or protective in effect and if the product on which the charge is imposed is not in competition with any domestic product"*.

Indeed, the Court considered that the statistics compiled were too broad to be of benefit to traders, and excluded the argument presented as a defence. The charge need not be levied at the border so long as it is levied by reason of crossing the border.

Application: This case is a real cornerstone of the notion of CEE, which gave rise to several rules developed bellow.

General principle: Any pecuniary charge, however small can constitute a CEE.

Commission v Italy (the 'Statistical Levy' case) (Case 24/68) [1969] ECR 193

Here, the Court recalls that Article 30 only applies to pecuniary charges, whereas Articles 34 to 36 deal with non-pecuniary charges. However, it also tells us that the amount of the charge is not important. For example, in this case the small charge of 10 lire on each importer was sufficient to breach Article 30.

General principle: Any CEE is prohibited, regardless its designation and mode of application.

Commission v Italy (the 'Statistical Levy' case) (Case 24/68) [1969] ECR 193
This broad definition of CEE encompasses most of the charges that have the equivalent effect that a custom duty would have while being covered behind another denomination or system of collecting the charges. This rule, set up by the Court, ensures that the real objective of Article 30 is achieved.

General principle: A charge can be qualified as a CEE even if its purpose is not protectionist.

Sociaal Fonds voor de Diamantarbeiders v Chougol Diamond Co (Cases 2 & 3/69) [1969] ECR 211
Facts: A charge was applied by Belgium on the importation of diamonds. As a result, the imported diamonds became less competitive. The applicant argued that these measures were prohibited by Article 30 TFEU. Belgium replied that the purpose of this charge was not protectionist but rather aimed to fund additional social security benefits for Belgian diamond workers.
Preliminary question before the Court: Can a charge on importations and exportations be imposed on traders if its purpose is not protectionist but rather social?
Preliminary Ruling: The Court recalled that all custom duties or CEE were prohibited by Article 30, holding that: "*Customs duties are prohibited independently of any consideration of the purpose*

for which they were introduced and the destination of the revenue obtained therefrom".

Application: The intention of the Member State imposing duties on importations and exportations in its relation with other EU members is not taken into account. All of them are prohibited regardless if they are protectionist, benefit-oriented or social.

Charges that do not constitute a customs duty or a charge having equivalent effect

EU Law provides that no defence can be presented if a charge is qualified as a custom duty or a charge having equivalent effect. However, some charges on importations and exportations fall outside of the scope of Article 30; they are the charges that do not have equivalent effect of a custom duty.

General principle: A charge will not be regarded as CEE if EU Law itself requires an inspection on the good.

Commission v Germany (Case 18/87) [1988] ECR 5427

Facts: A charge was imposed in some German *Landers* to pay a veterinary checking for the trade of living animals. The Commission argued that this charge was equivalent to a custom duty. However, a Directive that ensured the good conditions of the international transport of animals required their inspection.

Preliminary question before the Court: In which situation a charge does not have the effect of a custom duty?

Preliminary Ruling: The Court held that a charge will not be declared CEE if the charge is "*attached to inspections carried out to fulfil obligations imposed by Community law*".

However, the Court added four conditions for such inspections to be authorized:

- The charge must not exceed the actual costs of the inspections;
- The inspections must be obligatory and uniform for all the relevant products in the Union;
- The inspections must be prescribed by EU law in the general interest of the Union; and

- The inspections must promote the free movement of goods, in particular by neutralising obstacles that could have arisen from unilateral inspection measures.

Application: This case permits a greater harmonization of norms on goods all over the Union. The strict conditions of this test also ensure that the inspection promotes the free movement of goods. The Court of Justice took the same position for inspections required by other international conventions (see **Commission v Netherlands** (Case 89/76) [1977] ECR 1355).

General principle: A charge corresponding to internal dues, treating domestic and imported goods the same will not be regarded as CEE.

Dansk Denkavit ApS v Danish Ministry of Agriculture (Case 29/87) [1988] ECR 2965

Facts: An EU Directive required Member States to check samples on feeding stuffs that contained additives. A levy was consequently charged to cover the costs of the control. However, this process was applied using the same criteria for domestic products.

Preliminary question before the Court: Are internal dues covered by Article 30 and therefore prohibited as having effect of custom duties?

Preliminary Ruling: The Court held that internal dues are part of an internal system treating fairly imported and non-imported goods were falling outside of the scope of Article 30.   It stated that: *"Article 30 of the Treaty must be interpreted as meaning that a national*

measure which subjects the importation of feedingstuffs containing additives to prior authorization constitutes a measure having an effect equivalent to quantitative restrictions on imports within the meaning of Article 30 of the Treaty".

Application: Internal dues fall outside of the scope of Article 30; they do not have the effect of custom duties. These types of charges belong to internal taxes rather than duties for goods having crossed the border. Internal dues are rather covered by Article 110 TFEU (see bellow). The main reason of this decision is certainly because all the goods were subjected to such a charge, regardless to where they were coming from. Conversely, in an earlier case, the Court held the reverse solution by because of the discrimination between domestic and imported goods (see **Bresciani v Amministrazione Italiana delle Finanze** (Case 87/75) [1976] ECR 129)

General principle: A charge will not be regarded as CEE if it constitutes a payment for service rendered.

The Court of Justice made clear, through its constant case law, that a charge for a genuine service that will benefit to importers or exporters cannot be classified as CEE. It is merely a payment for a service rendered. It was argued for the first time by the Italian government in the **Statistical levy** case, but the Court stated that the information compiled were too broad to benefit to traders. In the late 1980's, the Court of Justice finally recognized the legality of payment for service rendered in **Commission v Germany** (Case 18/87) [1988] ECR 5427. The Court listed the circumstances where a charge on imports will not constitute a customs duty or a CEE and hence not fall within Article 30. And it mentions clearly that it encompasses the situation where "*the charge constitutes payment for a service in fact rendered to the economic operator of a sum in proportion to the service*".

The Court of Justice added a further requirement in **W. Cadsky SpA v Istituto nazionale per il Commercio Estero** (Case 63/74) 1975. The Court requires that the service amounted to a specific and individual benefit to the trader, it stated: "*a charge does not breach Art 25 TEC (now Article 30) if it constituted consideration for a specific service actually and individually rendered to the trader, in an amount proportionate to that service. For that to be so there must be a specific and individual benefit to that trader*".
Threfore, in order for a payment in return to a service rendered to eschew the qualification of CEE, three conditions have to be satisfied according to the **"Customs Warehouses"** case.

General principle: The service rendered should be of benefit to the importer and the amount charged should be

commensurate to the service provided.

Commission v Belgium (the 'Customs Warehouses' case)
(Case 132/82) [1983] ECR 1649

Facts: Belgium charged for the use of a special warehouse within the country where customs clearance could be completed.

Preliminary question before the Court: Does the charge for use of public warehouses within the country where for imported goods, constitute a mere payment for service rendered?

Preliminary Ruling: The Court rejected the Belgian argument: *"Whilst it is true that the use of a public warehouse in the interior of the country offers certain advantages to importers it seems clear first of all that such advantages are linked solely with the completion of customs formalities which, whatever the place, is always compulsory"*. In other words, the Court qualified the charge as having equivalent effect to custom duties, therefore prohibited by Article 30. But, more importantly, the Court devised a test for a charge to be qualified as payment for service rendered (and then eschewing the scope of Article 30):

- It is consideration for a service rendered;
- It is of benefit to the importer; and
- The amount charged is commensurate with the costs of the service provided.

Application: Once again after **Statistical Levy**, the Court refuses the argument of a service benefiting to the traders. However this time it sets out a test to qualify a charge as payment for service rendered. Furthermore, the Court clarified the second condition on the benefit to the importer in its case **Bresciani.** In this case, the Court qualified the charge as CEE because the inspections were carried out in the public interest rather than as a service rendered to the importer. Therefore, the test appears to be restrictive and only very few charges will be qualified as payment for service rendered.

Article 110 TFEU: discriminatory internal taxation
The scope of article 110

Article 110 stipulates:
"(1) No Member State shall impose, directly or indirectly, on the

products of other Member States any internal taxation of any kind in excess of that imposed directly or indirectly on similar domestic products.

(2) Furthermore, no Member State shall impose on the products of other Member States any internal taxation of such a nature as to afford indirect protection to other products."

As stated above, if Article 30 concerns charges applied to product for having crossed the border, Article 110 regulates charges that are levied as a system of internal taxation within the state. Therefore, Article 110 supplements and strengthens the protection of free movement of good provided by Article 30. Without Article 110, Member States could hypocritically let imported goods in without any charge at the border in order to comply with Article 30, to better tax them internally at higher levels of taxation than domestic products. These internal trade barriers increase the costs of importation and place the importer at a competitive disadvantage comparing to the domestic traders. These barriers are usually referred to as "taxes regulated by Article 110".

It is very important to distinguish between a charge under Article 30 and a tax under Article 110 mainly because they have different effects. Article 30 provides with a very strict scrutiny over Member States; any custom duties or CEE will be declared unlawful and this irrespectively of whether or not it is discriminatory or protectionist. However, a tax under Article 110 is permissible as far as it is not discriminatory or protectionist. Therefore, Article 110 is much more flexible and leaves a certain autonomy for Member States to determine their own internal taxation policies. At an early stage, the Court of Justice recognized the direct effect of Article 110 in order to ensure its enforceability **(see lfons Lütticke GmbH v Hauptzollamt Saarlouis** (Case 57/65) [1966] ECR 205).

General principle: A charge constitutes an internal tax as far as it is part of a general system of internal dues that are not applied solely because the good has crossed the border.

Commission v France ('Reprographic Machinery') (Case

90/79) [1981] ECR 283

Facts: The case concerned an internal tax on reprographic machinery such as offset printing machines, microfiche scanners and photocopiers. Only 1% of the reprographic equipment put into the French market came from domestic products. The remaining 99% was imported. The Commission argued that this meant that, in practice, the levy was *de facto* borne by importers alone and so constituted a CEE.

Preliminary question before the Court: the question was to know if the levy constituted either a charge under Article 30 or a tax under Article 110?

Preliminary Ruling: The Court started by holding that the levy constituted a tax under Article 110. The levy was part of a general system of internal dues because of the reason for which the levy was imposed, the purpose for which the money was to be used and the fact that it formed part of a wider tax scheme.

Application: In this case, the Court clarifies the line between charges and taxes under Article 30 and 110.

Article 110(1) prohibits discrimination of similar products

Article 110 is divided into two paragraphs. The first paragraph prohibits discrimination between imported goods and similar domestic goods whereas the second paragraph prohibits protectionism between products, though not similar, being at competition. The prohibition of discrimination of Article 110(1), in concrete terms, forces Member States to subject imported and domestic similar goods to the same taxation regime.

(i)   Similarity of goods

General principle: Two goods are similar if at the same stage of production or marketing, the products had similar characteristics and met the same needs from the point of view of consumers.

Rewe- Zentrale des Lebensmittel-Großhandels GmbH v Hauptzollamt Landau/Pfalz (Case 45/75) [1976] ECR 181
Facts: This case involved a monopoly on alcohol. A particular

beverage was subjected to a specific tax. The applicants argued that their beverages were similar to the one considered as having a monopoly, therefore all these goods should be subjected to the same taxation regime.

Preliminary question before the Court: What is the meaning of "similar goods" under Article 110?

Preliminary Ruling: The Court of Justice held that: "*A comparison must be made between the taxation imposed on products which, at the same stage of production or marketing, have similar characteristics and meet the same needs from the point of view of consumers. In this respect, the classification of the domestic product and the imported product under the same heading in the common customs tariff constitutes an important factor in this assessment*".

Application: By establishing this test, the Court clearly shows that the nature of the goods is not the most important factor in determining their similarity. It devised a rather pragmatic test that focuses on the production, marketing and the use of the goods.

The Court later underlined the importance of the similar and comparable use of the goods (see **Commission v France ('Spirits')** (Case 168/78) [1980] ECR 347).

General principle: Goods are similar as far as being used similarly by consumers, even though they have been manufactured differently.

Commission v Denmark (Case 106/84) [1986] ECR 833

Facts: In Denmark, wine made from grapes was taxed at a higher level than wine made from fruits. In addition to this, the wine made from grape was exclusively imported to Denmark. In contrast wine made from fruit was mainly produced in Denmark. Both of these wines were table wine used by consumers as a beverage accompanying meals.

Preliminary question before the Court: the question was to know whether or not goods manufactured differently but being similarly used can be qualified as similar goods?

Preliminary Ruling: The Court upheld the similarity of goods: *"With regard to wine of the table-wine type, it should be noted in the first place that wine made from grapes and wine made from other fruit are manufactured from the same kind of basic product, namely agricultural produce, and by the same process, namely natural fermentation. Their organoleptic properties, in particular their taste and their alcohol content, are similar ... Moreover, in view of their similar characteristics the two categories of beverages can meet the same needs from the point of view of consumers inasmuch as they can be consumed in the same way, namely to quench thirst, as refreshments and at meal times".*

Application: The Court in **Commission v Denmark** presents an extensive test for similarity of goods, preventing Member States to differentiate between similar products on the way they had been manufactured.

(ii)   Discrimination

An internal tax, in order to be declared unlawful under Article 110(1) must be applied to similar goods, as it has been presented. In addition to this, the application of the tax must be discriminatory.

In practice, it generally means that the State is taxing the imported good at a higher level than the domestic one. However, the Court of Justice recognized, based on anti-discrimination Law of individuals, two types of discrimination: direct and indirect.

- **Direct discrimination**

Direct discrimination is easily identifiable; it implies a higher taxation of imported goods, as mentioned in the example above. This results on placing the importer at a disadvantage in its competition with domestic traders. For example, in **Commission v Italy ('Regenerated Oil')** (Case 21/79) [1980] ECR 1, the Italian government had an ecological policy of charging lower tax on the sale of regenerated oil than that imposed on normal oil. However, this benefit was only available to domestic oil producers. Therefore, the Court of Justice consequently declared the tax as directly discriminatory. Direct discrimination cannot be legitimately justified. A direct discrimination will always be prohibited by the Luxembourg Court.

- **Indirect discrimination**

General principle: A tax is indirectly discriminatory when although being facially neutral; it has a disproportionate impact on imported goods in practice.

A straightforward example of indirect discrimination can be found in the case **Commission v Denmark** (Case 106/84) [1986] ECR 833. In this case, wine made from grapes (exclusively imported to Denmark) was taxed at a higher level than wine made from fruits. In contrast wine made from fruit was mainly produced in Denmark. These rates were not officially determined by the taxation system regarding the origin of the goods but rather on their manufacturing. However, since grapes fruits were exclusively imported, it was consequently having a disproportionate impact on imported goods. The Court held that the tax was indirectly discriminatory.

Humblot v Directeur des Services Fiscaux (Case 112/84) [1985] ECR 1367

Facts: This case was about the French regime of taxation that was depending on the engine size of cars. Behind 16CV, the tax was approximately 1000 Francs, whereas over 16 CV the tax was 5000 francs. The tax was not mentioning the origin of the cars, but only the size of their engine. However, in practice, French manufacturers were only producing cars up to 16CV. The applicant claimed that this amounted to indirect discrimination.

Preliminary question before the Court: Can a facially neutral tax be declared discriminatory because it places imported goods in practice at significant disadvantage?

Preliminary Ruling: The Court of Justice held indirect discrimination for having promoted French cars over imported cars with bigger engines. This encouraged the consumer to buy a French car rather than a foreign car.

Application: In this case, once again, the Court relies on the production in practice. If the disadvantaged goods are exclusively imported, the test of discrimination will always be satisfied. However, exclusively does not mean mostly imported (see **Commission v France** previously mentioned). Even if the 99% of the production is imported, if the remaining one percent comes from domestic production, the discrimination will not be upheld.

Commission v Greece (Case 132/88) [1990] ECR I-1567

Facts: Greek legislation imposed a tax on cars increasing on the basis of the cylinder capacity of the car. The increase in the taxes became more pronounced at 1,201cc and again at 1,801cc. Indeed, one of the taxes, which was payable when the car was first registered, rose by 50% between 1,800cc and 1,801cc. Greece justified the measure on social policy, but indeed only produced cars up to 1,600cc. The tax was apparently neutral, because applied similarly for domestic and imported goods. However it was disproportionately affecting importing goods that were more likely to trigger higher levels of taxes.

Preliminary question before the Court: Can a facially neutral tax be declared discriminatory because it places imported goods in practice at significant disadvantage?

Preliminary Ruling: In this case the Court of Justice accepted the Greek justification based on social policy declaring that it was not, as such, contrary to Article 110. It also stated that the Commission failed to prove the protective nature of the Greek taxation system. According to the Court, consumers could still choose cars between 1,600cc and 1,800cc that were exclusively imported and not disproportionately affected by the tax. Or they could choose to buy cars below 1,600cc that were composed of both imported and domestically manufactured.

Application: It should be noted that in this case, even though there is indirect discrimination, the Court acknowledges the justification because the disparity in the levels of taxation was not as extreme as they were in **Humblot**. In addition to this, **Commission v Greece** also shows that justifications are not only limited to purely economic policies.

General principle: An internal tax is not discriminatory, and therefore permissible, if it is applied systematically to categories of products irrespective of their origins, even if it applies mainly to imported products in practice.

Commission v France ('Reprographic Machinery') (Case 90/79) [1981] ECR 283

Facts: The case concerned an internal tax on reprographic machinery such as offset printing machines, microfiche scanners and photocopiers. Only 1% of the reprographic equipment put into the French market came from domestic products. The remaining 99% was imported. The Commission argued that this meant that, in practice, the levy was *de facto* borne by importers alone and so constituted a CEE.

Preliminary question before the Court: Can an internal tax under Article 110, be *de facto* discriminatory because the market is mostly composed of imported goods?

Preliminary Ruling: The Court held, declared permissible the internal tax under Article 110 as being non-discriminatory. It stated that the tax related to: *"a general system of internal dues applied systematically to categories of products in accordance with objective criteria irrespective of the origin of the products"*.

Application: The criterion for indirect discrimination requires the strict exclusivity of imported goods, this case reminds us that "mostly composed of imported goods" is not enough.

General principle: Indirect discrimination of imported goods can be objectively justified by the specificity of the raw materials used or the production processes employed.

Chemial Farmaceutici SpA v DAF SpA (Case 140/79) [1981] ECR 1

Facts: Italy was differentiating between synthetic and fermented alcohol. Synthetic alcohol was charged 10 times more than fermented alcohol according to the Italian internal taxing regime. However, Synthetic alcohol was exclusively imported to Italy. Therefore, imported goods were undeniably placed at a competitive disadvantage.

Preliminary question before the Court: Can indirect discrimination on goods be legitimately justified?

Preliminary Ruling: The Court of Justice first acknowledged that Italy was indirectly discriminating against imported goods. However, it was justifiable according to the Court because it drew a distinction between the two types of alcohol that aimed to promote agricultural products and avoid alcohol from petroleum derivatives.

The Court stated: "*In its present stage of development community law does not restrict the freedom of each member state to lay down tax arrangements which differentiate between certain products on the basis of objective criteria, such as the nature of the raw materials used or the production processes employed. Such differentiation is compatible with community law if it pursues economic policy objectives which are themselves compatible with the requirements of the treaty and its secondary law and if the detailed rules are such as to avoid any form of discrimination, direct or indirect, in regard to imports from other member states or any form of protection of competing domestic products*".

Application: The justification can be invoked as far as the Member State presents objective reasons other than economic. It can be based on the protection of environment, public health or the promotion of craft production for example.

Article 110(2) prohibits protectionism of non-similar products at competition

Article 110 (2) prohibits protectionist measures promoting domestic goods over imported goods at competition. The goods at stake are not similar but at competition. The Court of Justice, in its case **Commission v France ('Spirits')** clarified Article 110(2) as it follows: *"without being similar within the meaning of the first paragraph, are nonetheless in competition, even partial, indirect or potential, with certain products of the importing country"*.

General principle: the test lies in the substitutability of the products affected by the protectionist measure; if one product is rendered more expensive, are consumers likely to switch to the other product?

Commission v UK ("Wine and Beer") (Case 170/78) [1980] ECR 417 and **[1983]** ECR 2265

Facts: UK imposed a higher rate of tax on wine compared to beer. Wine and beer have always been at competition and since the accession of the UK in the European Communities; its tax burden had become approximately five times that of beer. The Commission argued that wine and beer were at competition and therefore the protectionist measures taken by the UK were prohibited by article 110(2).

The Court delivered a first judgement accepting the Commission's argument and declaring the measures incompatible with Article 110(2).

Preliminary question before the Court: Can wine and beer be qualified as goods at competition under article 110 (2)?

Preliminary Ruling: the Court of Justice, in a second judgement of 1983, concluded that the comparison had to be made between beer and the cheapest and lightest type of wine, because they were the only goods at competition. It held that the abusive increase of tax on wine labelled it as a luxury product which had a significant impact on the decision of the consumer to switch his habits from wine to beer.

Application: In this case, the Court extends the protection of imported goods from protectionists' measures, which places the test on the substitutability of the products.

Furthermore, it should be noted that the consequences of an infringement of Article 110(1) and Article 110(2) are not the same. Under Article 110(1), the State has to equalise (up or down) the tax of similar goods to end the breach. However, under Article 110(2), the Member State only has to "remove the protectionist aspect", which do not necessarily mean to equalise the tax. For example, in **Commission v UK ("Wine and Beer"),** after the judgement of the Court, UK only lowered the tax on wine and it was approved by the Commission.

Chapter 8: Free Movement of Goods II
Articles 34–36 TFEU

General ideology

In Chapter 7 we have examined how EU Law has sought to prevent Member States from imposing fiscal barrier (Article 28-30 and 110 TFEU). In this second chapter on freedom of goods, we will examine how EU Law prevents Member States from imposing non-fiscal barriers on goods (Articles 34 and 35 TFEU). Furthermore, the permissible derogations to these prohibitions will also be analysed (Article 36 TFEU). There is a potentially infinite variety of non-fiscal barriers, from security measures on the safety of a product to hygiene inspection or technical legislation. For instance, banning the advertisement of strong alcohol can constitute a non-fiscal barrier.

Article 34 TFEU provides:
"Quantitative restrictions on imports and all measures having equivalent effect shall be prohibited between Member States"

Article 35 stipulates:
"Quantitative restrictions on exports and all measures having equivalent effect shall be prohibited between Member States"

Any measure infringing Article 34 or 35 is *prima facie* contrary to EU Law. However, Article 36 presents the situations where Article 34 and 35 will not apply. These derogations can be based on various grounds. The Court of Justice of the European Union qualified article 34 and 35 TFEU as being of direct effect. It stated, in its case **Ianelli & Volpi SpA Meroni** (Case 74/76) 1977 ECR 595 that *"The prohibition of quantitative restrictions and measures having equivalent effect has direct effect and creates individual rights which national courts must protect"*. Regarding to the scope of Article 34 and 35, it should be noted that they are addressed to the Member States and therefore apply only to acts or omissions on their behalf. Thus, purely private bodies or individuals remain outside the ambit of these Articles.

However, the Court of Justice has extended the scope of Articles 34 and 35 to quasi-public bodies other than the mere central and local governments. Thus, it results from the CJEU's case law that the following entities have been held capable of infringing Articles 34 and 35:

- Semi-public bodies such as quasi-autonomous non-governmental organisations (QANGOS), see **Apple and Pear Development Council v K J Lewis ltd** (Case 222/82) 1983 ECR 4083.

- Nationalised industries. For example, the Post Office in **Commission v France** (Case 21/84) 1985 ECR 1355 has been held liable for a breach of Article 34.

- Regulatory agencies and professional bodies established under statutory authority, see **Royal Pharmaceutical Society of Great Britain, ex parte Association of Pharmaceutical Importers and Others** (Case 267/87) 1989 ECR 1295.

- The EU's institutions see **Denkavit** (Case 15/83 1984 ECR 2171).

Article 34 TFEU: restrictions on imports

Quantitative restrictions

The Court of Justice, in **Geddo v Ente Nazionale Risi** (Case 2/73) [1973] ECR 865 held that quantitative restrictions are "*measures which amount to a total or partial restraint ... of imports, exports or goods in transit*". This can involve quota systems or outright bans on imports for instance (as illustrated with the following cases).

General principle: A quantitative restriction is a measure that amounts to a total or partial restraint of imports of goods in transit such as bans or quotas on imports.

R v Henn and Darby (Case 34/79) [1979] ECR 3795
Facts: The United Kingdom introduced a ban on the importation of pornographic material. Importing pornographic material resulted on committing a statutory offense punishable on conviction. The applicant argued that this measure was a quantitative restriction prohibited by Article 34 TFEU under free movement of goods.
Preliminary question before the Court: Can a complete ban of the importation of a specific good constitute a quantitative restriction under Article 34 TFEU?
Preliminary Ruling: The Court of Justice of the European Union upheld that the domestic statutory offense breached Article 34 as constituting a quantitative restriction.
Application: In this case, the outright ban is the most obvious example of a quantitative restriction that is clearly contrary to the principle of freedom of goods. Usually, Member States will justify these bans by invoking the necessary protection of public morality or public health.

However, quotas on imports can also constitute quantitative restrictions. In this respect, the Member State sets a maximum amount of imports for certain products above which they will not be accepted at the border anymore. For instance, it is the case of a licencing system (see **International Fruit Company NV v Produktschap voor Groenten** (Cases 51-54/71) [1971] ECR 1107).

Measures equivalent to quantitative restrictions (MEQRs)

MEQRs cover a wide range of measures that can be qualified as disguised non-fiscal trade barriers. It is a pure jurisprudential extension of the concept of quantitative restrictions, as far as nothing in the Treaties mentions MEQRs. It has been established by the well-known **Dassonville** formula.

General principle: Trading rules that hinder Union trade directly or indirectly, actually or potentially are to be considered as measures having effect equivalent to quantitative restrictions.

Procureur du Roi v Dassonville (Case 8/74) [1974] ECR 837
Facts: Belgian Law required a certificate of origin for Scotch whisky. Benoit Dassonville, a Belgian trader, unable to provide the certificate of origin of his products, imported some whisky from France with forged documents. The importer was convicted for fraud.
However, he argued that the Belgian measure requiring the certificates was infringing Article 34 TFEU.
Preliminary question before the Court: Can a measure that is not formally a quantitative restriction but that has the same effects, be introduced in compliance with Article 34?
Preliminary Ruling: The Court held that, though the measure was not formally a quantitative restriction, it has the same subsequent effect as to hinder trade and therefore should be prohibited under Article 34. It recognized for the first time that Article 34 encompassed MEQRs. The Court stated: *"All trading rules enacted by Member States which are capable of hindering, directly or indirectly, actually or potentially, intra-Union trade are to be considered as measures having an effect equivalent to quantitative restrictions"*.
Application: This case sets up a very important definition of MEQRs that has always been cited in cases involving Article 34 ever since. This approach of the CJEU extends significantly the scope of measure capable of breaching Article 34.
However, it should be reminded that Article 34 only deals with non-fiscal barriers, therefore a MEQR cannot be qualified as charge having the effect of a custom duty infringing Article 30 which deals with fiscal barriers (see **Ianelli & Volpi SpA Meroni** (Case 74/76) 1977 ECR 595).

The case **Dassonville** did not take into account the discriminatory nature of the impugned measures. However, Directive 70/50 drawn the distinction between distinctly applicable MEQRs and indistinctly applicable MEQRs. This distinction is crucial because it will determine whether or not the "mandatory requirements" apply.

(i) Distinctly applicable MEQRs

These are measures that do not apply equally to domestic and imported goods. Such measures discriminate against imports because they make importation more difficult or costly relative to the domestic product. For example, it can be a domestic rule that demands higher standard in terms of hygienic precautions for imported goods than domestic goods. The Court of Justice's case law reveals a broad variety of MEQRs which may be classified as distinctly applicable measures. The following cases give a sense of their main characteristics.

General principle: It is generally contrary to Article 34 to promote the consumption of a domestic product in the context of a "buy national" campaign.

Commission v Ireland ('Buy Irish') (Case 249/81) [1982] ECR 4005
Facts: The Irish Goods Council, a semi-public body was given the task of promoting domestic Irish goods. The Irish Ministry of industry even financed a massive advertising campaign. The European Commission, in a reasoned opinion, argued that these measures were infringing Article 34. The case was later referred to the Court on the basis of MEQRs hindering free trade.
Preliminary question before the Court: The question was to know whether or not a campaign inciting consumers to buy domestic products constituted a non-fiscal trade barrier under Article 34?
Preliminary Ruling: The Court held that the allegations of the Commission on the breach of Article 34 were valid. The launching of massive campaign advertising by Member States was incompatible with the EU principle of free movement of goods because it could influence actors of the market into discriminating against imported goods.
Application: This case appears to enlarge the scope of protection

of Article 34 against the wrongs of Member States of disguising trade barriers by actively promoting the consumption of domestic goods.

However, this case was limited by **Apple and Pear Development Council v K J Lewis ltd** (Case 222/82) 1983 ECR 4083. In this case, the Court of Justice upheld that it is not contrary to EU Law to promote domestic goods by pointing out the particular qualities of these goods.

General principle: Domestic measures requiring importers to present import licences are considered as barriers to trade.

Evans Medical & Macfarlan Smith (Case 2324/93) 1995 ECR I-563

Facts: This case concerned a British measure that required a licence to import poppy seeds into the UK. The government justified this requirement by the necessary protection of public health. Indeed, if the transformation of these poppy seeds could convert it into diamorphine, a very strong painkiller, it could also end on the streets as heroin substitute. This was a widespread phenomenon in the UK at the time.

Preliminary question before the Court: Does the requirement of import licences constitute a trade barrier under Article 34?

Preliminary Ruling: The Court held that the fact that certain Member States required licences only to imported goods were trade barriers contravening with Article 34. This is because the cost and time spent to apply for a licence could render the importation more difficult. It was restraining partially the effective importation of goods in transit.

Application: Evans prevents Member States to require formalities that would partially restraint the importation of goods in their territories. The Court went further in the case **Commission v UK UHT Milk** (case 124/81) 1983 ECR 203, by stating that Article 34 prevents the requirement of every licences, even if the granting of the licence would be a mere formality.

General principle: Additional hygiene inspections for

imported goods are prohibited by Article 34.

The main reason for this rule is that hygiene inspections carried out on imported goods may trigger delays and expenses in the delivery. On this question, two cases are illustrating the reluctance of the Court of Justice to authorize additional hygiene inspections on imported goods:

- In **Rewe-Zentralfinance** (case 4/75) 1975 ECR 843; the Court declared the German requirement of phytosanitary inspections on imported apples was contrary to Article 34.
- In **Commission v France (Italian Wines)** (Case 42/82) 1983 ECR 1013, the Court of Justice outlawed the thorough inspections imposed by France on imported Italian wines.

(ii) Indistinctly applicable MEQRs

Indistinctly applicable MEQRs apply to both domestic and imported goods without drawing a distinction between them (Article 3 of Directive 70/50). Nevertheless, these measures have the potential to hinder trade. They can sometimes still place imported goods at a disadvantage in practice but not always. The following cases illustrate the main examples of indistinctly applicable MEQRs.

General principle: Domestic rules requiring goods to be marked with their country of origin are generally incompatible with Article 34.

Commission v UK (origin-marking) (Case 207/83) 1985 ECR 1201
Facts: The Trade Description order 1981 in UK prohibited the supply or offer of many goods such as textile or cutlery if they were not marked with their country of origin. The inscription had to be clear and legible, as to be easily visible for consumers. However, the order applied to every goods, including domestic goods manufactured in the UK. The Commission alleged that this requirement hindered free trade and the principle of free

movement of goods.

Preliminary question before the Court: The question was to know whether or not the requirement of origin marking could be qualified as measure equivalent to quantitative restrictions.

Preliminary Ruling: The Court held that a breach of Article 34 had been committed by stating: "*The purpose of origin-marking is to enable customers to distinguish between domestic and imported products and this enables them to assert any prejudices which they may have against foreign products... The Treaty, by establishing a Common Market ... seeks to unite national markets in a single market having the characteristics of a single market. Within such a market, the origin-marking requirement not only makes the marketing in a Member State of goods produced in other Member States ... more difficult, it also has the effect of slowing down economic interpenetration of the Union*".

Application: This case can be explained by the fact that origin marking imposes an extra-burden on importers because they have to comply with national laws that they might not be aware of and that might takes them more efforts than domestic traders to comply with.

General principle: Packaging requirements specific to each Member States create non-fiscal barriers incompatible with free movement of goods.

The main reason for this rule is that it would place importers at a competitive disadvantage because they would have to develop special packaging processes solely for the importing State. In addition to this, if each Member State introduces different packaging requirements, an importer would have to develop 28 packages in order to trade with all the Member States of the Union. This results on unreasonable costs that hinder free trade and places barriers to free movement of goods. For example, in the case **Walter Rau v De Smedt** (Case 261/81) 1982 ECR 3961, Belgian legislation required a complex packaging in cube. This packaging required an expensive investment in both time and money. Consequently, the Court of Justice declared this requirement incompatible with Article 34.

General principle: A complete ban under national legislation on the use of a product is a measure equivalent to quantitative restrictions.

Toolex Alpha (Case C-473/98) 2000 ECR I-5681

Facts: Swedish legislation prohibited the sale, transfer or use of chemical products for industrial purposes such as trichloroethylene. Toolex, a chemical manufacturer used it in its manufacturing process. The company challenged the ban for breach of Article 34.

Preliminary question before the Court: Can a prohibition to use a good constitute a measure equivalent to quantitative restrictions?

Preliminary Ruling: The Court held that a complete prohibition to use a good is a measure equivalent to quantitative restrictions. A domestic prohibition to use a good is a *prima facie* violation of Article 34 until being legitimately justified.

Application: A complete domestic ban on the use of a specific good is one of the most obvious infringements to free movement of goods in terms of non-fiscal barriers. Such measure will always be considered as being *prima facie* prohibited by Article 34. However, the issue will be then to know whether or not it can be justified.

In a range of recent cases, the Court of Justice declared the prohibitions of use certain goods as contravening with the dispositions of Article 34, even when it could be lawfully imported and sold, as far as it cannot be used in the country, consumers were deterred to buy them. However, in the majority of these cases, the prohibition was justified by the **Cassis de Dijon** principles, which will be examined now.

Defences: mandatory requirement for indistinctly applicable MEQRs

The point of differentiating distinctly and indistinctly applicable MEQRs lies on the fact that they do not give rise to the same defences. Indeed, the traditional position of the Court of Justice is to accept the mandatory requirements' defence only when the national legislation is indistinctly applicable. In this respect, The

Court of Justice, in the case **Gilli & Andres** 1 CMLR 146 (1981) stated:

"It is only where national rules, which apply without discrimination to both domestic and imported products, may be justified as necessary in order to satisfy imperative requirements relating in particular to the protection of public health, the fairness of commercial transactions and the defence of the consumer that they may constitute an exception to the requirements arising under Article 34".

To some extent, it aims to sanction the Members States that had been discriminatingly applying a measure equivalent to quantitative restrictions to importations only. The mandatory requirements arose in the late 1970's after the enacting of very complex consumer protection legislation in the Member States. Indeed, Article 36 did not cover many measures taken by the Member States qualifying as MEQRs. Therefore, these measures were incapable of being justified.

(i) The rule of reason

The Court of Justice, instead of waiting for a long and heavy reform of the Treaties, took a decisive action in the case **Cassis de Dijon.** Since the Court had no power to amend Article 36, it devised a parallel derogation to Article 34 enshrining the "rule of reason" approach.

General principle: indistinctly applicable MEQRs may be recognised as being necessary to satisfy mandatory requirements relating to objectives of general interest.

Cassis de Dijon case (Case 120/78) [1979] ECR 649
Facts: The facts involved a German measure that laid down a minimum alcohol level of 24 per cent per litre for certain spirits including cassis. A German company, Rewe-Zentral, applied to the body in charge of labelling the German spirits, to import Cassis de Dijon, a French blackcurrant liqueur of 15-20 per cent proof. The applicant company was informed that the liqueur was

not strong enough to be labelled as "German spirits". The applicant challenged the impugned Law for incompatibility with Article 34 TFEU. The German government argued that the Law had been enacted to protect public health and to ensure fairness in commercial transactions.

Preliminary question before the Court: The question was to know whether or not national law incompatible with Article 34 could be justified on grounds such as mandatory requirements relating to public health or fairness of commercial transactions for instance.

Preliminary Ruling: The Court of Justice laid down the "rule of reason" establishing new grounds for the derogation of Article 34 such as, *inter alia,* consumer protection or public health. The Court held: *"Obstacles to movement within the community resulting from disparities between the national laws relating to the marketing of the products in question must be accepted in so far as those provisions may be recognized as being necessary in order to satisfy mandatory requirements relating in particular to the effectiveness of fiscal supervision, the protection of public health, the fairness of commercial transactions and the defence of the consumer".*

However, as a matter of fact, the Court of Justice considered that in this case the derogations were not necessary, a clear labelling would have been sufficient.

Application. The new test set up by the Court called "Rule of reason" is also referred to as "objectives of general interests" or "overriding reasons in the general interests" in other cases.

More importantly, the Court, in its judgement, before mentioning potential grounds, added: *"in particular"* which means that the Court will be able to recognize other grounds later on. It has to be contrasted with Article 36 that relies on a closed list of grounds.

Consequently the Court of Justice has progressively recognized a range of other grounds for derogating to Article 34 under the mandatory requirements:

- The protection of public health (1979). See **Cassis de Dijon**.

- The fairness of commercial transactions (1979). See **Oosthoek's**

- **Uitgeversmaatschappij BV** (Case 286/81) [1982] ECR 4575
- The defence of the consumer (1979). See **Robertson and others** (Case 220/81) 1983 ECR 2349

- The improvement of working conditions (1981). See **Oebel** (Case 155/80) 1981 ECR 1993.

- The protection of the environment (1985). See **ADBHU** (Case 240/83) 1985 ECR 531.

- The protection of culture (1985). See **Cinéthèque** (Case 60 and 61/84) 1985 ECR 2065

- The diversity of press (1997). See **Filmapress** (Case C-368/95) [1997] ECR I-3689

- The maintenance of social security systems (1998). **Decker** (Caes C-120/95) 1998 ECR I-1831.

- Road safety (2000). See **Snellers Autos** (Case C-314/98) 2000 ECR I-8633.

- The protection of fundamental rights (2003). See **Schmidberger v Austria** (Case C-112/00) 2003 ECR 5659.

- Protection of children (2008). See **Medien v Avides Media** (Case C-244/06) 2008 ECR I-505.

- The "fight against crime" (2008). See **Commission v Portugal (Tinter film for car windows)** (Case C-205/06) 2008 ECR I-2245.

(ii) Mutual recognition

Cassis de Dijon dealt with the mutual recognition principle which implies that provided they have been lawfully produced and marketed in one Member State, there is no valid reason why goods should not be introduced into any other Member State.

Craig, in a commentary on this case, stated: *"The judgment encapsulated the principle of mutual recognition (where the goods have been lawfully and marketed in one of the MSs, there is no valid reason why they should not be introduced into any other MS) unless the mandatory requirements are satisfied under the rule of reason"*.

According to **Barnard,** this principle replaces dual recognition of a product (home and host states) with single regulation (home state) which the host state must respect. Consequently, there is no need for much harmonisation legislation anymore. The author concludes that: *"Cassis therefore promoted the Union interest of market regulation at the cost of potentially eroding the diverse national standards adopted by democratically elected national governments that may create a regulatory gap"*.

(iii) Proportionality

In order to restrict free movement of goods by requiring product requirements, Member States have to show that it is justified by the rule of reason under the **Cassis de Dijon** principles. However, the Court of Justice added a further condition for the national rule to be accepted: the steps taken should be proportionate.

General principle: A barrier trade, in order to be justified by the mandatory requirements, has to be proportionate to a legitimate aim.

Walter Rau Lebensmittelwerke v De Smedt PVBA (1983) Case 261/81
Facts: A Belgian rule required butter to be marketed in cub-shaped packages to avoid confusion with butter was an indistinctly applicable MEQR as it required foreign margarine to be repackaged before being sold in Belgium. Walter Rau argued that

the law was incompatible with Article 34 TFEU.

Preliminary question before the Court: Did this law violate Art 34 TFEU preventing restrictions on the free movement of goods between EU Member States?

Preliminary Ruling: The Court of Justice held that the barrier to trade could be justified by the consumer protection under the mandatory requirement. However, the Luxembourg Court concluded that the law could not be justified, as it was not proportionate to the aim of preventing confusion between margarine and butter. The Court stated: *"It cannot be reasonably denied that in principle legislation designed to prevent butter and margarine from being confused in the mind of the consumer is justified. However, the application by one member state to margarine lawfully manufactured and marketed in another member state of legislation which prescribes for that product a specific kind of packaging such as the cubic form to the exclusion of any other form of packaging considerably exceeds the requirements of the object in view. Consumers may in fact be protected just as effectively by other measures, for example by rules on labelling, which hinder the free movement of goods less".*

Application: In this case, the Court adds a further condition to the justification of a barrier to trade under the mandatory requirement: the rule must be proportionate to a legitimate aim.

Article 35 TFEU: restrictions on exports

Article 35 is a perfect mirror of Article 34 except that it applies to exports. It prohibits quantitative restrictions and MEQRs on exports. However, there is much less case law than for imports, this is mainly because Member States generally promote exports. The Court also made a distinction between measures distinctly and indistinctly applicable. However, there are some fundamental differences between the operation of Article 34 and 35, hence they are analysed separately.

(i) Distinctly applicable MEQRs

They are measures that clearly discriminate against exports. The discrimination is disadvantaging goods indented to be exported in comparison with goods marketed domestically.

General principle: Domestic bans on exports are infringing Article 35 TFEU.

On this issue, the Court of Justice has delivered a range of decisions leading to the following conclusion: Article 35 prohibits general bans on exports. For instance, in the **case R v Ministry of Agriculture, Fisheries and Food, ex p Hedley Lomas (Ireland) Ltd** (Case C-5/94) [1996] ECR I-2553, the Court declared that the general ban to export living animals to Spain was incompatible with Article 35. This solution has been upheld despite the Irish argument of the protection of animal health. In **R v Thompson "old coins case"** (Case 7/78) [1979] ECR 2247, the Court came up with the same conclusion on old coins having been prohibited for exportation.

General principle: Requiring licencing for exports hinders free movement of trade.

Bouhelier (Case 53/76) 1977 ECR 197
Facts: A French Law required watchmakers to possess a licence for exporting their products. This rule was introduced to maintain a certain standard of quality of watches exported. The applicant argued that this contravened with Article 35 and free movement of goods.
Preliminary question before the Court: Does the requirement of a licence to export constitute an infringement to Article 35 TFEU?
Preliminary Ruling: The Court held that requiring licences for exports hindered free movement of trade and infringed Article 35. The Court drew particular attention to the fact that the rule was imposed only on exporters and not on trader marketing their products in France. The Court concluded that it led to *"arbitrary discrimination between the two types of products which constitutes an obstacle to intra-Union trade"*.
Application: In this case, the Court extended the Article 35 prohibition of MEQRs on exports to licencing requirements. Since

then, the Luxembourg Court applied this principle in other cases such as **Belgium v Spain (Rioja wine exports)** (Case C-388/95) 2000 or **Jersey potatoes** (Case C-293/02) 2005.

(ii) Indistinctly applicable MEQRs

These domestic measures do not distinguish between goods intended for the national markets and goods intended for export.

General principle: Indistinctly applicable MEQRs fall outside the scope of Article 35 and are therefore permissible in the light of free movement of goods.

P.B. Groenveld BV v Produktschap voor Vee en Vlees (Case 15/79) [1979] ECR 3409

Facts: The Dutch Processing and Preparation of Meat Regulation (1973) prohibited any manufacturer of having in stock or processing horsemeat. The measure applied indistinctly to goods intended to be exported and goods marketed domestically. Groenveld, A Dutch sausage manufacturer, challenged the Dutch legislation as being incompatible with Article 35.

Preliminary question before the Court: The question was to know whether or not Article 35 TFEU prohibited indistinctly applicable quantitative restrictions or MEQRs.

Preliminary Ruling: The Court held that there was no breach of Article 35 because the Dutch Law made no distinction between domestic sales and exports of sausages. The Court concluded in its judgement: *"Article 35 will only apply to measures that have as their specific object or effect the restriction on the patterns of export and thereby the establishment of a difference in treatment between the domestic trade of a Member State and its export trade in such a way as to provide a particular advantage for national production or for the domestic market of the state in question at the expense of the production or of the trade of other Member States. This is not in a case of prohibition ... which is applied objectively to the production of goods of a certain kind without drawing any distinction depending on whether or not such goods are intended for the national market of for export"*

Application: In the case of indistinctly applicable MEQRs, there is simply no breach of Article 35. This is the main difference between the effect of Article 34 and Article 35.

Defences: Article 36 TFEU derogations

Article 36 provides that:

"The provisions of Articles 34 and 35 shall not preclude prohibitions or restrictions on imports, exports or goods in transit justified on grounds of public morality, public policy or public security; the protection of health and life of humans, animals or plants; the protection of national treasures possessing artistic, historic or archaeological value; or the protection of industrial and commercial property. Such prohibitions or restrictions shall not, however, constitute a means of arbitrary discrimination or a disguised restriction on trade between Member States".

The derogations listed in Article 36 are available to avoid the application of both Article 34 and Article 35. However, the question arose to know whether or not the Court of Justice could add new grounds to this list.

General principle: The list of grounds in Article 36 TFEU is exhaustive and no grounds can be added to.

Commission v Ireland ('Irish Souvenirs') (Case 113/80) [1981] ECR 1625

Facts: Irish rules required imported jewellery that incorporated motifs suggesting that they were souvenirs from Ireland, such as a shamrock motif, to bear an indication of the country in which it was made and the word "foreign". The defence of the Irish government was that consumers wanted to buy souvenirs that had been made in the country they were visiting and needed such origin-marking to distinguish such items. It claimed derogations to Article 34 under Article 36 for the protection of consumers and the protection of cultural diversity.

Preliminary question before the Court: Is the list of Article 36 derogations exhaustive or can the Court add new grounds to this list?

Preliminary Ruling: The Court held that the Article 36 list of grounds was exhaustive and could not be extended by case law: *"The exceptions listed in Article 36 cannot be extended to cases other than those specifically laid down. In view of the fact neither the protection of consumers nor the protection of creativity and cultural diversity in is included amongst the exceptions set out in Article 36, those grounds cannot be relied upon as such in connection with that Article".*

Application: The Court here enshrines a restrictive interpretation of Article 36 and rejects grounds such as the protection of consumers or culture that have been later recognized by the **Cassis de Dijon** case. In another case, arguments for the recognition of grounds based on economics or fairness of transaction have been rejected as well, see **Campus oil Ltd** (Case 72/83) 1984 ECR 2727

However, the main restriction to the application of Article 36 lies on the last sentence of its text: *"Such prohibitions or restrictions shall not, however, constitute a means of arbitrary discrimination or a disguised restriction on trade between Member States".* In other words, the derogations cannot be relied upon if the measure employed by the Member State constitutes arbitrary discrimination or a disguised restriction on trade. A further requirement of proportionality has been added by the Court of Justice in the case **ATRAL** (Case C-14/02) 2003 ECR I-4431: *"An exception to the principle of the free movement of goods may be justified under Article 36 only if the national authorities show that it is necessary in order to attain one or more objectives mentioned in that article and that is in conformity with the principle of proportionality".* Article 36 recognizes 6 grounds of derogation that will be examined in turn.

(i) Public morality.

General principle: The prohibition of supply or offer of footages having a pornographic content belongs to the protection of public morality.

R v Henn and Darby (Case 34/79) [1979] ECR 3795

Facts: This case concerned a UK ban on the import of pornographic films and magazines. Henn and Darby imported a consignment of pornographic films that was denied access at the UK border. The applicant argued that this measure constituted a quantitative restriction contrary to Article 34. In addition to this, the UK government was not arbitrarily discriminating against imported goods as there was no lawful trade in such goods in the UK.

Preliminary question before the Court: The question was known whether or not the prohibition of sales of pornographic product based on public morality was valid?

Preliminary Ruling: The Court of Justice held that the UK was able to rely on the public morality derogation under Article 36. The Court of Justice stated that *"it is for each Member State to determine in accordance with its own scale of values and in the form selected by it the requirements of public morality"*.

Application: Before declaring a restriction of the use of a good in a Member State as prohibited, one should verify it is not likely to be justified on the ground of public morality.

(ii) Public policy.

General principle: Public policy is a valid justification for a restriction on trade if the fundamental interests of society required such rule.

R v Thompson "old coins case" (Case 7/78) [1979] ECR 2247

Facts: This case concerned a ban from the UK to export old coins to prevent them to be destroyed. The important point was that the export ban went hand in hand with an equivalent ban on silver coins being melted down or destroyed in the United Kingdom itself. These measure was challenge on the basis of its incompatibility with Article 35. The UK justified this restriction on exports by the fundamental interest of society protected by public policy.

Preliminary question before the Court: The question was to know whether or not a policy protecting the right to mint coinage could be accepted as a valid public policy?

Preliminary Ruling: The Court of Justice accepted than the ban on export, supplemented by another internal measure prohibiting the destruction of coins, was necessary for the State to protect the right to mint coinage. According to the Court, the ling coinage involved a fundamental interest of society.

Application: In this case the Court acknowledges a right to Member States to restrict trade when it can be justified by the necessary protection of the fundamental interest of society.

This ground provides the Member States with a possibility to restrict the consumption of alcohol, drugs, or other addictions that might be harmful to society. For instance, the Court of Justice acknowledged this defence, presented by the Finnish government, in the case **Ahokainen & Leppik** (Case C-434/04) 2006 ECR I-9171. In this case, a Finnish Law prohibited the importation of alcohol above 80% proof without licence. However, despite a great potential width, this ground has rarely been successfully invoked in practice.

(iii) Public security.

The leading case on this issue is **Campus Oil Ltd v Minister for Industry and Energy** (Case 72/83) [1984] ECR 2727. In this case, a domestic quantitative restriction was implemented by Ireland to avoid becoming over-reliant on import of petrol. It was argued that becoming over-reliant on import of petrol raised concerned of public security. The Court of Justice accepted this derogation under Article 36. This was because petroleum products are of fundamental importance for the existence of the State. It is an essential good to public services. According to the Luxembourg Court, an interruption of supplies of petroleum products can seriously affect public security as a result.

(iv) The protection of health/life of humans, animals or plants.

Article 36 TFEU also mentions the protection of health and life of humans, animals or plants. It is the derogation most commonly used. It has been successfully invoked in the case **Toolex** that involved the importation of chemical products presenting an important risk of causing cancer. The Court of Justice concluded on this issue that "*the health and life of humans rank foremost among the property or interests protected by Article 36*".

In practice, the protection of health and life of humans, animals or plants has been frequently used concerning the importation of drugs or additives having supposedly adverse effect on public health. Finally, the protection of animals has been invoked in the case **R v Ministry of Agriculture, Fisheries and Food, ex p Hedley Lomas (Ireland) Ltd** (Case C-5/94) [1996]. This case involved a ban on the exportation of living animals to Spain. However, it was refused by the Court of Justice for lack of evidence. Finally, the case **Criminal proceedings against Ditlev Bluhme "Læso brown bee"** (Case C-67/97) 1998 concerned a ban on the importation of bees in Island to protect the biodiversity. Indeed, the importation of other species of bees than the Læso brown bee, the main colony on the island, would have triggered a risk of extinction. The justification based on the protection of health and life of humans, animals or plants was accepted by the Court. It stated that: "measures to preserve an indigenous animal population with distinct characteristics contribute to the maintenance of biodiversity through ensuring the survival of the population concerned; their aim is thus to protect the life of those animals".

(v) The protection of national treasures possessing artistic, historic or archaeological value.

The protection of national treasures possessing artistic, historic or archaeological value has been very rarely invoked in the CJEU's case law. In addition to this, no case has yet succeeded on this ground. However, it is still an available derogation that could be use in very particular situations.

(vi) The protection of industrial and commercial property.

Finally, the last ground mentioned by Article 36 TFEU is the protection of industrial and commercial property.For instance, in the case **Belgium v Spain (Rioja wine exports)** (Case C-388/95) 2000 Spanish Law required Rioja wine to be bottled in the region of Rioja. The Spanish government argued that it was crucial to preserve the worldwide high quality reputation of this type of wine that belonged to the protection of industrial and commercial property. The Court accepted this defence stating that some goods: "*May enjoy a high reputation amongst consumers and constitute for producers who fulfil the conditions for using them an essential means of attracting custom*".

Selling arrangements

The interpretation of Article 34 was so wide in the **Dassonville Formula** that it led importers and retailers to challenge a range of national law which impact to free movement of goods was controversial. Something had to be done to narrow the scope of Article 34. Therefore, the Court of Justice intervened in **Keck and Mithouard (1993)** by drawing a distinction between:

- Product requirements concern domestic rules regulating the goods themselves. It can be for instance, a domestic requirement on the content of goods; a provision providing that the chocolate sold in Member State should not present a percentage of cacao exceeding 95%. As presented above, product requirements are *prima facie* prohibited by Article 34 and the **Dassonville Formula** unless justified by one of the grounds of either Article 36 or the **Cassis de Dijon** principles.

- Selling arrangements do no deal with the goods themselves but rather with how, when and where they are marketed. For instance, in **Criminal Proceedings Against Tankstation't Heukste vof and JBE Boermans** (Cases C-401 & C-402/92) [1994] ECR I-2199, domestic rules regarding the closure of all petrol stations at night applying to all traders operating in the national territory did not fall within Article 34. Selling arrangements do not fall under Article 34 and therefore do not need any justification. Distinguishing between product requirements is sometimes a difficult task. The Court of Justice drew a line in the **Mars** case.

Verein gegen Unwesen in Handel und Gewerbe Köln v Mars GmbH (Case C-470/93) [1995] ECR I-1923
Facts: Mars sold ice creams 10% bigger than the usual once and marked of their wrappers '10%' with a coloured flash on the end of the wrappers. The German association for the protection of consumers challenged this measure on the basis that it created the impression that the 10% increase was free. The defendant argued that any prohibition on the selling of these ice creams would be an MEQR contrary to Article 34, in other words a product requirement.
Preliminary question before the Court: the question was to know if a measure on the selling of goods concerning their wrappers constituted a product requirement or a selling arrangement.
Preliminary Ruling: The Court upheld the defendant's argument that the measure would be a product requirement as long as the wrapper was part of the product. The manufacturer would have to change the wrappers and thereby incur additional costs.
Application: In this case, the Court of Justice confirms that any measure relating to the product itself, even if it concerns its wrapping remain a product requirement and do not enjoy the selling requirement's exclusion from the application of Article 34.

An early case before the adoption of **Keck** is **Cinéthèque SA v Fédération Nationale des Cinémas Français** (Cases 60 & 61/84) [1985] ECR 260. In this case, a selling arrangement was considered as a MEQR. This case involved a ban on the sale or hire of video-films during the first year in which the film was released. The ban did not concern a requirement on the product itself but rather how, when and where it could be marketed. The Court considered that it was hindering importations but it could be justified as a mandatory requirement because proportional to achieve the legitimate aim of protecting cinematographic production.

General principle: Restrictions or prohibitions on certain selling arrangements affecting in the same manner, in law and in fact, the marketing of domestic and imported products, do not hinder trade between Member States and are therefore falling outside Article 34's ambit.

Criminal Proceedings Against Keck and Mithouard (Cases C-367 & C-268/91) [1993] ECR I-6097

Facts: The case involved a French Law prohibiting the resale of products at a lower than the purchase price. This law intended to prevent powerful companies to abuse from their dominant positions. Two supermarket managers, Keck and Mithouard, were prosecuted for having sold goods at a lower price than the purchased one. Consequently, the applicants argued that the French Law hindered trade, and was a measure equivalent to quantitative restriction under Article 34.

Preliminary question before the Court: The question was to know whether or not, restrictions or prohibitions on certain selling arrangements affecting in the same manner, in law and in fact, domestic and imported products, were prohibited by Article 34.

Preliminary Ruling: The Court of Justice introduced the concept of selling arrangement, drawing a distinction with product requirements and excluding the former from the scope of Article 34. The Court, in its judgement, stated that: "*Contrary to what has previously been decided, the application to products ... of national provisions restricting or prohibiting certain selling arrangements is not such as to hinder, directly or indirectly, actually or potentially, trade between Member States within the meaning of the Dassonville judgement, so as long as those provisions apply to all traders operating within the national territory and as long as they affect in the same manner, in law and fact, the marketing of domestic products and those from other Member States. Where these conditions are fulfilled, the application of such rules to the sale of products from another Member State meeting the requirements laid down by that State is not by nature such as to prevent their access to the market or to impede to access any more than impedes the access of domestic products. Such rules therefore fall outside the scope of Article 34*".

Application: In this case, the Court of Justice delivers a decisive decision that is significantly reducing the scope of its previous jurisprudence **Dassonville.** It excludes from the application of Article 34 a range of laws that are not hindering free trade between Member States or affecting the principle of equal treatment of imported and domestic goods.

However, **Keck and Mithouard (1993)** only applies to certain selling arrangements that must satisfy the following two conditions in order to avoid in infringement of Article 34:

1. It must apply to all affected traders operating within the national territory;

2. It must affect the marketing of domestic and imported products in the same manner in law and in fact.

Following **Keck and Mithouard,** the Luxembourg Court applied the concept of selling arrangements to many situations.

General principle: Requiring that goods have to be sold through specific outlets is a selling arrangement falling outside the scope of Article 34.

For example, many Member States require a specific licence for shops to sell alcohol; this has been considered as a selling arrangement in **Quietlynn Limited and Brian James Richards v Southend Borough Council** (Case C-23/89) 1990.

Furthermore, the Court of Justice came up with the same conclusion in **Commission v Greece (processed milk)** (Case C-391/92) 1995 ECR I-1621 where the sale of processed milk for infants limited to pharmacies was qualified as a selling arrangement.

In those cases, the court of Justice took a formalistic approach considering that a measure restricting trade that was not a product requirement was consequently a selling arrangement. In the case **Semeraro Caso Uno Srl v Sindaco del Commune di Erbusco** c418/93 [1996] ECR I-2975 the Court of Justice concluded that the measure was a selling arrangement excluded from Article 34 application, without even considering the importer's argument that it caused inequality.

In the contrary, S. Weatherill argued that the correct approach to Article 34, and the other Treaty Articles was to focus upon market access, and not just factual and legal equality, therefore Weatherill proposed a new test. This academic argument in favour of market access claims that: "*measures introduced by authorities in a Member State which apply equally in law and in fact to all goods and services without reference to origin and which impose no direct or substantial hindrance to the access of imported goods or services to the market of that Member State escape the prohibition of Article 34 TFEU*".

The Court of Justice based its reasoning on the "market access" approach in the instance **Konsumentombudsmannen (KO) v. Gourmet International Products AB** (GIP) (Case C-405/08) 2001. The ECJ at the time held that: "*It should be pointed out that, according to paragraph 17 of its judgment in Keck and Mithouard, if national provisions restricting or prohibiting certain selling arrangements are to avoid being caught by Article 30 of the Treaty, they must not be of such a kind as to prevent access to the market by products from another Member State or to impede access any more than they impede the access of domestic products*".

General principle: domestic rules regulating the price of specific goods constitute selling arrangements.

This situation implies the regulation of national Law on minimum and maximum prices for certain goods. These measures are mainly applied to prevent retailers from selling goods at a loss. Before **Keck and Mithouard** these measures were qualified as equivalent to quantitative restrictions infringing Article 34. However, price controls have since been reclassified as selling arrangements which do not violate Article 34, see **Belgapom** (Case C-63/94) 1995 ECR I-2467.

Chapter 9: Free Movement of Workers
Article 45 TFEU

General ideology

Free movement of worker is one of the four essential freedoms of the EU internal market (Article 3 TEU). This freedom is very controversial since Member States have usually allocated immigration and the control of aliens to their most sovereign attributions. The particular groups who benefit from this freedom under EU Law include workers, the self-employed and companies. The latter two groups may either "establish" themselves in another Member State, for the purposes of setting up a business, or provide "services" there on a temporary or intervallic basis. Workers may move to other Member States in order to take up employment. Thus the basic freedom is further divided into "free movement of workers", "freedom of establishment" and "freedom to provide services". In this chapter, we will only examine free movement of workers employed by an employer, this excludes the self-employed or companies which will be studied later.

The scope of Article 45

Free movement of worker is enshrined by Article 45 TFEU which provides as follows:

"1. Freedom of movement for workers shall be secured within the Union.
2. Such freedom of movement shall entail the abolition of any discrimination based on nationality between workers of the Member States as regards employment, remuneration and other conditions of work and employment.
3. It shall entail the right, subject to limitations justified on grounds of public policy, public security or public health:
(a) To accept offers of employment actually made;
(b) To move freely within the territory of Member States for this purpose;

(c) To stay in a Member State for the purpose of employment in accordance with the provisions governing the employment of nationals of that State laid down by law, regulation or administrative action;

(d) To remain in the territory of a Member State after having been employed in that State, subject to conditions which shall be embodied in regulations to be drawn up by the Commission.

4. The provisions of this article shall not apply to employment in the public service."

Article 45 TFEU presents two main objectives. It has been summarized by the Court of Justice in its case **Lyyski** (Case C-40/05) 2007 ECR I-99: *"The Treaty provisions relating to freedom of movement for persons are intended to facilitate the pursuit by Union workers of occupational activities of all kinds throughout the Union, and preclude measures which might place them at a disadvantage when they which to pursue an economic activity in the territory of another Member State".*

Firstly, it aims to allow for workers to move freely from one EU Member State to another for the purposes of employment. This is to the benefits to both employees and employers. Employees can move freely from Member States of high unemployment and low wages to areas of low unemployment and higher wages. Employers also benefit because they have a greater choice of potential workers to choose from. Moreover, migrant workers will generally be very motivated to do their best since they settle down in a foreign country and take risks. An influx of workers can also help to solve a "skill shortage". This was the case for example with the UK that needed constructing workers in the 1990's and has therefore hosted an important influx of Eastern European workers to solve its problem.

Secondly, article 45 TFEU prohibits discrimination on grounds of nationality against workers who have migrated. This objective is related to Article 18 TFEU that prohibits any discrimination on the basis of nationality within the scope of application of the Treaties. This implies a perfectly equal treatment of migrant workers compared to nationals, including the same employee's rights, an equal access to public services, social welfare. There would be a massive disincentive to move if employers and governments of other Member States were able to discriminate against migrant workers.

Secondary legislation has supplemented Article 45 TFEU in order to ensure its enforceability. In this respect, Regulation 492/2011 conferring rights of equal treatment relating to employment, tax and social advantages for workers and certain members of their families has been enacted. In addition to this, Directive 2004/38 deals with right of entry and residence of Union workers.

The scope of Article 45 has always been interpreted by the Court of Justice in the light of the economic purpose of the former EEC. Under Article 2 of the Rome Treaty, the Court was generally applying free movement of workers to relationship of an economic nature. However, this economic nature has been broadly interpreted by the Court of Justice. For instance, the CJEU declared the professional categories of sports subjected to the application of Article 45 TFEU. In **Walrave & Koch v Association Union Cycliste Internationale** (Case 36/74) [1974] ECR 1405, the Court defined the term professional: *"the sport activity has to be of an economic nature having the character of a gainful employment"*. This case concerned professional cyclists. Likewise, the activities of professional and semi-professional footballers who are in gainful employment have also been held to fall within Article 45 TFEU (see, for example, **Union Royal Belge des Sociétés de Football Association ASBL v Jean Marc Bosman** (Case C-415/93) [1995] ECR I-4921).

General principle: A measure infringing Article 45 TFEU must constitute a restriction on the worker's mobility such as a limitation of his access to the labour market.

Graf (Case C-190/98) 2000 ECR I-493
Facts: An Austrian Law provided workers, who had been working at least three years for the same employer, with a termination payment. However, this payment could be forfeited if the employee left prematurely for no important reasons.
The applicant, Volker Graf, resigned to go to work in Germany

and his former company refused to pay up the termination payment. Graf argued that this was contrary to Article 45 and free movement of workers.

Preliminary question before the Court: Does the refusal to pay a termination payment constitute an obstacle to mobility?

Preliminary Ruling: The Court held that there was no breach of Article 45 TFEU as far as Austrian legislation imposed no obstacle on the worker's mobility. Although he was not entitled to get the termination payment, the worker was completely free to leave the company and work in the Germany. The Court stated that *"Provisions which, even if they are applicable without distinction, preclude or deter a notional of a Member State from leaving his country of origin in order to exercise his right to free movement therefore constitute an obstacle to that freedom. However, in order to be capable of constituting such an obstacle, they must affect access of workers to the labour market"*.

Application: In this case, the Court clarifies the scope of Article 45 and subjects its application to a real restriction on the worker's mobility. Therefore, before declaring a domestic measure incompatible to Article 45, one will have to show that the impugned measure placed an obstacle on the worker's mobility.

General principle: Article 45 (2) has horizontal direct effect and applies to employment in the private sector.

Angonese (Case C-281/98) 200 ECR-4139

Facts: Roman Agonese, was an Italian citizen speaking, in addition to his native language, fluently German, Polish and Slovene. He applied for a job in a private Bank located in the Italian region of Bolzano. The required language, German and Italian, had to be attested by a certificate of Bolzano university. However, the applicant had been studying languages and translation in Vienna, and the bank refused his certificate. The applicant claimed that this measure was infringing his right to freedom of movement under Article 45(2).

Preliminary question before the Court: The question was to know whether or not Article 45(2) had horizontal direct effect applying to employment in the private sector?

Preliminary Ruling: The Court of Justice accepted the

applicant's argument; the bank's insistence on accepting only the certificate issued in Bolzano constituted a form of discrimination based on nationality and was therefore prohibited by Article 45(2). **Application:** Article 45 applies both to public bodies belonging to the Member States but also to private employer. Furthermore, this provision of primary legislation can be directly enforced by individuals before national Courts.

Finally, regarding to the *rationae loci* of Article 45, the Court of Justice adopted an extensive approach. Indeed, Article 45 applies logically throughout the territories of the Member States but also beyond to workers sufficiently linked to companies established within the territory of any Member State but temporarily working outside the Union's territory. In the case SARL Prodest (Case 287/83) 1984 ECR 3153 the Court of Justice held that: *"The principle of non-discrimination applies to the case of a national of a Member State who is employed by an undertaking of another Member State even during a period in which the employee temporarily works outside the territory of the EU"*.

Definition of "worker"

(i) A Union definition

Nothing in the Treaty is providing a definition for "worker" for the purposes of free movement of workers. However, it was important to find a Union definition to ensure uniformity of application of freedom of movement. Once again, the Luxembourg Court had to clarify the situation. As stated above, **Walrave & Koch** indicates that, to be a worker, a person must be engaged in an economic activity having the character of gainful employment. In addition to this, the Court of Justice, in the case **Lawrie-Blum**, presented the main features of an employment relationship.

General principle: An employment relationship implies the performance of services for and under the direction of another person for which the former receives remuneration.

188

Lawrie-Blum v Land Baden- Württemberg (Case 66/85) [1986] ECR 2121

Facts: An English citizen went to Germany to train to be a teacher. During the admission process, she was refused on the ground that she was not a German national. The preparatory service required her to take classes eleven hours a week in exchange of remuneration. The applicant argued that she had been victim of discrimination based on nationality which affected her access to the labour market as to infringe Article 45 TFEU.

The German authorities replied that the applicant was a mere trainee not capable of being qualified as a "worker" under EU Law.

Preliminary question before the Court: What are the main features of an employment relationship according to EU Law?

Preliminary Ruling: The Court of Justice held that there was a valid employment relationship because the applicant was paid in exchange of a service for and under the direction of the defendant. The CJEU stated: *"Objectively defined, a "worker" is a person who is obliged to provide services to another in return for monetary reward and who is subject to the direction and control of the person as regards the way in which the work is done ... The essential feature of an employment relationship ... is that for a certain period of time a person performs services for and under the direction of another person in return for which he receives remuneration".*

Application: This case, combined with **Walrave & Koch**, provides with a general definition of the notion of "worker" under Article 45 TFEU.

(ii) Part-time and low-paid employees

The Court of Justice has been flexible on the interpretation of gainful employment. It had to tackle this issue since several Member States have been raising claims that part-time and low-paid employees were not "workers".

General principle: As far as the employment relationship is established, the qualification of worker is not affected by the

fact that the latter is poorly paid or working part-time.

Levin v Staatssecretaris van Justitie (Case 53/81) [1982] ECR 1035

Facts: A British national went to Netherlands with her husband to settle down there. The couple was financially independent but the Dutch authorities asked the applicant to find a job. Therefore the applicant worked as a part-time chambermaid in a Dutch hotel for 20 hours a week for which she was paid the equivalent of 20euros. These wages were bellow the Dutch minimum wage and the authorities therefore denied her the quality of worker.

The applicant then challenged the Dutch decision claiming that the amount of money paid was not important as far as the employment relationship was established.

Preliminary question before the Court: The question was to know whether or not the fact that the individual was working part-time or poorly paid could influence the qualification of worker under Article 45 TFEU.

Preliminary Ruling: The Court held that there was a breach of Article 45 because the applicant was in an employment relationship. The fact of employment, rather than the wages or the time of work by week, was what mattered. In this respect, the Court concluded: *"Whilst part-time employment is not excluded from the field of application of the rules on freedom of movement for workers, those rules cover only the pursuit of effective and genuine activities, to the exclusion of activities on such a small scale as to be regarded as marginal or ancillary"*.

Application: This case confirmed that individuals working part-time are considered as workers, no matter how much they are paid for their work as far as they are in an employment relationship.

General principle: An individual is considered as worker as far as the effective and genuine nature of the employment relationship is asserted, regardless whether or not the worker supplements his income by recourse to social security benefits provided by the Member State.

Kempf v Staatssecretaris van Justitie (Case 139/85) [1986] ECR 1741

Facts: In this case, Kempf, a German national was working as a music teacher in the Netherlands. However, he was working only 12 hours a week. Since his income was not sufficient to live on, he asked for a supplement from the public general income support, which positively received his demand. Later on, he claimed for a resident permit that was rejected on the ground that he was not able to support himself. The applicant challenged this decision for violation of his freedom of movement.

Preliminary question before the Court: Can an individual earning a very small income, assisted by public financial support, be qualified as worker under Article 45 TFEU?

Preliminary Ruling: The Luxembourg Court declared that the fact that the applicant was supported by public financial assistance was not excluding him from the provisions of Article 45. The Court held that: "*A person in effective and genuine part-time employment cannot be excluded from Article 45 merely because the remuneration he derives from it is below the level of minimum means of subsistence and he seeks to supplement by other lawful means of subsistence. In that regard it is irrelevant whether those supplementary means of subsistence are derived from property or from the employment of a member of his family ... or whether, as in this instance, they are obtained from financial assistance drawn from the public funds of the member state in which he resides, provided that the effective and genuine nature of his work is established*".

Application: In its conclusion, the Court explains that an individual working part-time should be considered workers no matter how they supplement their income as to support themselves (property, family help or public financial assistance).

Along these two cases, the CJEU's approach on the qualification of worker appears to be very generous. However, it should be noted that some situations will be excluded from the scope of Article 45. For example, the Court of Justice rejected the missions of reintegration part of socio-occupational programs because they were not economic activities of a genuine and effective nature (see **Bettray v Staatsecretaris van Justitie** (Case 344/87) [1989] ECR 1621). Generally, participants to these programs, in exchange of household work, are given accommodation and pocket money. It has been qualified by the Court as being marginal and ancillary. However, in a recent case in similar facts the Court recognized that the relationship satisfied the **Lawrie-Blum** test but left it to the domestic Courts to determine whether or not the effective and genuine nature of the economic activity was established (see **Torjani v Centre Public d'Aide Sociale de Bruxelles (CPAS) (Case C-456/02) [2004] ECR I-7573**).

(iii) Trainees

According to **Lawrie-Blum**, discussed above, students undertaking vocational trainings are "workers" enjoying Article 45 TFEU rights. More recently, the Court held that a trainee spending time of his legal training in a Law firm in London who received an allowance was carrying an economic genuine and effective activity that had to be regulated by Article 45, regardless the fact that the allowance paid constituted only an assistance allowing trainees to meet their minimum needs (See **Kranemann** (Case C-109/04) 2005 ECR I-2421).

(iv) Job-seekers

The question is to know if Article 45 TFEU could be applied to work-seekers? A literal reading of Article 45 seems to indicate that not. Job-seekers by definition are not participating in any economic activity. However, the Court of Justice has rarely made a literal interpretation of the treaties. It prefers to promote a purposive approach that looks at the real objectives of the provision at stake.

General principle: Job-seekers have the right to move freely to other Member-States in order to find employment for a period allowing them to appraise themselves of the work situation.

R v Immigration Appeal Tribunal, ex parte Antonissen (Case 292/89) [1991] ECR I-745

Facts: A Belgian citizen challenged a deportation order made against him following a prosecution for possession of cocaine. He has been unsuccessfully looking for work in the UK during two years. Under UK Law, deportation was possible after 6 months of unemployment.

The applicant challenged the measure as contravening with his freedom of movement under Article 45 TFEU.

Preliminary question before the Court: Do job-seekers have a right to move freely to other Member States for the purposes of seeking employment?

Preliminary Ruling: The Court of Justice held that job-seekers have a right to move to other Member-States to look for work. In this respect, the Court stated that: *"Article 45(3) must be interpreted as enumerating, in a non-exhaustive way, certain rights benefiting nationals of Member States in the context of free movement of workers ... that freedom also entails the right for nationals of Member States to move freely within the territories of other Member states and to stay there for the purposes of seeking employment"*. However, in the present case, the Court considered that the 6-month period to stay in order to seek employment was not, as such, jeopardising the effectiveness of the principles of free movement. According to the Court, it was leaving job-seekers reasonable time to find work.

Application: In this case, the Court acknowledges that job-seekers have certain rights arising from Article 45 TFEU, such as, *inter alia*, the right to move freely to other Member States for the purposes of seeking employment. As a matter of fact, the Court considered in this instance that 6 months were sufficient enough to comply with Article 45.

Furthermore, another issue about the rights of job-seekers to social benefits in the hosting Member State arose. We will see later that migrant workers have the same right to social and tax advantages as nationals of the hosting Member State (Article 7(2) of Regulation 492/2011). On this issue, the CJEU's jurisprudence has significantly evolved. At first, the Court held that job-seekers had no rights to social or tax advantages (**Lebon** (Case 316/85) 1987 ECR 2811. However, that ruling has been overturned by **Collins** (Case C-138/02) 2004 ECR I-2703. In this case, the Court of Justice held that job-seekers were entitled to claim some social and tax advantages, such as job-seeker's allowance. It does not mean that job-seekers will automatically receive these benefits, but they are at least entitled to apply for them without suffering discrimination on grounds of nationality.

The worker's relatives

(i)   Family members

Article 45 TFEU does not expressly provide that workers can bring their family to stay in the hosting Member State. However, freedom of movement in practice would be undermined if family members had no such rights. Why would migrant workers move to other Member States if they had to leave their family behind them?

Hence, Regulation 1612/68 enshrined a right to install the spouse or husband for married couples and their children either under 21 years old or still dependent on them. Article 10(2) of the Regulation extends this possibility to any other family member dependent on the worker or living under his or her roof in the country he or she came from.

Furthermore, the Court of Justice had to interpret whether or not this provision should apply to unmarried cohabiting couples in the case **Netherlands State v Reed** (Case 59/85) [1985] ECR 1283. The Court of Justice held that the term "spouse" in Article 10 was confined to a person who is married to the worker. However, in this case, the Court based its approach on Union citizenship to finally allow the partner to accompany the worker. The Court used this trick to avoid the Regulation to be indirectly discriminatory for thousands of homosexual couples for example in the countries were they still have no rights to marry.

Therefore, Article 10 of Regulation 1612/68 has been repealed by Directive 2004/38. Article 2(2) of the Directive now defines family members as it follows:

" Family member means:
(a) A spouse;
(b) The partner with whom the Union citizen has contracted a

registered partnership, on the basis of the legislation of a Member State, if the legislation of the host Member State treats registered partnerships as equivalent to marriage and in accordance with the conditions laid down in the relevant legislation of the host member State.

(c) The direct descendants who are under the age of 21 or are dependants and those of the spouse or partner as defined in point (b).

(d) The dependent direct relatives in the ascending line and those of the spouse or partner as defined in point (b)."

It should be noted that Article 2(2) b only applies to registered partnership. This means firstly that cohabiting couples that do not registered their partnership, regardless for how many years they have been living together, would not enjoy these rights. Secondly, the registered partnership must be recognised as the equivalent of marriage by the legislation of the host Member State. In the UK for example, the equivalent of registered partnership is civil partnership. However, six Member States do not recognize the validity of registered partnership at all, these are: Bulgaria, Latvia, Lithuania, Poland, Romania and Slovakia.

(ii)   Other beneficiaries

Article 3 of Directive 2004/38 confers the right for the worker to install in the hosting Member State with "other beneficiaries", providing with two new categories:

- Other family members, not falling into Article 2(2) scope that are dependents or household of the worker or whose serious health problems require the personal care of such a person.
- Partners having with the worker "*a durable relationship, duly attested*". This targets unmarried cohabiting couples that have not registered their partnership. It applies to both heterosexual and homosexual couples. Article 3(2)(b) was necessary to ensure that Directive 2004/38 would not be indirectly discriminatory to homosexuals unable to get

their union officially recognized in the six countries mentioned above.

Beneficiaries are not able to benefit from the rights conferred on family members under Article 2(2). However, under Article 3, Member States have a duty to facilitate their entry and residence.

Equality in social and welfare rights

On this issue, the main provisions are contained in secondary legislation. Indeed, Regulation 1612/68 and Regulation 492/2011 were passed to clarify the social and welfare rights of workers.

(i)   Rights of employment

First of all, Article 3 and 4 of Regulation 1612/68 regulate the eligibility of workers for employment:

"Article 3
1. Under this Regulation, provisions laid down by law, regulation or administrative action or administrative practices of a Member State shall not apply:
• Where they limit application for and offers of employment, or the right of foreign nationals to take up and pursue employment or subject these to conditions not applicable in respect of their own nationals; or
• Where, though applicable irrespective of nationality, their exclusive or principal aim or effect is to keep nationals of other Member States away from the employment offered.
This provision shall not apply to conditions relating to linguistic knowledge required by reason of the nature of the post to be filled".

However, requiring a standard of linguistic knowledge for teachers is not infringing Article 3 according to the Court of Justice in **Goroener v Minsiter for Education** (Case 379/87) 1989 ECR 3967.

"Article 4

1. Provisions laid down by law, regulation or administrative action of the Member States which restrict by number or percentage the employment of foreign nationals in any undertaking, branch of activity or region, or at a national level, shall not apply to nationals of the other Member States."

For instance, Article 4(1) was infringed in **Commission v France** (Case 167/73) 1974 ECR 359, where French legislation imposed an overall ratio of three French employees to one migrant worker for the crew of merchant ships.

Article 7 of Regulation 1612/68 enshrines the prohibition of every forms of discrimination, direct or indirect, against migrant workers:

"Article 7
1. A worker who is a national of a Member State may not, in the territory of another Member State, be treated differently from national workers by reason of his nationality in respect of any conditions of employment and work, in particular as regards remuneration, dismissal, and should he become unemployed, reinstatement or re-employment."

It should be noted that once discrimination is committed, it can be justified under the grounds presented in Article 45(3) and (4). These derogations will be examined more in details in the next section. In addition to this, above the derogations presented by Article 45, discrimination can usually also be justified on the basis that it was necessary to preserve overriding national interests. However, this last justification can only apply to indirect discrimination.

- **Direct discrimination**

Direct discrimination concerns national legislation which expressly discriminates against workers because of their nationality. It is clearly prohibited by Article 45(2) TFEU. It can be for example an express Law mentioning that no migrant workers should be hired as carpenters. Another example of direct discrimination can be found in **Commission v France** (discussed above) which imposed a quota on migrant workers. Direct discrimination is *prima facie* prohibited but can still be justified under Articles 45(3) and 45(4).

- **Indirect discrimination**

Indirect discrimination is established when a facially neutral provision has the effect of disproportionally disadvantaging migrant workers or conversely advantaging nationals. In this case, the impugned law is in breach of Article 45(2). The case **O'Flynn** provides with a definition of indirect discrimination of migrant workers.

General principle: A domestic provision, although applying irrespective of nationality, that is liable to affect substantially higher proportion of migrant workers is indirectly discriminatory.

O'Flynn v Adjudication officer (Case C-237/94) 1996 ECR I-2617
Facts: A provision of UK Law provided the cover of the burial or cremation of deceased persons if the ceremony was happening in the UK. The applicant was an Irish national working in the UK which had been denied this benefit because the burial of his father took place in Ireland. The applicant claimed for unequal treatment of workers under Article 45 (2).
Preliminary question before the Court: The question was to know whether or not a domestic provision indirectly disadvantaging migrant workers in practice could be classified as discrimination under Article 45 (2).
Preliminary Ruling: The Court of Justice held that the UK provision was discriminatory because a greater proportion of nationals than migrant workers would satisfy the burial requirement. It concluded that: "*Conclusions imposed by national law must be regarded as indirectly discriminatory where, although applicable irrespective of nationality, they affect essentially migrant workers or the great majority of those affected are migrant workers, where they are indistinctly applicable but*

can be more easily satisfied by national workers than migrant workers, or there is a risk that they may operate to the particular detriment of migrant workers ... It is not necessary to find in this respect that the provision does in practice affect substantially higher proportion of migrant workers. It is sufficient that it is liable to have such an effect".

Application: In this case, the Court of Justice provides with an exhaustive definition of indirect discrimination which encompasses several types of measures that might disproportionately disadvantage migrant workers. It should be noted that there is no need to prove the actual substantial disadvantage, as far as such measure is liable to have such an effect.

Another example can be found in the case **Sotgiu v Deutsche Bundespost** (Case 152/73) [1974] ECR 153. This case involved a promotion called "separation allowance" for workers' families not residing with them. The allowance was of 10 DM for workers whose families were residing in Germany and only 7.5DM for worker whose families were residing abroad. This German provision was held indirectly discriminatory by the Court of Justice as long as it substantially affected higher proportion of migrant workers because their family, national of other Member States, were more likely to reside abroad.

(ii)   Social and tax advantages

Article 7 Regulation 1612/68 provides that migrant workers should be afforded the same social and tax advantages as domestic workers. This provision has been interpreted widely by the CJEU's case law.

General principle: The equal access to social and tax advantages must include all forms of social advantages, whether or not attached to the contract of employment.

Forini v SNCF (Case 32/75) 1975 ECR 1085
Facts: The applicant was the widow of an Italian national that had

worked in France from 1962 until he was killed in an industrial accident in 1968. The applicant decided to stay in France with her four children and decided to apply for reduced rail travel. It was refused by the French authorities on the ground that she was unemployed. Therefore, French authorities restricted the scope of Article 7 (2) to employed migrants.

Preliminary question before the Court: The question was to know whether or not "social advantages" in the meaning of Article 7 Regulation 1612/68 had to be related to a contract of employment.

Preliminary Ruling: The Court held that the rights to social advantages of the family of the worker continued even after his death and it was not necessary to attach them to a contract of employment. The Court stated that: *"The reference to "social advantages" in Article 7(2) cannot be interpreted restrictively. It therefore follows that, in view of the equality of treatment which the provision seeks to achieve, the substantive area of application must be delineated so as to include all social and tax advantages, whether or not attached to the contract of employment"*.

Application: In this case, the Court delivers a very extensive interpretation of Article 7 Regulation 1612/68. The right to equal social and welfare benefits continues even after the death of the worker.

The following case, **Lair**, established a right to funding and maintenance for education.

General principle: Migrant workers have a right to funding and maintenance for education if either they can show some continuity between the course and the previous employment or if they have involuntarily become unemployed and have to undertake retraining.

Lair v Universität Hannover (Case 39/86) [1988] ECR 3161
Facts: Lair was a French national that had spent five years in Germany alternating between short-term jobs and involuntary unemployment. She finally secured a job at Hanover University, where she claimed for a maintenance grant to pursue education. This was refused on the ground that she had not been employed

for the last five years (rule that was applied distinctly to migrant workers only). The applicant challenged this refusal arguing that she had the same right to access social and tax advantages than domestic workers under Article 7 Regulation 1612/68.

Preliminary question before the Court: The question was to know whether or not migrant workers had a right to funding and maintenance for education in the hosting Member State, and if so under which conditions.

Preliminary Ruling: The Court of Justice upheld that Article 7(2) of Regulation 1612/68 provided workers with maintenance grants in order to pursue education. Moreover, the German requirement of the five years employment applying only to foreigners was discriminatory and contrary to Article 7(2). However, this grant should only be provided if the worker can show that the course was somehow connected to the previous employment, the Court stated: *"Migrant workers are guaranteed certain rights linked to the status of "worker" even when they are no longer in an employment relationship. In the field of grants for university education, such a link between the status of "worker" and a grant awarded for maintenance and training with a view to the pursuit of university studies does, however, presuppose some continuity between the previous occupational activity and the course of study; there must be a relationship between the purpose of the studies and the previous occupational activity. Such continuity may not, however, be required when a migrant has involuntarily become unemployed and is obliged by conditions on the job market to undertake occupational retraining in another field of activity."*

Application: Thus, in order to be entitled to funding and maintenance for education, the worker should prove that there is some continuity between his/her course and the previous employment, except in the case of involuntary unemployment.

As an example of the meaning of "continuity", the Court of Justice, in the case **Mateucci** (Case 235/87) 1988 ECR 5589 upheld that the continuous requirement was satisfied. In this case, a teacher in eurhythmics followed a singing and voice-training course. In **Ninni-Orache** [2003] ECR I-13187, the Court of Justice had to clarify the concept of involuntary unemployment.

An Italian national applied for a maintenance grant for courses in languages at an Austrian university after losing her job as a waitress. There was obviously no continuity between the course and the previous employment but she had a right to funding and maintenance for education because she had been obliged to undertake occupational retraining by the conditions of the market.

(iii) Access for worker's children to education

Former Article 12 of Regulation 1612/68 is now Article 10 of Regulation 492/2011 stipulates:

"The children of a national of a Member State who is or has been employed in the territory of another Member State shall be admitted to that State's general educational, apprenticeship and vocational training courses under the same conditions as the nationals of that State, if such children are residing in its territory. Member States shall encourage all efforts to enable such children to attend these courses under the best possible conditions".

The Court has extensively interpreted Article 10 that only mentions a right to be equally *"admitted"*. In **Casagrande** (Case 9/74) 1974 ECR 773, the Court of Justice held that Article implied *"general measures to facilitate attendance"* including grants and loans to undertake such courses.

General principle: there is no age restriction under Article 10 for the worker's children, regardless whether or not they are dependent on their parents, to benefit educational rights.

Gaal (Case C-7/94) 1995 ECR I-1031
Facts: The son of a Belgian worker installed in Germany began a German biology degree at a German university. He applied for funds when he was 22. The German authorities refused his application since he was over 21.
Preliminary question before the Court: Does Article 10 imply a condition of age for worker's children to benefit the rights that it contained?
Preliminary Ruling: The Court of Justice held that the term

"children", in the purpose of Article 10, was not subject to any conditions of age. The applicant could then rely on Article 10 to challenge the refusal to award the scholarship. The Court stated: *"Article 10 encompasses financial assistance for those students who are already at an advanced stage in their education, even if they are already 21 years of age or older and are no longer dependants on their parents. Accordingly, to make the application of Article 10 subject to an age limit or to the status of dependant child would conflict not only with the letter of that provision, but also with its spirit"*.

Application: The term *"children"* under Article 10 is not limited to age restrictions and applies to children of workers, regardless whether or not there are still dependants on their parents.

Children of workers enjoy these rights regardless if their parents are still working in the hosting Member State or not. The worker can be dead, retired, unemployed or even working in other Member State as far as *"he has been employed"* in the hosting Member State. This solution results on a logical application of Article 10(1) that was confirmed by the Court of Justice in **Michel S** (Case 76/72) 1973 ECR 457.

Derogations to free movement of workers

(i) The public service exemption Article 45(4) TFEU

In virtue of Article 45(4), Member States are allowed to exclude foreign nationals from working in the public service. However, this rule has been restrictively interpreted by the Court of Justice to prevent Member States to abuse it in order to undermine free movement of workers.

Firstly, the Court, in the case **Sotgiu** (discussed above) has held that Article 45(4) only applies to access to employment but not to conditions of employment. Secondly, in **Lawrie-Blum** the Court stated that the public service exemption applied only to certain public functions, not all employment in the public service. The derogation should only apply to the posts that require: *"a special* *relationship of allegiance to the State on persons occupying them and reciprocity of rights and duties which form the foundation of the bond of nationality"*. For example, in this case a teacher was not found having a special relationship of allegiance to the State.

General principle: The powers conferred by public law to public functions, for the purpose of safeguarding the general interests of the Member State, must be regularly exercised by their holders.

Colegio de oficales de la marina mecante Espanola (Case C-405/01) 2003 ECR I-10391
Facts: In this case, there was a dispute about the post of ship's master, which was exclusively reserved to Spanish nationals. The Spanish government invoked the public service exemption under Article 45(4). It argued that the ship's master had a number of public order powers on the board in case of emergency.
Preliminary question before the Court: The question was to know whether or not the post of ship's master could be qualified as a public service function under Article 45(4).
Preliminary Ruling: The Court of Justice recognized, in this instance, that Article 45(4) applied because the ship's master had powers to enforce public safety *"conferred by public law for the purposes of safeguarding the general interests of the flag State"*. However, more importantly, the Court held that it was necessary that these powers were used on a regular basis and did not represent a minor part of the activity. In this respect, it stated that:
"The scope of Article 45(4) must be limited to what is strictly necessary for safeguarding the general interests of the Member state concerned, which cannot be imperilled if rights under powers conferred by public law are exercised only sporadically, even exceptionally, by national of other Member States".
Application: Colegio de Oficiales introduced further limitations on the scope of Article 45(4), subjecting it to the necessity of safeguarding the general interests of the State.

(ii) Justification to non-discriminatory rules

Justification to non-discriminatory rules is a pure product of the

CJEU's jurisprudence. It allows Member States to justify restrictions on the free movement of workers. However, the national rule at stake has to satisfy four criteria:

- It is non-discriminatory
- It is justified by imperative requirements of the general interest
- It is the most suitable solution to the objective pursued
- It is necessary and proportionate to achieve a legitimate aim

This test is also known as the "four part test". The following case is an example of its application.

Clean Car Autoservice (Case C-350/96) 1998 ECR I-2521

Facts: The Austrian registration service of companies required that companies' managers had to reside in Austria to be validly registered. A company appointed a German manager residing in Berlin and applied to register. The application was rejected and the Austrian authorities justified it on two points. First, this measure was necessary to ensure that the manager was effectively the person in charge of this function. Second, to ensure that he could be served with notice of any fines.

Preliminary question before the Court: Can the Austrian requirement of residence for companies' registration be justified as a non-discriminatory rule?

Preliminary Ruling: The Court applied the four part test and upheld that the measure was non-discriminatory because applying to every companies operating in Austria, regardless of the nationality of their managers and that it was justified by the imperative requirements of general interests regarding to the reasons given by the defendant. However, the Court considered that the national rule was neither the most suitable option nor proportional and necessary. For example, in response to the argument about the imposition of fines, the Court stated that *"fines could be served at the company's registered office instead"*.

Application: This case shows that the Court expects the four criteria to be satisfied all together. The fact that the national rule appears to satisfy the first criteria of non-discrimination is not enough to declare the rule justified. The Court applies the four part test strictly; one has to thoroughly check that all the criteria are effectively met (see also **Allue and Conan** (Case 33/88) [1989] ECR 1591).

Chapter 10: Union's citizenship

The historical rise of EU citizenship

The original EC Treaty of 1957 made no reference to any form of European citizenship. It is a notion that arose along with the European construction. The Union's citizenship is a strong symbol of integration. Indeed, before the EU citizenship, no such supra-national citizenship had ever between developed. The principle of citizenship was established by the Treaty on the European Union that entered into force in 1993. The Treaty of Maastricht amended the EC Treaty. Article 8 TEU (now Article 20 TFEU) conferred on all individuals holding nationality of one of the Member States additional status of Union citizen. It stipulates:

"1. Citizenship of the Union is hereby established. Every person holding the nationality of a Member State shall be a citizen of the Union. Citizenship of the Union shall be additional to and not replace national citizenship.
2. Citizens of the Union shall enjoy the rights and be subject to the duties provided for in the Treaties".

This principle includes the rights to enter, reside and exit freely within the territory of the Union. In addition to this, at least for a residence of maximum three months, those rights are not subjected to economic activity. Almost 20 years later, Directive 2004/38, the so-called Citizenship Directive, clarified the scope of EU citizenship. It defines more in detail the right to residence and its derogation but also the status of family members. All the primary provisions about citizenship form nowadays part 2 of the TFEU (Articles 18-25). It should be noted that the negotiations of the Single European Act 1986 discussed the elimination of all border controls in the EU. However, the UK and Ireland were opposed. The remaining Member States resolved this by signing the Schengen Agreement. It abolished internal border controls amongst the signatory Member States and introduced common visa controls. The Treaty of Amsterdam has now incorporated the Schengen Agreements into the Treaties. However, frontier controls remain when persons enter the UK and Ireland.

The nationality requirement (Article 20 TFEU)

The main condition to acquire EU citizenship is to possess the nationality of one of the Member States. This requirement stems from the text of Article 20 (reproduced above). On the attribution of nationality, the Luxembourg Court stated in **Micheletti** (Case C-369/90) 1992 ECR I-4239: "*it is for each Member State, having due regard to Union law to lay down the conditions for the acquisition and the loss of nationality*". The Union's citizenship is undeniable if the individual has a dual nationality of two Member States (see **Garcia Avello v Blegium** (Case C-148/02) 2003 ECR I-11613). However, the question of individuals holding the nationality of one of the Member States and that of a non-Member State was more delicate. The Court tackled this issue in the **Micheletti** case.

General principle: Dual nationals having a non-Member State nationality acquire EU citizenship as long as their second nationality is of one of the Member States.

Micheletti (Case C-369/90) 1992 ECR I-4239
Facts: Mario Micheletti was born in Argentina to Italian parents. He had a dual Italian-Argentinian nationality. He wanted to set up in Spain as a dentist but was refused entry on the basis of the nationality of his country of birth: Argentina. However, under Italian law, he acquired the nationality of this country by parental heritage, regardless of where he was born. The applicant then challenged the Italian provision as being contrary to his right of citizenship.
Preliminary question before the Court: The question was to know whether or not the fact of having a second nationality of a non-Member State could influence citizenship?

Preliminary Ruling: The Court of Justice held that the term nationality was wide enough to include dual nationals, even if one of the nationalities belonged to a non-Member State.

Application: In this case, the Court made a quite logical interpretation of Article 20 TFEU that indicates that citizenship is automatically conferred to nationals of Member States, irrespective if they have other nationalities.

Concerning the loss of nationality, the Court of Justice, in **Rotmann** (Case C C-135/08) 2010 ECR I-1449, recalled that Member States were generally free to decide on matters such as acquisition and loss of nationality. This is a traditional principle of public international Law. On this point, the Court stated that it was *"legitimate for a Member State to which to protect the particular relationship of solidarity and good faith between it and its nationals and also the reciprocity of rights and duties, which form the bedrock of the bond of nationality".* However, the Court added that it was incumbent on the national Courts to scrutinize the proportionality of such revocation. These Courts, if relevant, should take into account the consequences of such revocation and the potential subsequent loss of EU citizenship for the individual and his or her family.

Citizens' rights of free movement and residence (Article 21(1))

Article 21(1) provides as follows:
"1. Every citizen of the Union shall have the right to move and reside freely within the territory of the Member States, subject to the limitations and conditions laid down in the Treaties and by the measures adopted to give them effect".

The Court of Justice, in the case **Kaur** (Case C- 192/99) 2001 ECR I-1237 confirmed that as it is the case for nationality, the Member States are free to determine the conditions regulating the right of residence. The right of residence in the EU stems from the right of residence in the Member State. In this case, the exceptional situation of a British national with no rights of residence could not rely on Article 21 TFEU. Can Article 21(1) be relied upon before national Courts? The Luxembourg Court replied to this question in **Baumbast v Secretary of State of the Home Department** (Case C-413/99) 2002 ECR I-7091

Although Union citizenship is subject to limitations and conditions, this did not deprive it of direct effect. All limitations and conditions must be applied in compliance with EU Law and particularly the principle of proportionality. This case is crucial as it confirms the legal enforceability for nationals of every Member States to move freely, stay and even reside in other Member States. It apparently obviates the need for individuals to present an economic activity (which is so difficult to satisfy under the traditional provisions on free movement: Article 45, 49 and 56). Thus, individuals of the following categories have been recognized the right of residence stemming from their Union citizenships: unemployed, students, retired, children or disabled incapable of working. The details and conditions of these rights will be examined below in a section on Article 7 of Directive 2004/38.

Furthermore, the citizens having a right to reside in other Member States can invoke Article 18 TFEU that prohibits discrimination. In this respect, foreign nationals are entitled to the same social and tax advantages as of nationals of the host State. Article 18 states that: *"Within the scope of application of the Treaties, and without prejudice to any special provisions contained therein, any discrimination on grounds"*.

However, the major threshold in these cases of citizenship, devised by the Court of Justice in the case **Grzelczy** (Case C-184/99) 2001 ECR I-6193, is that *"beneficiaries of the right of residence must not become an unreasonable burden on the public finances of the host Member State"*. This broad solution has raised many uncertainties regarding to its interpretation. Nevertheless, in the following cases, it should be noted that the CJEU kept this safeguard for exceptional situations. Indeed, we will see that the Court of Justice has awarded child-raising allowances, minimum-subsistence allowances, student loans and grants without classifying their holders of "unreasonable burdens".

General principle: EU Law compels Member States to treat equally all Union citizens irrespective to their nationalities.

Martinez Sala (Case C-85/96) ECR I-2691

Facts: A Spanish national lived in Germany and has been working there intermittently for approximately 10 years. She then did not work for 4 years, was in receipt of social security and gave birth to a child in 1993. After having applied for a child-rearing benefit, this was refused by the German authorities mainly on the ground of her nationality. That applicant contested the decision for incompatibility to Article 18 taken in conjunction with Article 21(1) TFEU.

Preliminary question before the Court: The question is to know whether or not EU citizenship gives right to an equal access to social benefits for domestic and foreign nationals in the host Member State.

Preliminary Ruling: The Court held that the applicant was an EU citizen, lawfully residing in Germany, and therefore was entitled to claim for equal access to social benefits, under Article 18 taken in conjunction with Article 21(1). The Court stated that "*Article 21(1) attaches to the status of Citizen of the union the rights and duties laid down by the Treaty, including the right, laid down in Article 18, not to suffer discrimination on ground of nationality within the scope of application rationae material of the Treaty. A citizen of the European Union ... lawfully resident in the territory of the host Member State, can rely on Article 18 in all situations which fall within the scope rationae materiae of Union Law*".

Application: This case is the earliest case of discrimination taken in conjunction with citizenship. It is the first step of the broad recognition of equal treatment for EU citizens residing lawfully in other Member States.

General principle: Citizenship rights can be invoked in the citizen's home State.

D'Hoop v Office National de l'Emploi (Case C-224/98) 2002 ECR I-6191

Facts: The applicant, a Belgian national, had undertaken her secondary school in France. She then came back to Belgium for a degree. On graduating, she applied for a "tideover allowance" devised for recent graduates having undertaken their schooling in Belgium. This was refused by the Belgian authorities that invoked the fact that she had left for France. The applicant challenged this decision for incompatibility with Article 18 taken in conjunction with Article 21(1).

Preliminary question before the Court: Can citizen's rights be invoked in the citizen's home State?

Preliminary Ruling: The Court of Justice held that citizen's rights can be relied upon in the citizen's home State. This has to be in relation to discrimination for having left to another Member State under free movement rights. In this case, the Luxembourg Court concluded that the applicant was entitled to the "tideover allowance".

Application: D'Hoop provides nationals to rely upon Union citizens' rights in their home States. The main reason for this decision is that the reverse solution would amount to hinder free movement rights.

General principle: Children of Union citizens are entitled to invoke their rights of residence that are only effective if their primary carers are also allowed to reside with them in the host State.

Zhu and Chen v Secretary of State for the Home Dept (Case C-200/02) 2004 3 WLR 1453

Facts: A couple of Chinese nationals went to Ireland in order to give birth to their daughter. According to Irish Law, any child born on the island acquired Irish nationality. Subsequently, the mother of the child took her to Cardiff in Wales to live there. Consequently the question of their entitlement to residence arose.

Preliminary question before the Court: the question was to know whether or not an infant child could rely on her status as a Citizen of the Union, and if her primary carer was entitled to live with her.

Preliminary Ruling: The Court of Justice held that, since the child was an Irish national, she was entitled to reside in any Member State of the Union. Furthermore, the Court considered, that her mother, as being her primary career, was allowed to live with her. The Court stated: "*A young child can take advantage of the rights of free movement and residence guaranteed by EU Law. The capacity of a national of a Member State to be the holder of rights guaranteed by the Treaty ... cannot be made conditional upon the attainment by the person concerned of the age prescribed for the acquisition of legal capacity to exercise those right personally ... A refusal to allow the parent, whether a national of a Member State or a national of a non-Member State country, with is the career of a child ... to reside in that child in the host Member State would deprive the child's right of residence of any useful effect*".

Application: The Court of Justice, in **Zhu and Chen**, delivered a very generous decision ensuring the enforceability of rights of residence for citizens' children and their careers. In doing so, the Court did not place time limit except that the career can only stay for the duration of the child's residence; "*the carer must be in a position to reside with the child in the host Member State for the duration of such residence*".

Citizens' rights of entry, residence and exit

The rights of EU citizens' to exit their Member State and enter other Member States to reside their family and set up home there is are regulated by Directive 2004/38. This Directive repealed Directive 68/360, however it was of a significant relevance when introducing the new Directive and some of its case law has been incorporated. For instance, in the case **Royer v Belgium** (Case 48/75) 1976 the Court of Justice held that the right of nationals of a Member State to enter territory of another Member State and reside there was conferred directly by the EC Treaty and its application (Directive 68/360). The main articles of the new Directive will be examined in turn.

(i)   Right of exit: Article 4

Article 4 deals with the right of a citizen to leave his home Member State to reside to another Member State. No further conditions or formalities such as exit visas or justifications should be placed on the migrant.

Article 4 provides as it follows:
" ... *all Union citizens with a valid identity card or passport and their family members who are not nationals of a Member State and who hold a valid passport shall have the right to leave the territory of a Member State to travel to another Member State.*
2.   No exit visa or equivalent formality may be imposed on the persons to whom paragraph 1 applies.
3.   Member States shall, acting in accordance with their laws, issue to their own nationals, and renew, an identity card or passport stating their nationality".

(ii)   Right of entry: Article 5

All Union citizens with a valid ID card or passport have a right to enter any Member State in order to take up residence there. Article 5(1) stipulates that:

"*Without prejudice to the provisions on travel documents applicable to national border controls, Member States shall grant Union citizens leave to enter their territory with a valid identity card or passport and shall grant family members who are not nationals of a Member State leave to enter their territory with a valid passport*".

The host State cannot require an entry visa for Union citizens. However, it can be required for non-EU nationals allowed to enter the territory as member of a citizen's family without necessary travel documents. This is regulated by Article 5(4):

"*Where a Union citizen, or a family member who is not a national of a Member State, does not have the necessary travel documents or, if required, the necessary visas, the Member State concerned shall, before turning them back, give such persons every reasonable opportunity to obtain the necessary documents or have them brought to them within a reasonable period of time or to corroborate or prove by other means that they are covered by the right of free movement and residence"*.

(iii) Right of residence up to three months: Article 6

European citizens shall be entitled to reside up to three months in any Member State with no further requirement that a valid ID card or passport. Additional conditions or formalities are strictly prohibited. Article 6 provides: "*Union citizens shall have the right of residence on the territory of another Member State for a period of up to three months without any conditions or any formalities other than the requirement to hold a valid identity card or passport"*. However, in the case **Salah Oulane** (Case C-215/03) 2005 the Court stated that a Member State may not refuse to recognise the right of residence on the sole ground that a person did not present one of these documents. Any document or evidence proving unequivocally that a person is an EU citizen should be accepted by a host Member State.

(iv) Right of residence for more than three months: Article 7

Article 7 of the Directive presents three situations where an EU citizen is entitled to reside in the host State for more than three months:

- The citizen is a worker or self-employed having an economic activity or;
- The citizen has sufficient resources and comprehensive sickness insurance cover in order to not become a "burden" on the social assistance system of the host State or;
- The citizen is studying or undertaking vocational training, has sufficient resources and comprehensive sickness insurance.

Article 7(3) provides that the right of residence for more than three months is not affected in the following situations:

"... a Union citizen who is no longer a worker or self-employed person shall retain the status of worker or self-employed person in the following circumstances:

(a) he/she is temporarily unable to work as the result of an illness or accident;

(b) he/she is in duly recorded involuntary unemployment after having been employed for more than one year and has registered as a job-seeker with the relevant employment office;

(c) he/she is in duly recorded involuntary unemployment after completing a fixed-term employment contract of less than a year or after having become involuntarily unemployed during the first twelve months and has registered as a job-seeker with the relevant employment office. In this case, the status of worker shall be retained for no less than six months;

(d) he/she embarks on vocational training. Unless he/she is involuntarily unemployed, the retention of the status of worker shall require the training to be related to the previous employment".

Some English cases are illustrative of the application of these principles. For instance, in **De Brito v Home secretary** (2012) EWCA Civ 709, the Court of Appeal held that a worker who has been declared permanently unable to work for health reasons fell outside the scope of Article 7(3) which only mentioned "temporarily" incapacitated. In this context, the term "worker" is explained with more details in Chapter 9 on free movement of workers.

(v) Retention of residence rights: Article 14

Article 14 provide as it follows:

"1. Union citizens and their family members shall have the right of residence provided for in Article 6, as long as they do not become an unreasonable burden on the social assistance system of the host Member State.

2. Union citizens and their family members shall have the right of residence provided for in Articles 7, 12 and 13 as long as they meet the conditions set out therein.

In specific cases where there is a reasonable doubt as to whether a Union citizen or his/her family members satisfies the conditions set out in Articles 7,12 and 13, Member States may verify if these conditions are fulfilled. This verification shall not be carried out systematically.

3. An expulsion measure shall not be the automatic consequence of a Union citizen's or his or her family member's recourse to the social assistance system of the host Member State.

4. By way of derogation from paragraphs 1 and 2 and without prejudice to the provisions of Chapter VI, an expulsion measure may in no case be adopted against Union citizens or their family members if:

(a) the Union citizens are workers or self-employed persons, or

(b) the Union citizens entered the territory of the host Member State in order to seek employment. In this case, the Union citizens and their family members may not be expelled for as long as the Union citizens can provide evidence that they are continuing to seek employment and that they have a genuine chance of being engaged".

These provisions have been confirmed by the cases **Antonissen** and **Collins**. They are examined in details in Chapter 9 on workers.

(vi) Right of permanent residence: Articles 16-21

The right of permanent residence has been described by the Court in the case **Lassal** (Case C-162/09) 2010 ECRI-9217, as being *"a key element in promoting social cohesion and the feeling of Union citizenship"*. The main condition to acquire permanent citizenship, under Article 16(1), is to *"have resided legally in the host State for a continuous period of years"*.

The necessary lawful nature of the residence has been interpreted restrictively. For instance, time spent imprisoned in a prison cannot be considered as "a legal residence" giving rise to the right of permanent residence (see **Carvalho v Home Secretary** 2010 EWCA Civ 1406).

Article 17 presents certain exemptions of the traditional 5 years requirement. Permanent residence rights may be acquired before the completion of the 5 years legal residence laid down in Article 16, for workers or self-employed persons who:

- At the time they stop working, have reach the age laid down by the law of that Member State for entitlement to an old age pension or workers who cease paid employment to take early retirement, provided that they have been working in that Member State for at least the preceding 12 months and have resided there continuously for more than three years.

- Have resided continuously in the host State for more than two years and stop working there as a result of permanent incapacity to work. If such incapacity is the result of an accident at work or an occupational disease entitling the person concerned to a benefit payable in full or in part by an institution in the host Member State, no condition shall be imposed as to length of residence.

- After three years of continuous employment and residence in the host State, work in an employed or self-employed capacity in another Member State, while retaining their place of residence in the host Member State, to which they return, as a rule, each day or at least once a day.

Regarding to the continuous nature of residency, Article 16(3) provides that: "*Continuity of residence shall not be affected by temporary absences not exceeding a total of six months a year, or by absences of a longer duration for compulsory military service, or by one absence of a maximum of twelve consecutive months for important reasons such as pregnancy and childbirth, serious illness, study or vocational training, or a posting in another Member State or a third country*".

In terms of continuity, Article 17 (4) (a) stipulates that: *"If, however, the worker or self-employed person dies while still working but before acquiring permanent residence status in the host Member State on the basis of paragraph 1, his family members who are residing with him in the host Member State shall acquire the right of permanent residence there, on condition that: (a) the worker or self-employed person had, at the time of death, resided continuously on the territory of that Member State for two years"*.

The Court of Justice, in **Givane** (Case C-257/100) ECR I-345 that involved death of the citizen, considered that the residence had to immediately precede the death to give rise to rights of family members. If the individual left the host Member State between the employment period and the death; the permanent right of residence will not be granted. Finally, Article 16 (4) states that once acquired, the permanent residence can be lost through absence from the host State for a period exceeding two years.

The rights of a citizen's family members

Directive 2005/38 extends the provisions of free movement of citizens to their family members. It gives effectiveness to a citizen's right to move freely. The reverse solution would amount to a significant financial as well as emotional disincentive to go abroad for work or studies.

Article 2 of the Directive defines the scope of the citizen's family:

" "Family member" means:
(a) the spouse;
(b) the partner with whom the Union citizen has contracted a registered partnership, on the basis of the legislation of a Member State, if the legislation of the host Member State treats registered partnerships as equivalent to marriage and in accordance with the conditions laid down in the relevant legislation of the host Member State;
(c) the direct descendants who are under the age of 21 or are

dependants and those of the spouse or partner as defined in point (b);
(d) the dependent direct relatives in the ascending line and those of the spouse or partner as defined in point (b)"

Article 2 (2) mentions the spouse, the partner, the direct descendants or the dependants; all of them will be examined below.

(i)   The spouse

The general principle concerning "spouse" was laid down by the Court of Justice in the case **Netherlands v Reed** (Case 59/85) 1986 ECR 1283: *"In the absence of any indication of a general social development which would justify a broad construction, and in the absence of any indication to the contrary in the Legislation, it must be held that the term spouse refers to a marital relationship only"*. Despite many criticisms from the doctrine to a traditional approach on marriage, this solution was confirmed recently in **Hadj Ahmed** (Case C-45/12) 2013.

General principle: The spouse in a marital relationship with an EU citizen keeps the right of residence until the divorce is officially pronounced, regardless if they both live on their own and plan to divorce at a later date.

Diatta v Land Berlin (Case 267/83) 1985 ECR 567
Facts: A Senegalese woman married a Frenchman. They lived together in Germany. One year later, they began to live apart. The couple intended to get a divorce, but the woman was working and wanted to stay in Germany on her own. When she applied for a new resident permit, it was refused on the grounds that she was no longer a member of a citizen's family. The applicant challenged this decision claiming that she was still a family member entitled to a right of residence.
Preliminary question before the Court: The question was to know whether or not the non-EU national in a marital relationship with an EU citizen, knowing that the couple was separated and both were living on their own, was still a citizen's family member.

Preliminary Ruling: The Court of Justice held that the applicant was still a family member. Despite being separated, since the divorce was not pronounced yet, the applicant had not yet lost her right of residence. The Court stated: *"the marital relationship cannot be regarded as dissolved so long as it has not been terminated by the competent authority, It is not dissolved merely because the spouse live separately, even where they intend to divorce at a later date. Moreover, if co-habitation of the spouses were a mandatory condition, the citizen could at any time cause the expulsion of his spouse by depriving her of a roof".*

Application: The right of residence will still be valid for all "spouses" married to Union citizens until the divorced is pronounced. Individuals in such situations should be aware of the current state of their right at this time.

Furthermore, the Court upheld in **Metock and Others** (case C-127/08) 2008 ECR I-6241 that the location and timing of the marriage do not influence the acquisition of the status of spouse.

General principle: The rights of free movement of family members cannot be invoked when the spouse of the EU citizen is living in a Member State other than that in which the citizen is residing.

Lida (Case C-40/11) 2013 1 CMLR 47, 2013 2 WLR 788
Facts: The applicant is a Japanese national that has married a German national. The couple had children together. While the wife went to Austria to work there and bring her daughter with her, the husband asked to renew his resident permit in Germany where he wanted to stay. He was refused the permit on the ground that he did not qualify for the status of family member under Directive 2004/38 anymore.

Preliminary question before the Court: Does the non EU-national spouse of an EU citizen, keep a right of residence, even though they do not live in the same Member State?

Preliminary Ruling: The Court held that although he was still a spouse, the applicant did not qualify anymore for the status of family member under Directive 2004/38. This was because Article 3 (1) required him to "accompany or join" his wife in

Austria.

Application: This decision can appear harsh. However, the main purpose of the extension of free movement to the citizen's family members is to promote free movement and avoid families to be separated. If the spouse does not want to accompany or join his/her married partner in a Member State, there is no point to guarantee such rights to family members anymore.

Article 13 (2) of Directive 2004/38 deals with the status and rights of ex-wives or ex-husbands or their equivalent in a registered partnership that are non-EU national. These individuals are not deprived of all their EU rights. Article 13 (2) states:

"2.   Without prejudice to the second subparagraph, divorce, annulment of marriage or termination of the registered partnership referred to in point 2(b) of Article 2 shall not entail loss of the right of residence of a Union citizen's family members who are not nationals of a Member State where:
(a) prior to initiation of the divorce or annulment proceedings or termination of the registered partnership referred to in point 2(b) of Article 2, the marriage or registered partnership has lasted at least three years, including one year in the host Member State; or
(b) by agreement between the spouses or the partners referred to in point 2(b) of Article 2 or by court order, the spouse or partner who is not a national of a Member State has custody of the Union citizen's children; or
(c) this is warranted by particularly difficult circumstances, such as having been a victim of domestic violence while the marriage or registered partnership was subsisting; or
(d) by agreement between the spouses or partners referred to in point 2(b) of Article 2 or by court order, the spouse or partner who is not a national of a Member State has the right of access to a minor child, provided that the court has ruled that such access must be in the host Member State, and for as long as is required."

Finally, the Court of Justice had to tackle the issue of marriages of convenience, which is traditionally viewed as an abuse of rights. In the case **Akrich** (Case C-109/01) 2003 ECR I-9607, the Luxembourg Court affirmed that: *"The marriage must be a* *genuine one and not a marriage of convenience".*

(ii)   Registered partners

This category of family members includes the partners in registered partnerships. Conversely, it excludes the boyfriends and girlfriends in partnerships that are not legally registered. According to Article 2 (2) b, the status of partner is only conferred to individuals who have contracted a registered partnership on the basis of the legislation of a Member State that treats it as equivalent to marriage. The reference to *"in the legislation of a Member State"* means that a partnership registered in a non-EU country would not count. For instance, the equivalent of the EU notion of registered partnership is the civil partnership.

Many fears about potential discrimination arose on the consequences of this article. Mainly for the LGBTI minority that would not have been entitled to the same right as those of heterosexual "spouses" because of the second condition that implies that the host State recognizes the registered partnership as equivalent to marriage. As stated earlier, six countries do not recognize registered partnership at all.

Fortunately, the individuals in such situations will be able to rely on Article 3(2) b which refers to *"partner with whom the Union citizen has a durable relationship"*. This option is much wider and permitted to avoid potential situations of inequalities. It will be discussed more in details in the next section on the other family members.

(iii)   Descendants

Directive 2004/38 includes direct descendants as family member as long as they are under 21 of age or *"dependant"*. This provision has been interpreted by the Court as to encompass a citizen's children, grandchildren, and step-children (see **Baumbast** mentioned above). However, there is still a question mark on the issue of adopted children, as neither the Directive nor the CJEU's case law have yet answered this question.

(iv)   Dependants

The test on dependency relies on factual factors, the main question is: does the citizen provide financial support? There is no requirement that the citizen was under legal obligation to provide financial support. There is no condition neither of necessity for the dependant. What matters is the actual fact that the citizen is supporting financially the dependant. As stated above, in the **Lebon** case the Court holds that:

"The status of dependent of a worker's family is the result of a factual situation. The person having that status is a member of the family who is supported by the worker and there is no need to determine the reasons for recourse to the worker's support or to raise the question whether the person concerned is able to support himself by taking up paid employment".

Finally, in **Lebon** the Court also concluded that a member of the citizen's family does not cease to be dependent simply because they make a claim for a social welfare benefit.

(v)   Other Family Members (OFM)

Article 3(2) of the Directive identifies the rights of other beneficiaries of the citizen's family:

"2.   Without prejudice to any right to free movement and residence the persons concerned may have in their own right, the host Member State shall, in accordance with its national legislation, facilitate entry and residence for the following persons:
(a) any other family members, irrespective of their nationality, not falling under the definition in point 2 of Article 2 who, in the country from which they have come, are dependants or members of the household of the Union citizen having the primary right of residence, or where serious health grounds strictly require the personal care of the family member by the Union citizen;

(b) the partner with whom the Union citizen has a durable relationship, duly attested".

It should be noted, however, that these individuals do not have the rights conferred to the traditional family members. The Other Family Members (OFMs) only have rights to get entry and residence facilitated by the host State. They are people such as nephews, siblings, uncles, cousins, aunts, nieces that do not fall within the traditional family members categories.

Derogations to free movement of citizens

Freedom of movement is not an absolute right for citizens. It can be restricted on the grounds of public security, public health or public policy. Article 27 of Directive 2004/34 gives further guidance:

"1. Subject to the provisions of this Chapter, Member States may restrict the freedom of movement and residence of Union citizens and their family members, irrespective of nationality, on grounds of public policy, public security or public health. These grounds shall not be invoked to serve economic ends.
2. Measures taken on grounds of public policy or public security shall comply with the principle of proportionality and shall be based exclusively on the personal conduct of the individual concerned. Previous criminal convictions shall not in themselves constitute grounds for taking such measures.
The personal conduct of the individual concerned must represent a genuine, present and sufficiently serious threat affecting one of the fundamental interests of society. Justifications that are isolated from the particulars of the case or that rely on considerations of general prevention shall not be accepted".

(i)   Public policy

Public policy may be invoked to restrict free movement of EU citizens. However, it does not only imply criminal conducts. For instance in **Van Duyn**; the applicant was denied entrance to the UK for being member of the Church of Scientology. Throughout the CJEU's case law, it was considered that activities such as prostitution or the promotion and use of drugs can constitute dangers to public policies.

General principle: Repressive measures to freedom of movement cannot be taken if they constitute special measures against foreign nationals that are not equally taken by the host State against its own nationals.

Adoui and Cornuaille v Belgium (Case 115/81) 1982 ECR 1665
Facts: Two French women employed as waitresses in a bar in Belgium were in fact prostitutes. The Belgian authorities refused their application for residence permits because they were "seating all day semi-naked behind windows"; which was a minor penalty in Liège.
Preliminary question before the Court: The question was to know whether or not a Member State could adopt a restrictive measure on EU citizens which was not adopted against its nationals to combat such conducts.
Preliminary Ruling: The Court of Justice held that the restrictive measures could not be justified on the ground of public policy as long as such measures were not taken against nationals in comparable situations. The Court stated: *"Conduct may not be considered as being of sufficiently serious nature to justify restrictions on the admission to or residence within the territory of a Member State of a national of another Member State in a case where the former Member State does not adopt, with respect to the same conduct on the part of its nationals repressive measures or other genuine and effective measures intended to combat such conduct".*
Application: This decision prevents Member States to take special repressive measures against foreigners on the ground that they should get additional sanctions with respect to their residence status. In this case, the Member State is not protecting fundamental interests of its society anymore; hence it cannot rely on this ground.

(ii) Public security

This ground is usually reserved to combat serious crimes, separatist movements, terrorism etc.

The fight against crime is generally belonging to public policy, whereas public security involves a risk of the survival of the nation or a threat of disturbance of the peaceful coexistence of nations. However in the case **Tsakouridis** (Case C-145/09) 2010 ECR I-11979, the Court held that a group of narcotics importing very harmful drugs at a large scale could reach that minimum level of intensity. In another recent case, **Ministre de l'Intérieur v Aitor Oteiza Olazabal** (Case C-100/01) 2002, the Court had to deal with the ETA a autonomist organization seeking for the independence of the Basque area of northern Spain and southern France. The Court of Justice stated:

"The defendant in the main proceeding ... has been sentenced in France to 18 months' imprisonment and a four year ban on residence for conspiracy to disturb public order by intimidation or terror ... he formed part of an armed and organised group whose activity constitutes a threat to public order in French territory. Prevention of such activity may, moreover, be regarded as falling within the maintenance of public security".

Finally, Article 27 (2) of the Directive subjects restrictions taken on grounds of public security and public policy to *"the personal conduct of the individual concerned"*. In this respect, in the case **Bonsignore** (Case 67/74) 1965ECR 297, the Court held that a deportation could not be justified on the ground that it will serve as an example to others. The case **Calfa** is one of the most illustrative example of the personal conduct requirement in the CJEU's case law.

General principle: The personal conduct of the citizen against whom the restriction is taken has to be sufficiently serious as to represent a major threat to the fundamental interests of society.

Calfa (Case C-348/96) 1999 ECR I-11

Facts: An Italian national was caught by Greek police in possession of prohibited drugs. As required by Greek Law, she was convicted to three months imprisonment and expelled for life from the country. The automatic expulsion, only revocable by the Ministry of Justice, could be revoked for particular reason such as family reasons. The applicant challenged this decision arguing that Greek authorities were not empowered to expel EU citizens where a comparable measure could not be taken against Greek nationals.

Preliminary question before the Court: Is the personal conduct of the applicant representing a sufficiently serious threat affecting one of the fundamental interests of society?

Preliminary Ruling: The Court of Justice noted that an automatic expulsion was contrary to the personal conduct requirement because it was an mechanical measure that did not take into account the actual conduct of the defendant and the danger that he or she represented. The Court stated: *"The existence of a previous criminal conviction can ... only be taken into account in so far as the circumstances which gave rise to that conviction are evidence of personal conduct constituting a present threat to the requirements of public policy ... an expulsion order could be made against (an EU citizen) only if, besides her having committed an offense under national laws, her personal conduct created a genuine and sufficiently serious threat affecting one of the fundamental interests of society"*.

Application: This decision is explained by the fact that Greek Law had this automatic sanction against every individual arrested in possession of drugs, no matter whether they were caught by police with a huge quantity with the intention to sell it or if they had a small amount of recreational drug for personal use.

(iii)   Public health

Article 29 of Directive 2004/38 presents the public health ground as it follows:

"1.   The only diseases justifying measures restricting freedom of movement shall be the diseases with epidemic potential as defined

by the relevant instruments of the World Health Organisation and other infectious diseases or contagious parasitic diseases if they are the subject of protection provisions applying to nationals of the host Member State.

2. Diseases occurring after a three-month period from the date of arrival shall not constitute grounds for expulsion from the territory.

3. Where there are serious indications that it is necessary, Member States may, within three months of the date of arrival, require persons entitled to the right of residence to undergo, free of charge, a medical examination to certify that they are not suffering from any of the conditions referred to in paragraph 1. Such medical examinations may not be required as a matter of routine".

The CJEU provides no case law on the scope of this article. Some parts remain unclear regarding to their interpretation.

Citizens' political rights (Article 22-25 TFEU)

Article 22(1) TFEU confers every EU citizen residing in Member States, of which they are not nationals, a right to vote in and even stand as a candidate at "municipal elections". This rule is driven by the equality principle: nationals and foreigners should access these rights in the same conditions. However, the minimum age or other capacity requirements to vote are left to the internal rules of Member States, provided that those are applied equally to all EU citizens.

Article 22 (2) provides with the same rule in elections to the European Parliament in the host State.

General principle: It is not incompatible with EU Law for Member States to add a residency requirement to Article 22 (2), even if it excludes their nationals living in overseas countries and territories to vote and to stand as a candidate in elections to the European Parliament.

Eman & Sevinger (Case C-300/04 2006 ECR I-8055
Facts: Dutch nationals were residing in Aruba, a Caribbean island

classed as an overseas territory of the Netherlands. However, the applicants were not entitled to register for the European Parliament elections under a Dutch Law that was excluding this right to Dutch people residing in the Dutch Antilles and Aruba. The complainants contested that this decision was contrary to their citizens' right under Article 22(2) TFEU.

Preliminary question before the Court: The question was to know whether or not a Member State could add a residence requirement to Article 22 (2) excluding its nationals residing in overseas territories.

Preliminary Ruling: The Court held that Article 22 (2) did not apply to a citizen residing in overseas countries and a territory, who wishes to exercise his right to vote in the Member state of which he is a national. The Luxembourg Court concluded that: *"the criterion linked to residence does not appear, in principle, to be inappropriate to determine who has the right to vote and to stand as a candidate in elections to the European Parliament".*

Application: This decision was certainly influenced by the **Menlnychenkov v Ukraine** decision of the ECtHR (2004), which held that the residency requirement to vote was not in itself, unreasonable or arbitrary and could be justified on several grounds.

Article 23 TFEU confers diplomatic protection to EU citizens residing in non EU countries if there is no consular office from that person's own State in that country. Finally, Article 24 TFEU deals with the rights to bring claims to the EU institutions. It encompasses, *inter alia*, the right to petition the European Parliament or to apply to the Ombudsman.

Chapter 11: Freedom of establishment
Articles 49–55 TFEU

The scope of freedom of establishment and its related Articles

Freedom of establishment is one of the major pillars of the internal market. It permits a company, firm or self-employed person to install in another Member State permanently or semi-permanently for the purposes of performing an economic activity there. The main sources of primary legislation regulating freedom of establishment are provided by Articles 49-55. The Court of Justice has significantly developed these principles. In addition to this, secondary legislation has been introduced in respect of the mutual recognition of professional qualifications awarded by Member States. Freedom to provide (or receive) services, Articles 56-62 TFEU, supplements freedom of establishment. However, it will be examined separately in the next chapter.

The main provision regulating freedom of establishment is Article 49 TFEU, it provides that:

"Within the framework of the provisions set out below, restrictions on the freedom of establishment of nationals of a Member State in the territory of another Member State shall be prohibited. Such prohibition shall also apply to restrictions on the setting-up of agencies, branches or subsidiaries by nationals of any Member State established in the territory of any Member State.
Freedom of establishment shall include the right to take up and pursue activities as self-employed persons and to set up and manage undertakings, in particular companies or firms within the meaning of the second paragraph of Article 54, under the conditions laid down for its own nationals by the law of the country where such establishment is effected, subject to the provisions of the Chapter relating to capital".

Article 54 extends the prohibition of restrictions on freedom of establishment to companies: *"Companies or firms formed in accordance with the law of a Member State and having their registered office, central administration or principal place of business within the Union shall, for the purposes of this Chapter, be treated in the same way as natural persons who are nationals of Member States.*

"Companies or firms" means companies or firms constituted under civil or commercial law, including cooperative societies, and other legal persons governed by public or private law, save for those which are non-profit-making".

These two articles permit to make two conclusions. Firstly, the prohibition of restrictions on freedom does not only apply to the primary establishment of companies (incorporation) but also to the setting of secondary forms of companies, such as branches, agencies and subsidiaries. Secondly, the main principle governing the free establishment of self-employed is equal treatment of all self-employed EU citizens established in a Member State, without consideration to their nationalities. The Treaties do not provide any definition of self-employment. However, the Court of Justice, in the case **Jany v Staatssecretaris van Justitie** (Case C-268/99) [2001] ECR I-8615 held that a person acts is self-employment where he or she acts:

- Outside any relationship of subordination concerning the choice of the activity performed, working conditions and conditions of remuneration.
- Under he or she's own responsibility.
- In return for remuneration paid directly and in full.

The objective of EU Law was to extinguish all forms of restrictions on freedom of establishment within a set transitional period. It required the European institutions to introduce secondary legislation to achieve this objective. However, it has not been achieved in practice and a lot of restrictions remained in the Member States. Therefore, the Court intervened to ensure the progressive extinction of all forms of restrictions on freedom of establishment. It strengthened Article 49 by providing it with direct effect.

General principle: Article 49 has vertical direct effect; it can be invoked in disputes between individuals and Member

States before national Courts.

Reyners v The Belgian State (Case 2/74) [1974] ECR 63
Facts: A Dutch national graduated from law school in Belgium. When he tried to apply for the bar exam in Belgium, this was refused by the Belgian authorities because he was not a Belgian national. The applicant challenged this decision under Article 49 TFEU.
Preliminary question before the Court: Can Article 49 TFEU be directly invoked by individuals against Member States before national Courts?
Preliminary Ruling: The Court of Justice held that Article 49 was directly effective, although the subsequent Directives had not been adopted. The Court stated that: "*In laying down that freedom of establishment shall be attained at the end of the transitional period, Article 49 TFEU imposes an obligation to attain a precise result, the fulfilment of which had to be made easier by, but not dependant on, the implementation of a programme of progressive measures. The fact that this progression had not been adhered to leaves the obligation itself intact beyond the end of the period provided for its fulfilment*".
Application: This decision provides Article 49 with an effective enforceability. It supplements the prior failures in trying to achieve a complete abolishment of restrictions on freedom of establishment. However, a question mark still remains on the horizontal direct effect of Article 49 where invoked against private parties.

Distinguishing between establishment and services

The distinction between these two freedoms lies on the degree of presence in the host Member State. It is either someone is simply providing services or is actually established in the host State. Freedom of establishment, for instance, would entail a company setting up a new branch in the host State in the purposes of performing a particular economic activity. Conversely, freedom to provide services entails a presence on a temporary basis which does not require any physical presence.

Article 57 TFEU defines the concept of service: "*Without prejudice to the provisions of the Chapter relating to the right of establishment, the person providing a service may, in order to do so, temporarily pursue his activity in the Member State where the service is provided, under the same conditions as are imposed by that State on its own nationals*".

The Court first declared that it was clear and obvious that activities carried out on a permanent basis were not governed by the provisions regulating freedom of services (see **Steymann v Staatssecretaris van Justitie** [1988] ECR 6159)

General principle: Establishment is characterized by the existence of a base in the host State as well as the regularity, periodicity or continuity of the activity performed.

Gebhard v Consiglio dell'Ordine degli Avvocati e Procuratori di Milano (Case C-55/94) [1995] ECR I-4165
Facts: A German lawyer called Mr Reinhard Gebhard from Stuttgart, lived in Milan, Italy. He called himself an "*avvocato*" and set up chambers to practice as a lawyer. He was suspended by the Milan Bar Council, because he had not been registered. Italian lawyers complained he used the title of 'avvocati' in his practice with mainly German customers in Milan.
Preliminary question before the Court: The question was to know if an EU citizen performing a permanent activity as a self-employed in another Member State where this person is settled could rely on the provisions protecting freedom of establishment.
Preliminary Ruling: The Court held that the applicant's activity fell within the scope of the provisions on freedom of establishment. According to the Court, he was pursuing a professional activity on a stable and continuous basis in another Member State where he was established on a professional base. The Court stated: "*The concept of establishment within the meaning of the Treaty ... is a very broad one, allowing a EU national to participate, on a stable and continuous basis, in the economic life of a Member States other than his State of origin and to profit therefrom, so contributing to economic and social*

interpenetration with the Union, in the sphere of activities of self-employed persons. The temporary nature of the activities in question has to be determined in the light, not only of the duration of the provision of the service, but also of its regularity, periodicity and continuity".

Application: In this case, the Court provides clarity about the distinction between establishment and services. The main criteria to determine establishment are regularity, periodicity or continuity of the activity performed.

Matters falling outside Article 49's ambit

Under the two following exceptions, restrictive measures are not prohibited by Article 49 as falling outside of its ambit.

(i)   Article 51 TFEU – the exercise of official authority

Article 51 TFEU stipulates:
"The provisions of this Chapter shall not apply, so far as any given Member State is concerned, to activities which in that State are connected, even occasionally, with the exercise of official authority. The European Parliament and the Council, acting in accordance with the ordinary legislative procedure, may rule that the provisions of this Chapter shall not apply to certain activities".

This provision does not clearly establish a general definition for official authority is not. The Advocate General in **Reyners v The Belgian State** (discussed above) identified: *"Official authority is that which arises from the sovereignty and majesty of the state; for him who exercises it, it implies the power of enjoying the prerogatives outside the general law, privileges of official power and powers of coercion ove*r citizens". In this case, the Court of Justice considered that the official authority exception extended only to activities which in themselves involve a direct and specific connection with the exercise of official authority. The profession of *"avocat"* (French equivalent of barrister), did not involve a direct connection with the exercise of official authority whereas, as a parallel, the function of judge would. The Court of Justice has interpreted Article 51 exception narrowly. Successively, the functions of road traffic experts, commissioner of insurance companies were held not to fall within the official authority exception. Thus, official authority is an exception that will be rarely used in practice. This is mainly because the restrictive interpretation of Article 51 confined it to the highest functions enjoying executive prerogatives of the State (judges, police, State officials etc.).

(ii)   Internal situations

The question here is to know if Article 49 can be applied within the home Member State? This question is frequently raised in the particular situation of a national returning to his home State to practise a vocation as self-employed after having obtained less stringent qualifications in another Member State.

General principle: Article 49 does not apply to purely internal situations with no cross-border element.

Knoors v Secretary of State for Economic Affairs (Case 115/78) [1979] ECR 399
Facts: This case involved a Dutch national who had obtained his qualification and experience in Belgium. When he came back to the Netherlands and applied for an authorisation to carry on his trade from there, it was refused by Dutch authorities because he lacked the Dutch qualifications.
Preliminary question before the Court: Can Article 49 be applied to purely internal situations with no cross-border elements?
Preliminary Ruling: The Court of Justice held that Article 49 couldn't be relied upon in purely internal situations. The applicant could not rely on Article 49 as, in each Member State, that Article only concerns the nationals of other Member States.
Application: This decision of the Court of Justice identifies the situation of nationals returning to their home State having difficulties to make their qualifications recognized as belonging to the purely internal situations exception of Article 49 application.
This solution has been confirmed by the case **Nino** (Joined cases

C-54/88, C-91/88 and C-14/89) [1990] ECR I-3537.

Restrictions under Article 49

What constitutes a restriction under Article 49? The most obvious examples of restrictions to Article 49 are probably measures that directly discriminate on the basis of nationality (as it was the case in **Reyners**). In this case, a measure restricting the applicant's freedom of establishment was taken solely because of his nationality, even though he had the required qualifications from the host State. However, the Court of Justice, throughout its case law, expanded the prohibition of restrictions beyond direct discrimination.

General principle: Restrictions under Article 49 are not only composed of directly discriminatory measures on the grounds of nationality but also of any forms of indirect or disguised discriminations.

Thieffry v conseil l'Ordre des Avocats a la Cour de Paris (Case 71/76) [1977] ECR 765

Facts: The facts of this case involved a Belgian national with a Belgian doctorate (Belgian equivalent of a PhD) who had practised as a lawyer in his home State. He obtained a certificate of equivalence from French Universities for his degree and passed the exam entrance to practice as an *"avocat"*. However, the Parisian bar refused him admission to the training stage for lack of degree in French Law. The applicant challenged this decision has hindering his right to freedom of establishment protected by Article 49 TFEU.

Preliminary question before the Court: The question was to know whether or not the scope of the prohibition of restrictions on freedom of establishment could be expanded beyond directly discriminatory measures.

Preliminary Ruling: The Court held that the applicant had suffered an unjustifiable restriction on his freedom of establishment. It concluded that the refusal of a candidate to the bar exam on his lack of qualifications where they were officially recognized as being equivalent by the competent authority in the host State, was a restricting freedom of establishment. On this point, the Court took into consideration the General Programme for the abolition of restrictions on freedom of establishment of the Council that proposed to eliminate any forms of *"disguised discrimination"*.

Application: In **Thieffry**, the Luxembourg Court thereby expanded the scope of Article 49 beyond direct discrimination based on nationality to include any indirect or disguised forms of discrimination. This solution prevents Member States to take restrictive measures against individuals' establishment whose equivalence of qualification is generally recognized.

Derogations justifying restrictions to freedom of establishment

(i) The public interest derogations

In this section "public interest" refers to the traditional derogations of public policy, public security and public health. This derogation to Article 49 TFEU is identified by Article 52, which provides:

"1. The provisions of this Chapter and measures taken in pursuance thereof shall not prejudice the applicability of provisions laid down by law, regulation or administrative action providing for special treatment for foreign nationals on grounds of public policy, public security or public health.

2. The European Parliament and the Council shall, acting in accordance with the ordinary legislative procedure, issue directives for the coordination of the abovementioned provisions".

The public interest derogations are the same as for free movement of persons, provided by Directive 2004/38. A similar application should be made for self-employed EU citizens. For companies, Directive cannot be invoked as long as it concerns only individuals.

However, for both companies and self-employed, the general principles of EU Law apply when assessing the derogation, and particularly proportionality. In this respect, in the case **Commission v UK (Open Skies)** (Case C-466/98) [2002] ECR I-9427 the Court mentioned a traditional solution: *"The public policy derogation under Article 52 TFEU presupposes the need to maintain the discriminatory measure in order to deal with a genuine and sufficiently serious threat affecting one of the fundamental interests of society. There has to be a direct causal link between the threat, which must be current, and the measure adopted to deal with it".*

(ii) Imperative requirements in the general interest

Restrictions on freedom of establishment, which are not directly discriminatory, can also be justified by imperative requirements in the general interest. This derogation has been devised by the CJEU. They are the equivalent of mandatory requirements under free movement of persons. They are also referred to as *"overriding reasons in the public interest"*. The main case law relating to free movement of persons is also relevant to imperative requirements for freedom of establishment. See *inter allia* **Cassis de Dijon**, **Gilli & Andres**, **Cinéthèque**, **Walter Rau** (all of these cases are discussed in details in Chapter 8). The test to satisfy for a restriction to freedom of establishment was enshrined by the Court in **Gebhard** (discussed above). In this latter, the Court of Justice held that in order to be justified by imperative requirements, the national rule amounting to a restriction on freedom of establishment had to satisfy four criteria:
- It is non-discriminatory. In other words the measure is not directly discriminatory.
- It is justified by imperative requirements of the general interest.
- It is the most suitable solution to the objective pursued.
- It is necessary and proportionate to achieve a legitimate aim.

Here, the Court of Justice took the same approach as the one taken for the justification to non-discriminatory rules under free movement of citizens.

Basic rights of establishment of companies

Article 54 extends the prohibition of restrictions on freedom of establishment under Article 49 from self-employed to companies. But this Article also applies to firms. Firms are businesses which are not officially registered as companies. Either they are sole proprietorships owned by one person, or they are partnerships. In both cases the owners' liabilities are not limited. Partners and Proprietors are personally liable, jointly and severally for the debts of the business. Companies (including firms) and self-employed enjoy the same rights under freedom of establishment. However, the main additional requirement presented by Article 54 is that it requires companies to be profit making. Conversely, a self-employed EU citizen established performing a non-profit activity still enjoys the protection of Article 49.

(i) The rights of the Member State of incorporation

All EU companies and firms have a right of incorporation in every Member State. However the Member State in which the company is incorporated retains the right to determine the conditions of incorporation of that company and the conditions under which the company may transfer its central administration to another Member State. According to the Court of Justice **in R v H.M. Treasury, ex parte Daily Mail and General Trust plc** (Case 81/87) [1988] ECR 5483, Article 49 as such did not confer a right to transfer central management and control to another Member State while keeping the advantages of the status being incorporated in the initial Member State.

(ii) The rights of a company to set up agencies, branches and subsidiaries

A stated above, the prohibition of restrictions on freedom of establishment of companies does not only apply to the primary establishment of companies (incorporation) but also to secondary forms of incorporation, such as setting up branches, agencies and subsidiaries. This solution provides traders with a wide choice of 28 Member States to incorporate their companies or setting up subsidiaries. They could chose to incorporate a company in one country, without any intention to make business there, and set up a range of branches in other countries where the rules of incorporations or the taxes appear to be more advantageous for them. Whilst this possibility has been qualified as a crucial component of the single market, some Member States attempted to stop this practice invoking abuses of EU rights.

General principle: Under freedom of establishment, companies and firms have a right to choose from the most advantageous Member States to register for incorporation and set up branches. However, it can be limited by justified restrictions to prevent abuses or fraudulent use of EU rights.

Centros Ltd v Erhvervs-og Selskabsstyrelsen (Case C-212/97) [1999] ECR I-1459

Facts: Centros, a company incorporated in the UK was acquired by two Danish nationals. One of them, appointed director, wanted to base his activity in Denmark, where he resided. The company then applied to set up a branch in Denmark, however, this was refused by the Danish authorities. The Danish Trade and Companies Board accused the shareholders of having acquired the company abroad and setting up one of its branch in Denmark solely to benefit the requirement of the minimum share capital that was less stringent in the UK. The Board mentioned an abuse of rights under free establishment.

Preliminary question before the Court: Does the refusal to set up a branch in a Member State, although the company has been lawfully incorporated in another Member State, constitute a restriction on freedom of establishment?

Preliminary Ruling: The Court held that the refusal to set up a branch in a Member Stat, although the company has been lawfully incorporated in another Member State, constitutes a restriction on freedom of establishment. However, this restriction could be justified to prevent nationals from abusing EU law or fraudulently taking advantage of it.

Furthermore, the Court of Justice concluded that incorporating a company and setting up its branches in the Member States where the rules on company Law appear to be the least restrictive is not an abuse of the right of free establishment in itself.

Application: In this case, the Court of Justice refuses to qualify such conducts of abuse of freedom of establishment while conferring a safeguard to Member States that can justify restrictions in practice if it effectively belongs to fraudulent intentions.

(iii) The mutual recognition of companies by Member States

The mutual recognition of companies by Member States comes along with the principle of harmonisation of EU Law throughout the Union. The non-recognition of the legal capacity of companies incorporated in other Member States would be a significant barrier to free establishment and free trade.

General principle: Freedom of establishment implies a right to obtain recognition of legal capacity for a company in other Member States than the one in which it has been previously incorporated.

Überseering BV v Nordic Construction Company Baumanagement GmbH (Case C-200/00) [2002] ECR I-9919
Facts: A company incorporated in the Netherlands had been acquired by two German nationals. The company's owners transferred its central administration to Germany. At this time, Germany did not recognize the legal capacity of companies having been incorporated abroad. The company did not even have the capacity to challenge this decision. The only solution for the owners was to reincorporate the company in Germany. This process was expensive in both time and money.
Preliminary question before the Court: The question was to know whether or not Member States had a duty to recognize the legal capacity of companies previously incorporated in other Member States.
Preliminary Ruling: The Court of Justice held that in order to be fully effective, freedom of establishment required Member States to recognize the legal capacity of companies previously incorporated in other Member States. Therefore, the German authorities had to recognize the legal capacity of the Dutch company in this case.

Application: Here, the Court of Justice ensures that no barriers such as a requirement of reincorporation will be placed on freedom of establishment of companies already incorporated in other Member States. It should be noted that this case did not engage with the validity of the incorporation in the home State. Therefore it shall be applied only to situations assuming that the company has been validly incorporated earlier under the laws of the home State.

Further rights under Article 49 for self-employed EU citizens

(i)   Entry, residence, and other social rights

These rights are conferred to self-employed EU citizens under free movement of persons (Directive 2004/38). Freedom of establishment implicitly includes a right to enter and reside for the purposes of establishing a business.   Article 24 of Directive 2004/38 particularly provides self-employed that are EU citizens the right to entry and residence within the Union for their family members.   In addition to this, the Court of Justice interpreted Article 49 TFEU as providing self-employed with a right to equal treatment regarding to certain social rights.

In this respect, in **Commission v Italy ("Italian Housing")** (Case 63/86) [1988] ECR 29, the Court of Justice declared that an Italian rule only promoting the lease or purchase of housing for nationals self-employed through financial help and not to self-employed from other Member States constituted a restriction on freedom of establishment. Thus, there should be no discrimination based on nationality regarding to the access of certain social rights for self-employed Union citizens.

(ii)   Professional qualifications

The refusal of equivalent qualifications by the host Member State can constitute a significant restriction on freedom of establishment. Indeed, most of the times, it will result on the impossibility for the self-employed to perform his activity in the host State. However, the task of EU Law on this issue was not an easy one. It had to find a compromise between achieving the objective fixed by the Council to remove all restrictions on freedom of establishment while respecting the requirements on appropriate qualifications maintaining high standards of professional competence. Article 53 TFEU provides the EU institutions with a framework to issue Directives in order to ensure a progressive mutual recognition of qualifications:

"In order to make it easier for persons to take up and pursue activities as self-employed persons, the European Parliament and the Council shall, acting in accordance with the ordinary legislative procedure, issue directives for the mutual recognition of diplomas, certificates and other evidence of formal qualifications and for the coordination of the provisions laid down by law, regulation or administrative action in Member States concerning the taking-up and pursuit of activities as self-employed persons".

The abolition of restrictions on freedom of establishment implied a necessary harmonisation on qualification as far as "lack of qualification" is the most commonly used justification of restrictions. Consequently, the Council adopted in 1961 the General Programme for the abolition of existing restrictions on freedom of establishment (already mentioned above). Consequently, secondary legislation, and precisely Directives, took over. The first mutual recognition directive was Directive 89/48 which stated: *"...in order to provide a rapid response to the expectations of nationals of Community countries who hold higher education degrees...".* It stems from this extract that this Directive was intended to regulate all professions requiring university level education. Then, other Directives have been issued (92/51, 2001/19), but they all have been replaced by Directive 2005/36. Directive 2005/36 enshrined the principle of mutual recognition for all professions that are not covered by specific Directives. It became the Directive applying in principle to all professions not covered by other specific Directives. For instance, Directive 98/5 regulates on the specific profession of lawyers, in this case the *lex specialis* applies.

However, the overall progress of these provisions was disappointing, a range of restrictions remained. Therefore, the Court of Justice, devised its own principle of principle of mutual recognition of equivalent qualifications. Firstly the Court dealt with qualifications obtained by self-employed in EU Member States striving to get them recognized in other Member States.

This was established by the **Thieffry** case (discussed above). The most relevant part of the Court's judgement is reproduced here:

"there is an unjustified restriction on that freedom where, in a Member-State, admission to a particular profession is refused to a person covered by the Treaty who holds a diploma which has been recognised as an equivalent qualification by the competent authority of the country of establishment and who furthermore has fulfilled the specific conditions regarding professional training in force in that country, solely by reason of the fact that the person concerned does not possess the national diploma corresponding to the diploma which he holds and which has been recognised as an equivalent qualification".

General principle: Member States, when awarding authorisations on establishment of self-employed EU citizens, must consider and compare foreign diplomas with the required national qualification. If both qualifications appear only partially equivalent, any other experience through which the person acquired knowledge should be taken into consideration.

Vlassopoulou v Ministerium fur Justiz, Bundes und Europaangelegenheiten Baden-Württemberg (Case 340/89) [1991] ECR 2357

Facts: This case concerned a Greek national having passed a Law degree in Greece. After having practised German Law in Germany for many years, she applied to the German bar. This was refused by the German authorities on the grounds that she lacked a German diploma. The applicant challenged this decision arguing that it hindered her freedom of establishment.

Preliminary question before the Court: The question was to know whether or not a Member State could reject an application for establishment solely because the self-employed EU citizen lacked a national degree.

Preliminary Ruling: The Court of Justice held that the German refusal amounted to a restriction on freedom of establishment. Member States had to take into consideration the foreign diplomas and compare them to those required by national qualification. However, if they are only partially equivalent, Member States should take into account the acquired knowledge and qualifications outside of the degree, either through course study or by practical experience. In this case, the Court considered indeed that the applicant's qualifications were equivalent to those required by national qualification.

Application: This case, also known as the **Vlassopoulou principles**, compels Member States to compare the equivalence of foreign degrees and provide them with guidance on how to process it. The Court enlarged the scope of the **Vlassopoulou principles** in its case **Férnandeza de Bobadilla v Museo Nacional del Prado** (Case C-234/97) [1999] ECR I-4773. It held that these principles could even be relied upon for nationals returning in their home State after having acquired a degree in another Member State.

Finally the question of mutual recognition arose for situations where initial qualification was obtained in a non-EU State but subsequent practical experience was acquired in a Member State.

General principle: The recognition, by a Member State, of a degree obtained in a non-EU State does not give rise to automatic recognition in all Member States, even if the self-employed EU citizen has been practising in the former.

Tawil-Albertini v Ministre des Affaires Sociales (Case C-

154/93) [1994] ECR I-451

Facts: This case involved a French national that had obtained a dentistry qualification in Lebanon. This degree was recognized in Belgium as equivalent to national qualifications and he subsequently practised there for several years. The applicant then applied to practise in France but this was refused by French authorities that did not recognize the equivalence of the Lebanese diploma to French required qualifications. The applicant challenged this decision arguing that if Belgium recognized the equivalence of his qualifications, which were in Directive 78/686, consequently his qualification were equivalent to the French ones. In addition to this, he claimed that according to the **Vlassopoulou principles** French authorities should have taken into account his practical experience acquired in Belgium.

Preliminary question before the Court: The question was to know whether or not a self-employed EU citizen could claim for mutual recognition of equivalent qualifications where after having initially obtained his qualification in a non-EU State but had practised for many years in a Member State.

Preliminary Ruling: The Court held that the simple fact that one Member State accepted the equivalence of qualifications did not bind other Member States where those qualifications were not listed in the directive. Furthermore the court explained that according to the **Vlassopoulou principles**, Member State should take into account the relevant practical experience through which the applicant acquired knowledge, however this does not give rise to an automatic right of acceptance.

Application: In this case, the Court clarifies that an initial non-EU qualification carries no right of acceptance by Member States. In addition to this, even if it had been recognized as equivalent in one Member State, this does not entitles the self-employed EU citizen to practise in all Member States. This is because the objective of the Directives is only to facilitate the mutual recognition of equivalent qualification obtained within the Union.

Chapter 12: Freedom to Provide Services
Articles 56–62 TFEU

Freedom to provide services: Articles 56 and 57 TFEU

Freedom to provide services is the last fundamental freedom that we will examine. Articles 56-62 TFEU regulate its main principles. As stated on the Chapter on freedom of establishment, services and establishment share many similarities. This is because the distinction in the treaties is ambiguous but also because the Court of Justice has interpreted them similarly on many issues. However, the difference lies on the degree of the presence of the company or self-employed in the host State. While Article 49 entails a permanent physical presence in the host State for establishment, Article 56 on services applies where the provider is not punctually present.

The main EU provision on freedom to provide services is Article 56 TFEU. It is the equivalent of Article 49 for freedom of establishment. Article 56 prohibits restrictions imposed on EU citizens' right to provide and receive services freely. It states: *"Within the framework of the provisions set out below, restrictions on freedom to provide services within the Union shall be prohibited in respect of nationals of Member States who are established in a Member State other than that of the person for whom the services are intended"*

This Article applies if two conditions are met. The provider has to be an EU citizen that already has a place of establishment in a Member State. It covers self-employed EU citizens. The protection has been extended to companies or firms by Article 62 (extending Article 54):
"Companies or firms formed in accordance with the law of a Member State and having their registered office, central administration or principal place of business within the Union shall, for the purposes of this Chapter, be treated in the same way as natural persons who are nationals of Member States.
"Companies or firms" means companies or firms constituted under civil or commercial law, including cooperative societies, and other legal persons governed by public or private law, save for those which are non-profit-making".

Freedom to provide services without restrictions was a crucial step to achieve the objectives of a single market. This issue was marked by a similar evolution as of the combat for the abolition of restrictions imposed on freedom of establishment. The Council announced an objective of complete abolition of restrictions on freedom to provide services. In order to do so, it introduced a general programme for the abolition of restrictions on the freedom to provide services and to issue directives to implement that programme. Once again, the overall result of these attempts was disappointing.

Therefore, the Court of Justice, in **van Binsbergen v Bestuur van de Bedrijfsvereniging voor de Metaalnijverheid** (Case 33/74) [1974] ECR 1299 held that Article 56 was directly effective. As a result, this strengthened Article 56 and provided with concrete means to achieve the objectives announced by the Council. Article 57 defines the meaning of term *"Services"* contained in Article 56:

"Services shall be considered to be 'services' within the meaning of the Treaties where they are normally provided for remuneration, in so far as they are not governed by the provisions relating to freedom of movement for goods, capital and persons.
'Services' shall in particular include:
(a) activities of an industrial character;
(b) activities of a commercial character;
(c) activities of craftsmen;
(d) activities of the profession."

Thus, Article 56 has a very wide scope. It covers, *inter allia,* all commercial and financial activities but also medical treatment or legal advices. As a matter of fact, the termination of pregnancy in private clinics (see **Society for the Protection of Unborn Children v Grogan** (Case 159/90) [1991] ECR I-4685) or even prostitution (see **Jany v Staatssecretaris van Justitie**, mentioned above) have been held capable of being services.

(i)   Remuneration

First of all, Article 57 TFEU states that services, in the meaning of the Treaty, *"are normally provided for remuneration"*. It means that the service is rendered by a provider carrying a profit-making activity. Article 56 applies whenever a cross-border service is provided in return of remuneration.

General principle: Remuneration does not have to be paid by the recipient of the service; it can be paid by a third party.

Deliège v Ligue Francophone de Judo et Disciplines Associées ASBL (Cases C-51/96 and C-191/97) [2000] ECR I-2549

Facts: A Belgian national having been competing as an amateur in national and international judo competition complained that she had not been selected by the Belgian national team on many occasions, which as a result frustrated her career. She challenged an ultimate refusal for a tournament in Paris, alleging a breach of Article 56. The problem was that she was an amateur and did not get direct remuneration from the Belgian ministry of sports (receiving the service).

Preliminary question before the Court: Can amateur sportsmen rely on the protection of Article 56 when performing at a competition?

Preliminary Ruling: The Court of Justice held that sporting activities did not generally fall into Article 56 TFEU, but only to the extent that they constituted economic activity. However, athletes of the highest level participating in international tournaments were capable of attracting sponsorships, paying publics or TV rights. Therefore, this could be seen as a *"remuneration"* under Article 57, regardless if the remuneration was paid by the person receiving the service or by a third person. In this respect, the Luxembourg Court stated: *"For example, an organiser of such a competition may offer athletes an opportunity of engaging in their sporting activity in competition with others and, at the same time, the athletes, by participating in the competition, enable the organiser to put on a sports event which the public may attend, which television broadcasters may retransmit and which may be of interest to advertisers and sponsors. Moreover, the athletes provide their sponsors with* *publicity the basis for which is the sporting activity itself"*.

Application: The Court of Justice in **Deliège** makes a strict interpretation of Article 57 based on the legal maxim: *"Where the law does not distinguish, neither should we distinguish"*. Article 57 only requires the service to be remunerated; it does not matter whether the recipient of the service or a third party pays it.

(ii) Genuine and effective economic activity

Finally, the service provided must constitute a genuine and effective economic activity which is not merely marginal or ancillary. The Court interpreted this criterion in the same way as for free movement of workers (see **Kempf**). The Court of Justice enshrined it for services in the case **Steymann v Staatssecretaris van Justitie** (Case 196/87) [1988] ECR 6159, as a mere application of **Kempf**. Therefore, in **Her Majesty's Customs and Excise v Schindler** (Case C-275/92) [1994] ECR I-1039, the Court held that lottery constitutes a genuine and effective economic activity as far as tickets are delivered in exchange of remuneration.

Matters falling outside Article 56's ambit

Under the following exceptions, restrictive measures on freedom to provide services are not affected by Article 56's prohibition because they fall outside of its ambit.

(i) The official service exception

Article 62 TFEU provides that the official authority exception in Article 51 TFEU also applies to the freedom to provide services under Article 56 TFEU. It means that Article 56 does not apply to services connected in the Member States with exercise of official authority. On this point, the case law on freedom of establishment is relevant for services too. Indeed, in the cases **Commission v Greece** (Case C-306/89) [1991] ECR I-5863 and **Commission v Italy** (Case C-272/91) [1994] ECR I-1409, the Court of Justice mentioned that it ruled on the exception of official authority applying to both establishment and services.

The definition given by the Advocate General in **Reyners v The Belgian State** should be reminded: "*Official authority is that which arises from the sovereignty and majesty of the state; for him who exercises it, it implies the power of enjoying the prerogatives outside the general law, privileges of official power and powers of coercion over* citizens". Thus, when looking at the restrictive approach of the Court on this exception, it can be concluded that it is confined to the highest functions enjoying executive prerogatives of the State (judges, police, State officials etc.).

(ii)   Matters which fall under other provisions of goods, persons or capital

Article 57 TFEU identifies that Article 56 only applies to matters "*in so far as they are not governed by the provisions relating to freedom of movement for goods, capital and persons*". Consequently, Article 56 will only apply to situations not falling under other provisions of goods, persons or capital. However, the Court limited this approach in **Omega**.

General principle: Where freedom to provide services and another freedom are commonly restricted by the same measure, Article 56 will apply if the other
freedom at stake is entirely secondary to freedom to provide services.

Omega Spielhallen- und Automatenaufstellungs-GmbH v Oberbürgermeisterin der Bundesstadt Bonn (Case C-36/02) [2004] ECR I-9609
Facts: This case concerned a ban on laser-sport games in which players attempted to shoot each other with infrared laser guns in Germany. This ban imposed restrictions both on freedom to provide services for the "fields" where this activity was carried out but also on free movement of goods for the importers of the material required to play such games (guns, helmets etc.). The decision has been challenged for breach of Articles 49 and 56.
Preliminary question before the Court: The question here was to know which provisions were governing a measure that was both

hindering free movement of goods and freedom to provide services.

Preliminary Ruling: In this case the Court of Justice held that the impact on freedom of goods was entirely secondary to the restriction imposed on freedom to provide services. Indeed, the ban would cut off one part of the market for importers of the material however for providers of this service it resulted on a complete prohibition to perform their activities in the host State. Therefore, the situation fell into Article 56's scope.

Application: In **Omega**, the Court affirms that Article 56 should govern when the major impact of the restriction is clearly affecting freedom to provide services, regardless if it also hinders other freedoms.

(iii)   Purely internal situations

Article 56 only protects services *"in respect of nationals of Member States who are established in a Member State other than that of the person for whom the services are intended"*.

In this respect, The Court of Justice in **Procureur du Roi v Debauve** (Case 52/79) [1980] ECR 833, the Court of Justice pointed out that Article 56 does not apply to *"activities whose relevant elements are confined within a single Member State"*. For instance, in the case of **Deliège** the service provider and the recipient of the service were in two different States. The fact that the tournament was taking place in another Member state than the home State of the provider was enough.

However, when both the provider and the recipient of the service are in the same Member State, then there has to be a "cross-border element". This solution has been delivered by the CJEU in **Carpenter** (Case C-60/00) 2002 ECR I-6279 in which the Court stated: *"Services come within the meaning of "services" in Article 56 both in so far as the provider travels for that purpose to the Member State of the recipient and in so far as he provides cross-border services without leaving the Member State in which he is established"*.

As an illustration of this requirement the Court considered that there was a sufficient cross-border element in **Hubbard v Hamburger** (Case C-20/92) [1993] ECR I-3777. This case involved legal advice from a lawyer to a client both based in the UK, however the case involved a transfer of ownership from a third party based in Germany.

Restrictions on freedom to provide services

Article 56 prohibits restrictions on freedom to provide services specifically imposed on EU citizens providing services in outside their Member States. Combined with the provisions established by Article 57, it has long been established that EU Law considers as restrictions any discriminatory measure hindering freedom to provide services on grounds of nationality or residence. This was confirmed in **van Binsbergen v Bestuur van de Bedrijfsvereniging voor de Metaalnijverheid** (Case 33/74) [1974] ECR 1299 by the Court of Justice which stated: *"The restrictions to be abolished pursuant to Articles [56 and 57] include all requirements imposed on the person providing the service by reason in particular of his nationality or of the fact that he does not habitually reside in the State where the service is provided, which do not apply to persons established within the national territory or which may prevent or otherwise obstruct the activities of the person providing the service".*

However, the Luxembourg Court was initially reluctant to interpret Article 56 and 57 TFEU as to extend the prohibition to non-discriminatory measures which acted as obstacles to the provision of services (see **Société Générale Alsacienne de Banque SA v Koestler** (Case 15/78) [1978] ECR 1971). Nevertheless, this solution has later been overturned by the Court itself.

General principle: The prohibition of restrictions under Article 56 is not only confined to discriminatory measures but extends to indistinctly applicable measures imposing obstacles to the free provision of services.

Säger v Dennemeyer & Co Ltd (Case 76/90) [1991] ECR 421

Facts: A company based in the UK was specialised in advising German holders of patents. A German-based patent agent challenged the company's activities in Germany as lacking a licence required by German law. The company argued that German legislation requiring a particular licence, even though it was not directly discriminatory on the nationality of the provider, was hindering its freedom to provide services.

Preliminary question before the Court: Can indistinctly applicable measures constitute *"restrictions"* under Articles 56 and 57 TFEU?

Preliminary Ruling: The Court of Justice held that the prohibition in Article 56 was not confined to discriminatory measures but could also extend to indistinctly applicable measures.

The Court stated that: *"It should first be pointed out that Article [56] of the Treaty requires not only the elimination of all discrimination against a person providing services on the ground of his nationality but also the abolition of any restriction, even if it applies without distinction to national providers of services and to those of other Member States, when it is liable to prohibit or otherwise impede the activities of a provider of services established in another Member State where he lawfully provides similar services".*

Application: It is now beyond doubt that Article 56 TFEU applies to "traditional" restrictions to provide services which are not of a discriminatory nature.

Justification of restrictions

Contrary to the matters falling outside Article 56's scope, the measures concerned here are effective restrictions that can however be justified under the following grounds.

(i)   Derogations

Article 62 mentions the traditional justification of the public interest: public security, public policy and public health. These grounds have been discussed on last chapter on freedom of establishment. The approach of the Court of Justice on these derogations is the same as for freedom of establishment. The main rules can be invoked for both the justifications of restrictions on services and establishment. The following example illustrates the mere application of the previous case law on establishment.

Omega Spielhallen- und Automatenaufstellungs-GmbH v Oberbürgermeisterin der Bundesstadt Bonn (Case C-36/02) [2004] ECR I-9609

Facts: This case concerned a ban on laser-sport games in which players attempted to shoot each other with infrared laser guns in Germany. Pointes were recorded and prices were given to the best "killers". The German authority justified this ban on public policy.

Preliminary question before the Court: The question was to know whether or not a ban on a game simulating killings of humane beings could be restricted on the ground of public policy.

Preliminary Ruling: The Court of Justice recalled that public policy may be relied on only if the activity constitutes a genuine and sufficiently serious threat to a fundamental interest of society. As a matter of fact, the ban was justified on this ground. According to the Court, commercializing games simulating humane being killings was a threat for a peaceful society. It infringed the fundamental right to fundamental dignity.

Application: In this case the Court of Justice applied the principles established by **Commission v UK (Open skies)** to freedom to provide services. The Court in **Omega** is quite generous to qualify laser-games as a genuine and sufficiently serious threat to a fundamental interest of society.

(ii)   Imperative reasons

The Court developed another ground for justification. Imperative reasons permit to justify restrictions indistinctly applicable aiming to apply and enforce rules of professional conduct which were justified by the general good. Once again, the approach of the Court is the same as for other freedoms in terms of justification of indistinctly applicable restrictions on "overriding reasons relating to the public interest". Therefore, the previous case-law on this topic for other freedoms is equally relevant to services (*inter allia* **Bosman**, **Ghebard** or **Cassis de Dijon**).

General principle: Imperative reasons, such as the general good, permit to justify restrictions indistinctly applicable aiming to apply and enforce rules of professional conduct.

Commission v Germany (Insurance Services) (Case 205/84) [1986] ECR 3755

Facts: A German rule required that agents and intermediaries providing insurances had to be established in West Germany. The Commission, alleging a breach of Article 56 referred the case to the Court after having issued Germany an unsuccessful reasoned opinion. Germany argued that this restriction could be justified on the ground of imperative reasons as far as they were indistinctly applicable and necessary for the general interest.

Preliminary question before the Court: Can indistinctly applicable measures be justified on the ground of imperative reasons?

Preliminary Ruling: The Court of Justice held that the freedom to provide services may be restricted only by provisions which are justified by the general good and which are applied to all persons within the State. The Court stated: "*The freedom to provide services, as one of the fundamental principles of the treaty, may be restricted only by provisions which are justified by the general good and which are applied to all persons or undertakings operating within the territory of the state in which the service is provided in so far as that interest is not safeguarded by the provisions to which the provider of a service is subject in the member state of his establishment. In addition, such requirements must be objectively justified by the need to ensure that professional rules of conduct are complied with and that the interests which such rules are designed to safeguard are protected*".

Application: This case is one of the first cases mentioning imperative reasons to justify restrictions on freedom to provide services. It built a framework for the test delivered by the Court in **Säger**, few years later.

In **Säger** (mentioned above), the Court devised a test for imperative reasons:

- The restriction must be indistinctly applicable;
- It must be justified by the general interest;
- It was necessary so as to ensure compliance with professional rules and to protect the recipients of services; and
- It should not exceed what is necessary to attain these objectives.

These two last conditions embody the proportionality principle (generally applied to justifications of restrictions of freedoms).

The rights to provide and receive services granted by Article 56

(i) The right to move and reside to provide services

This right is enshrined by Article 56 and 57 which allow any provider of services to move and reside freely, on a temporary basis that is required by the notion of *"services"* itself, in Member States other than their home States without being subjected to restrictions or discrimination in comparison to domestic traders. As for free movement of persons and freedom of establishment, Directive 2004/38 regulates these right more in details. Thus, for service providers which are self-employed EU citizens, Article 6 and 7 confer them and their family members, the right to move and reside freely to toehr Member States where they provide services.

Service providers performing their activities in other Member States than their home State even have a right to bring their own workforce for the period of that the service is provided (see **Rush Portuguesa Lda v Office National d'Immigration** (Case C-113/89) [1990] ECR I-1417). This decision has been codified by Directive 96/71 (the "Posted Workers Directive").

(ii) The right to move and reside to receive services

Article 56 protection on the freedom to provide services also includes freedom to receive services. For example, a rule prohibiting EU citizens from choosing their providers for a particular service would amount to a breach of Article 56. In **de Coster v Collège des Bourgmestre et Echevins de Watermael-Boitsfort** (Case C-17/00) [2001] ECR I-9445, the Court upheld that the imposition of a municipal tax on ownership of satellite dishes was hindering freedom to receive services (particularly satellite television broadcast from other Member States). It has been problematic in the situation of nationals moving from their home States to other Member States in order to receive services.

General principle: Article 56 TFEU also prohibits restrictions imposed on freedom to move other Member States in order to receive services.

Luisi and Carbone v Ministero del Tesoro (Joined Cases 286/82 and 26/83) [1984] ECR 377

Facts: An Italian Law provided with a maximum amount of foreign currency each individual were allowed to take out of the country. Two Italian nationals were prosecuted under Italian Law for taking excess foreign currency out of the country. They had withdrawn a considerable sum in US dollar, French and Swiss francs and Deutshmarks from various Italian banks. They spent this money in France and Germany for medical care and tourism. The applicants challenged this rule as being incompatible to freedom to provide services.

Preliminary question before the Court: Does Article 56 prohibition of restrictions applies to freedom to receive services?

Preliminary Ruling: The Court held that the Italian law on the control of foreign currency taken out of the country was a restriction imposed on freedom to receive services in other Member States which is prohibited by Article 56 TFEU. The Court stated: " *The freedom to provide services includes the freedom, for the recipient of services, to go to another Member State in order to receive a service there, without being obstructed by restrictions… and that tourists, persons receiving medical treatment and persons travelling for the purposes of education or business are to be regarded as recipients of services* ".

Application: In **Luisi and Carbone**, the Court of Justice enshrined a necessary corollary of the freedom to provide services. The Court even gave examples of recipients of services: tourists, people receiving medical treatment and people travelling for the purpose of education or business. However, today Directive 2004/38 would also be applicable where a Union citizen and his family members move to another Member State to receive services.

(iii)   Social rights

The Court of Justice, throughout its jurisprudence, generously interpreted Article 56 as to entitle Foreign Service providers or recipients of services to access certain social rights as equal as nationals from the host State.

General principle: Recipients of services traveling in other Member States are entitled to equal compensatory benefits as to nationals of the host State for criminal acts committed against them.

Cowan v Tresor Public (Case 186/87) [1989] ECR 195
Facts: An English man travelled as a tourist to France. After having been assaulted in Paris he applied for compensation to the *Commission d'indemnisation des victimes d'infractions*. Under French Law, this compensation was available to victims of criminal conduct. However, only French nationals or permit holders could apply for it. The applicant challenged this decision claiming that it was contrary to his right to receive services.
Preliminary question before the Court: The question was to know whether or not EU citizens, recipients of services in other Member States, were entitled to social rights in the host State.
Preliminary Ruling: The Court of Justice upheld the applicant's argument that French legislation hindered his freedom to receive services. It amounted to a restriction imposed on freedom to travel to other Member States and receive services such as tourism, which was prohibited by Article 56 TFEU. The protection of EU citizens from harm is a necessary corollary to free movement and freedom to receive services.
Application: In this case, the Luxembourg Court based its

judgement in Article 18 TFEU that contains the duty of equal treatment of all EU citizens and the prohibition of discrimination based on nationality.

Since Directive 2004/38 was introduced, the situation is clearer. Article 24 now provides an equal treatment principle for Union citizens and their family members for all social rights. However, it should be noted that the host State is not bound to provide social assistance to EU citizens during the first three months of their residency.

(iv)   Professional qualifications

The principles developed by the Court of Justice on mutual recognition of equivalent qualifications presented in last Chapter on freedom of establishment are equally applicable to services. Now, Title II of Directive 2005/36 regulates the recognition of professional qualifications in respect of the free provision of services. In principle, the latter applies to every service that is not governed by a specific Directive. For example, legal services are regulated by a specific Directive; Directive 77/249 (Lawyers Services Directive).

The Services Directive

In 2000 at Lisbon, the European Council asked the Commission to set out a strategy for the removal of the remaining barriers to services. As a result, the Commission came up with the introduction of Directive 2006/123, also known as the Services Directive. Article 1(1) of the Directive presents its main objective:

"This Directive establishes general provisions facilitating the exercise of the freedom of establishment for service providers and the free movement of services, while maintaining a high quality of services".

Article 2(1) provides that the Directive applies to services supplied by providers established in a Member States. The

Directive's scope includes "*any self-employed economic activity, normally provided for remuneration*". On the notion of service secondary legislation merely incorporated the CJEU's definition of services (discussed above). However, Article 2(2) excludes a range of services such as non-economic services of general interest, audio-visual services, transport or private security.

The central principle set out by the Directive is contained in Article 16(1):
"*Member States shall respect the right of providers to provide services in a Member State other than that in which they are established.*
The Member State in which the service is provided shall ensure free access to and free exercise of a service activity within its territory".

Article 16 translates the solution of Article 56 that prohibits the imposition of restrictions on freedom to provide (and receive) services, except where it can be justified. The traditional derogations of public interest are then presented (public policy, security and health) but subjected to the respect of general principles of EU Law such as non-discrimination and proportionality. On this latter condition, Article 16 states that "*the requirement must be suitable for attaining the objective pursued, and must not go beyond what is necessary to attain that objective*".

At one point during the proposal stage, the Directive would have introduced a "*country of origin*" principle, requiring host State to allow service providers to operate in their territories in accordance of laws of their home States. This very ambitious provision was abandoned as being too contentious. Instead, the Services Directive merely codified the CJEU's case law on freedom to provide services. Its impact on the general aim of abolition of restrictions on freedoms was disappointing. In this respect, **Craig and De Burca** have described it as "*patchy, complicated and legally rather unsatisfactory*".

Chapter 13: Competition Law
Articles 101-102 TFEU

General ideology

From its early days, one of the most important tasks of the Union was to establish the single market. This objective is contained in Article 3 TFEU. In order to achieve such an end, EU's institutions had to build up an entire legal framework ensuring the sustainability of the single market. This has be done partly by enshrining and enforcing the "four freedoms" and partly by regulating the competition rules. Article 2 of the EC Treaty stated that EU's institutions had to ensure that: *"competition in the internal market is not distorted"*. Now, Article 3(1)(b) TFEU provides that: *"the establishing of the competition rules are necessary for the functioning of the internal market"*.

At first, having rules on competition might appear to be contrary to the spirit of free trade, and the drive towards a single market unfettered by any national barriers to trade. These rules seem to place restrictions on businesses. However, this is not the case, the Treaty-makers rather tried to protect small and medium businesses from abuses of large powerful businesses using unfair means.

EU competition law has two basic and complementary aims. First, it aims to promote a competitive market. This is crucial for a capitalist approach of economy in order to achieve economic prosperity and development. Second, EU competition combats the restrictions on the integration of the single internal market. The market should only be driven by fair competition; this is a necessary corollary to the integration of the single market. In order to do so, EU competition law introduced two concrete measures contained in Chapter I, Title VII (Articles 101-109) TFEU:

- Abolishing restrictive practices, decisions and agreements (Article 101 TFEU)

- Preventing large businesses to abuse their economic dominance in the market (Article 102 TFEU).

These Articles are the main provision of primary legislation, however secondary legislation implementing those measures has also been introduced. Regulation 1/2003 (the "modernisation regulation") ensures the enforceability of Articles 101 and 102, whereas Regulation 330/2010 grants for potential exemptions from Article 101.

The role of the Commission in EU competition Law is central. It has a traditional function of initiator of policies and legislative policies. But it also ensures the enforcement of competition Law relating to its function of "Guardian of the treaties". The Commission is charged of the prevention of breaches of EU competition law. It can launch investigations and impose fines on individuals, companies or Member States. However, under Regulation 1/2003, national courts and the National Competition Authorities of Member States are also now responsible for enforcing EU competition law.

Article 101 and 102 will be examined in turn. However, some points such as the institutions' powers or the concept of undertakings in the following section relating to Article 101 can be equally applied to 102.

Article 101 and provisions on restrictive practices

The scope and conditions of Article 101

Article 101 is concerned with restrictive trade practices. It prohibits a range of anti-competitive acts and practices which have as their object or effect the prevention, restriction or distortion of competition within the single market. Article 101(1) stipulates:

"1. The following shall be prohibited as incompatible with the internal market: all agreements between undertakings, decisions by associations of undertakings and concerted practices which may affect trade between Member States and which have as their

object or effect the prevention, restriction or distortion of competition within the internal market, and in particular those which:

(a) Directly or indirectly fix purchase or selling prices or any other trading conditions;

(b) Limit or control production, markets, technical development, or investment;

(c) Share markets or sources of supply;

(d) Apply dissimilar conditions to equivalent transactions with other trading parties, thereby placing them at a competitive disadvantage;

(e) Make the conclusion of contracts subject to acceptance by the other parties of supplementary obligations which, by their nature or according to commercial usage, have no connection with the subject of such contracts".

This provision clearly identifies the specific types of anti-competitive practices that are prohibited, they are:

- Any agreement or category of agreements between undertakings,
- Any decision or category of decisions by associations of undertakings,
- Any concerted practice or category of concerted practices.

Article 101 (2) sets out the legal effect of the prohibition: all agreements, decisions or concerted practices infringing Article 101 are void, and it also applies retrospectively.

Article 101 (3) excludes certain pro-competitive agreements, decisions or concerted practices from the scope of the first paragraph. These measures will be lawful if they satisfy the conditions of Article 101(3). The following case is an illustrative example of a restrictive practice prohibited by Article 101.

IAZ international Belgium and others v Commission (Case 96 82) 1983 ECR 3369

Facts: A Belgian Law required washing machines and dishwashers to meet certain standards in order to connect to the general supply of water. The standards had been agreed between the national association of water suppliers and another association to which few major washing machine and dishwashers suppliers were affiliated.

Preliminary question before the Court: The question was to know whether or not an agreement subjecting trade to minimum standards or requirements taken only concluded by the major suppliers of the market was infringing Article 101.

Preliminary Ruling: The court held that this had the effect of disadvantaging the suppliers who were not affiliated to the trade association. Therefore, it found a breach of Article 101.

The concept of undertaking

Both Article 101 and 102 are only applying to the anti-competitive activities of *"undertakings"*. Generally, this term is broadly interpreted by the CJEU. It gave a definition of *"undertaking"* in **Hofner & Else v Macroton GmbH** (Case C-41/90) [1991] ECR I-1979: *"...the concept of an undertaking encompasses every entity engaged in an economic activity, regardless of the legal status of the entity and the way in which it is financed and, secondly, that employment procurement is an economic activity"*

Thus, it seems that the definition of undertaking encompasses almost every types of entity regardless of its legal statute provided that it has a legal capacity and engages in economic activities. Therefore, individuals, multi-national corporations and other entities have been qualified as *"undertakings"*. The Court enlarged the notion to:

- An opera singer (**Re unitel Commission Decision** Case 78/516 1978 3 CMLR 306)
- A state-owned corporation (**Italian State v Sacchi** Case 155/73 1974 ECR 409)
- A trade association (**FRUBO v Commission** Case 71/74 1975 ECR 563)

General principle: The economic activity of undertakings should be driven by a profit motive.

Fenin v Commission (Case T-319/99) 2003 ECR II-357

Facts: Spanish public hospitals (the SNS) purchased supplies from FENIN, a Spanish association comprising the majority of firms marketing medical goods and equipment. The SNS was delayed payment for a delivery and FENIN complained for a breach of Article 102; abuse of dominant position.

Preliminary question before the Court: Can publically financed bodies offering free services to the general public could be classed as undertakings?

Preliminary Ruling: The Court held that the SNS could not be classed as undertaking because the purchases sold were used to other than an economic activity. Article 102 was excluded because the SNS was providing free service to the public that did not amount to an economic activity.

Application: In **Fenin**, the Court of Justice confirmed that the main criterion to class an undertaking, namely the economic activity, should be interpreted as a profit motive. Therefore, the activities of non-profit entities are excluded from the definition of undertaking.

Prohibited agreements

(i)   Agreements between undertakings

An agreement between undertakings always involves some form of collusion; otherwise it amounts to a unilateral act. This comes from the traditional approach of contract Law.

General principle: A contract imposed by national Law on undertakings cannot be classed as agreement under Article 101.

Commission and France v Ladbroke Racing Ltd (C-359/95P) 1998 4 CMLR 27

Facts: In this case, a French Law required companies engaged in off course betting to be in the control of *Paris Mutuel Urbain* (PMU). It forced undertakings of the market to conclude agreements with PMU in order to be allowed to trade on this market. Ladbroke, the applicant company, challenged these agreements as infringing Article 101.

Preliminary question before the Court: The question was to know whether or not a contract imposed by national Law on undertakings could be classed as an "agreement" under Article 101.

Preliminary Ruling: The Court of Justice held that the contracts at stake could not be classed as agreement under Article 101. Contracts imposed by national Law on undertakings could not be classed as "agreements" under Article 101.

Application: In this case, the court of Justice adopted a restrictive approach of agreements. This is because undertakings were not acting according to their own initiative, therefore the contract lacked collusion.

Agreements that may breach Article 101 may be of two different types; horizontal or vertical. A horizontal agreement is concluded between undertakings at the same level. It is usually an agreement between competing manufacturers or distributors. A vertical is one reached between undertakings at different levels of the process, for example between wholesalers and retailers. These agreements would usually benefit the consumer, however they are prohibited by Article 101 if they imply exclusive distribution or licensing agreements. The distinction is made by the Court of Justice in the case **Consten and Grundig** (Cases 56 and 58/64) 1966 ECR 429. It is crucial to distinguish between these two types of agreements in term of exemptions, because different rules apply to them. This point will be examined more in details bellow.

(ii) Decisions by association of undertakings

Many companies collectively act within trading associations. They are usually in charge of setting standards in trade that bind their members. It is usually beneficial to trade in general. However, when anti-competitive decisions are adopted, they may infringe Article 101. Some categories of decisions are obviously breaching Article 101. It is the case for example of decisions fixing prices or collective boycotts.

The prohibition even extends to non-binding decisions. It has been held by the Court of Justice in **NV IAZ International Belgium v Commission** (ANSEAU-NAVEWA Conformity Label) (Joined Cases 96-102, 104, 105, 108 and 110/82) [1983] ECR 3369 in which the Court stated:*"Article [101](1) of the treaty applies also to associations of undertakings in so far as their own activities or those of the undertakings affiliated to them are calculated to produce the results which it aims to suppress ... [A] recommendation, even if it has no binding effect, cannot escape Article [101](1) where compliance with the recommendation by the undertakings to which it is addressed has an appreciable influence on competition in the market in question".*

(iii) Concerted practices

Concerted practices are co-ordinated actions between undertakings that, without amounting to agreements, consciously substitute co-operation for competition.

General principle: Anti-competitive concerted practices are prohibited by Article 101 TFEU, regardless to their informal nature, as far as undertakings had the common wish to act collectively.

ICI v Commission ("Dyestuffs") (Case 48/69) [1972] ECR 619
Facts: Here, a decision by the major manufacturers of dyestuffs, required a collective raise of prices at the same time. The Commission concluded that it constituted a concerted practice and imposed fines on the undertakings. The manufacturers challenged this decision arguing that it was a mere parallel behaviour within an oligopoly. They claimed that this decision was not a formal agreement; therefore it could not be in breach of Article 101.
Preliminary question before the Court: The question was to know if Article 101 applied only to formal agreement or collective decisions or if it could be extended to informal concerted practices.
Preliminary Ruling: The Court of justice held that collusion is not only identified in formal agreements. As a matter of fact, a series of correspondences and documents asserted a common wish

to act collectively. The argument of the lack of formal agreement was rejected.

The Court stated: "*[A] form of coordination between undertakings which, without having reached the stage where an agreement properly so-called has been concluded, knowingly substitutes practical cooperation between them for the risks of competition. Although parallel behaviour may not by itself be identified with a concerted practice, it may, however, amount to strong evidence of such a practice if it leads to conditions of competition which do not correspond to the normal conditions of the market*".

Application: In **Dyestuffs**, the Court of Justice makes a logic application of Article 101 TFEU holding that concerted practices having an anti-competitive effect were prohibited regardless to their informal nature.

The object or effect of preventing, restricting or distorting competition

(i)   The meaning of object and effect

According to the wording of Article 101, it is clear that the terms "object" or effect are alternative and not cumulative requirements. In the **STM case**, The Court of justice held that it is first necessary to consider whether the object of the agreement is to harm competition. Then, if it is not the case, it is necessary to consider whether the effect of the agreement was to hinder trade.

The object of an agreement can be found by looking at its purpose in the economic context (**STM** case).

General principle: The object of the agreement is determined objectively regardless to the subjective intentions of the parties.

Competition Authority v Beef Industry Development Society Ltd [2008] ECR I-8637
Facts: This case involved an agreement concluded by certain undertakings of the beef processing market aiming to reduce beef and veal processors. Some undertakings agreed to stay out of the market in return of compensation from those which were to remain as processors. The undertakings acted without the subjective intention of restricting competition.
Preliminary question before the Court: Should the object of an agreement be determined subjectively or objectively?
Preliminary Ruling: The Court of justice held that the fact that the undertakings acted without subjective intention to restrict competition was irrelevant when determining whether the object of an agreement was to restrict competition contrary to Article 101(1). The subjective intentions of the parties were only relevant for Article 101(3).
Application: In this case, the Court recalls that the object of an agreement is appreciated objectively. The intention of the parties is not relevant when determining a breach of Article 101(1).

For example, horizontal agreements which may have as their object the restriction of competition, include agreements to fix prices, limit production output, limit sales or exchange on price information. Whereas examples of vertical agreements having an anti-competitive object include bans on parallel imports or passive selling. A ban on parallel imports prevents a distributor of buying a product form anyone other than the appointed dealer. As stated above, the effect of the agreement will only be analysed if its object is not clearly restricting competition. Determining the restrictive nature of the effect of an agreement requires not only the full analysis of an agreement but also the full analysis of the market in which the agreement is to operate.

The General Court provided guidance as to how to assess the effect of an agreement in **European Night Services v Commission** (Cases T-374, 375, 384 and 388/94) [1998] ECR II-3141: *"It must be borne in mind that in assessing an agreement under Article [101(1)] of the Treaty, account should be taken of the actual conditions in which it functions, in particular the economic context in which the undertakings operate, the products or services covered by the agreement and the actual structure of the market concerned ... unless it is an agreement containing obvious restrictions of competition such as price-fixing, market-sharing or the control of outlots .,, In the latter case, such restrictions may be weighed against their claimed pro-competitive effects only in the context of Article 101(3) of the Treaty, with u view to granting an exemption from the prohibition in Article 101(1) TFEU".*

The relevant market is identified by the demand substitution principle, which implies that the relevant market is comprised of interchangeable or substitutable products that the consumer would buy if the initial product is not available.

(ii)   Preventing, restricting or distorting competition

Article 101(1) sets out in paragraphs (a) to (e) a non-exhaustive list of restrictions that are prohibited. They include agreements, decisions or practices which:

- Directly or indirectly fix purchase or selling prices. Recommended prices are permitted so long as they are only recommended and not enforced in anyway. It also includes the fixing of any trading conditions.
- Export bans and bans on parallel imports.
- Subject to Article 101(3), limit or control production, markets, technical development or investment.
- Share markets or sources of supply. This is the case, for instance, of agreements to share markets or sources of supply between undertakings which should be rivals.
- Apply dissimilar conditions to equivalent transactions with other trading parties, thereby placing them at a competitive disadvantage.
- Make the conclusion of a contract subject to acceptance by the other party of supplementary obligations, which, by their nature or according to commercial usage, have no connection with the subject of the contract. These agreements are also known as tie-in arrangements.

(iii) The rule of reason

Some agreements, such as exclusive distributive agreements for instance, may have both pro-competitive and anti-competitive features. Defendants that allegedly concluded anti-competitive agreements, decisions or practices may invoke the "rule of reason" defence. In this case, if the pro-competitive effect of an agreement outweighs its anti-competitive effect, the EU courts may decide that there has been no infringement of Article 101.

General principle: According to the rule of reason approach, certain agreements, containing anti-competitive provisions, may be compatible to Article 101 if their pro-competitive nature is predominant.

Pronuptia de Paris GmbH v Pronuptia de Paris Irmgard Schillgallis (Case 161/84) [1986] ECR 353
Facts: This case involved a dispute about a franchise agreement. Such agreements generally contain a range of anti-competitive

restrictions. As a matter of fact, the franchise agreement obliged Pronuptia de Paris, as the franchisor, to supply the clothing, to assist with the commercial aspects of the Schilligallis' business and not to open any other Pronuptia shops in the cities in which the franchise operated. In return, Schilligallis, as the franchisee, undertook obtain her supplies only from Pronuptia de Paris and from suppliers approved by Pronuptia, to sell them only in the shops specified in the contract, not to move the shop to a new location without the agreement of Pronuptia.

Preliminary question before the Court: The question was to know how franchise agreements, having both competitive and anti-competitive objects and effects should be interpreted in the light of Article 101.

Preliminary Ruling: The Court of Justice held that the compatibility of franchise agreements depended on the provisions contained therein. In order to determine the compatibility of franchise agreements with Article 101, EU Courts should balance both the competitive and anti-competitive features of these agreements. The franchisor has to be able to communicate its know-how and provide assistance without running the risk that this would aid its competitors. It must also be able to protect its identity and reputation. As a matter of fact, the anti- competitive restrictions in such agreements enabled the franchiser to be able to do this. Therefore, the franchise agreement was compatible with Article 101.

Application: Franchise agreements' compatibility with Article 101 should be determined on a case-by-case basis.

(iv) The *"de minimis"* defence

An agreement, decision or practice has to have an "appreciable" effect on either competition or inter-State trade. Otherwise, if this effect is insignificant, the defendant might invoke the *"de minimis"* defence.

General principle: The effect of the agreement on competition or inter-State trade is not appreciable if the position of the undertaking in the market is weak or insignificant.

Völk v Vervaecke (Case 5/69) [1969] ECR 295

Facts: In this case, a German producer of washing machines had granted an exclusive distributorship to Vervaecke in Belgium and Luxembourg and guaranteed an absolute territorial protection against parallel imports. However, Volk's share in the washing machine market only represented 0.2% of the German production and 0/08% of the Union production.

Preliminary question before the Court: The question was to know whether agreements having insignificant effects on either competition or inter-State trade could breach Article 101 TFEU.

Preliminary Ruling: The Court of Justice held that the effect of the agreement on competition or inter-State trade was too *"de minimis"*. In other words, the effect has to be appreciable when determining whether or not an agreement breached Article 101. The Court stated: *"An agreement falls outside the prohibition in Article 101 TFEU when it has only an insignificant effect on the markets, taking into account the weak position which the persons concerned have on the market of the product in question"*.

Application: In **Völk** the Court of justice clarified the scope of the *"de minimis"* defence and provided with guidance as to how to satisfy it. For instance, the position of the undertaking in the market can be a factor.

The effect on trade between Member States

In order to establish a breach of Article 101, it is also necessary to prove that the agreement, decision or practice may affect trade between Member states. Here the wording of Article 101 is very important. The term *"may"*, does not imply that the agreement actually affected trade but only that it had the potential to do so.

The test to satisfy this condition was set out in **Société Technique Minière v Maschinenbau Ulm GmbH** (Case 56/65) [1966] ECR 337 (the S.T.M. case). The Court of Justice stated that: *"It must be possible to foresee with a sufficient degree of probability on the basis of a set of objective factors of law or of fact that the agreement in question may have an influence, direct or indirect, actual or potential, on the pattern of trade between Member States"*.

Accordingly, the mere potential to affect trade is sufficient. The types of restrictions that have been found to affect inter-States trade were for example contracts prohibiting distributors to sell their goods in other Member-State other that their own or agreements whereby producers agree to protect each other's national markets. For instance, in **Vereening van Cementhandelaren v Commission** (Case 8/72) 1972 ECR 977 a Belgian cartel in roofing felt industry has been held capable of affecting inter-States trade because competitors outside the cartel were at a potential disadvantage. However, it should be noted that the potential effect on trade must be "appreciable" and not insignificant or *"de minimis"*.

The institutions' powers

Both the Commission and the CJUE have a central role in the enforcement of Article 101. Firstly, under Regulation 1/2003 the Commission can impose fines in two situations. It can impose repressive measures on undertakings and associations of undertakings which have intentionally or negligently infringed Articles 101 or 102 TFEU. The maximum fine which can be imposed on each undertaking and association of undertakings participating in the infringement is 10% of its total turnover in the preceding business year. Article 24 of Regulation 1/2003 provides the Commission with further prerogatives. If the undertaking is reluctant to comply with the Commission's order to put an end to the infringement, this latter can impose periodic penalty payments not exceeding 5% of the average daily turnover in the preceding business year per day.

Furthermore, according to Article 23 of the Regulation, the Commission can also impose smaller fines to undertakings failing to co-operate with investigations. This involves the delivery of false information or the provision of incomplete records.

Secondly, the Court of Justice can award damages, through national Courts, for losses caused by a breach of Article 101 TFEU. This is a necessary corollary to ensure the enforceability of competition Law. In **Courage Ltd v Crehan** (Case C-453/99) [2001] ECR I-6297, the Court of Justice stated that:

"The full effectiveness of Article 101 of the Treaty and, in particular, the practical effect of the prohibition laid down in Article 101(1) would be put at risk if it were not open to any individual to claim damages for loss caused to him by a contract or by conduct liable to restrict or distort competition. Indeed, the existence of such a right strengthens the working of the Community competition rules and discourages agreements or practices, which are frequently covert, which are liable to restrict or distort competition. From that point of view, actions for damages before the national courts can make a significant contribution to the maintenance of effective competition in the Community".

Subsequently, Article 3 of Directive 2014/104 now provides individuals with a right to full compensation.

Exemptions

There are several ways to avoid an agreement being in breach of Article 101. It includes the use of exemption that can be granted individually or as "block exemptions".

For both individual and block exemptions, four conditions must be met in order for them to be granted:

- First, the agreement, decision or practice must improve the distribution of goods or alternatively promote technical or economic progress (see **Transocean Marine Paint Association v Commission** (Decision 77/454) 1975 2 CMLR D75).
- Second, a fair share of the resulting benefit must pass to the consumer (see **AEC v Berliet Decision** 68319 1968 CMLR D35).
- Third, the agreement must not impose restrictions unnecessary for the achievement of positive aims. This is the proportionality requirement. For instance, an absolute

territorial protection such as a ban on parallel imports would be generally considered unnecessary.

- Finally, there must not be any possibility of the restrictions eliminating competition in respect of a substantial part of the product in question.

Until recently, individual exemptions were granted by Decisions of the Commission. However, Regulation 1/2003 introduced a new mechanism involving the intervention of Member States. It is no longer necessary to notify the Commission. The undertakings themselves are in charge of identifying the potential exemptions and the national authorities are then responsible to determine on a case-by-case basis whether there is an infringement of Article 101.

Block exemptions were introduced by secondary legislation in reaction to the increasing applications for individual exemptions. First, it led to a huge number of applications that left the Commission overwhelmed. Second, businesses were in a state of uncertainty until the Commission issued a Decision. Block exemptions allow undertakings to assess for themselves whether a type of agreement is exempt. Block exemptions are introduced in the form of Regulations regarding to certain specific types of agreements. Provisions of relevant secondary legislation are:

- Regulation 1984/83 and Regulation 2790/99 on exclusive distribution agrecments and vertical restraints.
- Regulation 123/85 on motor vehicle distribution.
- Regulation 5566/89 on know-how licencing.
- Regulation 2568/200 on research and development.

The new block exemption Regulation 32790/99 creates a general exemption for all vertical agreements in their own rights. However, the application of this rule is limited by several exceptions.

Article 102 and abuse of dominant position

The concept of abuse of a dominant position: Article 102

As presented above, Article 101 deals with collusive behaviours between undertakings. Conversely, Article 102 is usually concerned with the actions of a single or few undertakings abusing a dominant position. However, Article 102 does not prohibit the dominant position in itself. A dominant position indicates that a particular undertaking in a market acts very efficiently. Efficiency is one of the objectives of competition Law. Rather, Article 102 prohibits any abuse of such positions capable of affecting trade between Member States. Abuse may include any anti-competitive behaviour which threatens competition in a market. For instance, an abuse can lie on the use of a dominant position to weaken or drive smaller competitors out of the market or by preventing potential competitors from entering the market. Article 102 provides:

"Any abuse by one or more undertakings of a dominant position within the internal market or in a substantial part of it shall be prohibited as incompatible with the internal market in so far as it may affect trade between Member States.

Such abuse may, in particular, consist in:

(a) Directly or indirectly imposing unfair purchase or selling prices or other unfair trading conditions;

(b) Limiting production, markets or technical development to the prejudice of consumers;

(c) Applying dissimilar conditions to equivalent transactions with other trading parties, thereby placing them at a competitive disadvantage;

(d) Making the conclusion of contracts subject to acceptance by the other parties of supplementary obligations which, by their nature or according to commercial usage, have no connection with the subject of such contracts".

According to the wording of Article 102, three conditions must be satisfied in order to establish its breach:

- One or more undertakings engaging in the practice complained of must have a dominant position in the relevant market.
- The practice at stake amounts to an abusive behaviour
- Inter-state trade is affected as a result of the practice

As we have seen earlier, the Commission is charged with overseeing the enforcement of competition Law under the judicial review of the CJEU and the General Court. Recently, Regulation 1/2003 also empowered national competition authorities and Courts to play a role.

The definition of dominance

"*Dominance*" is not defined anywhere in primary legislation. However it was originally the case in the EC Treaty which stated that dominance was established when undertakings held a position "*shielding them against effective competition in a substantial part of the common market*". The CJEU then intervened in several cases to clarify the situation.

General principle: Dominance results for undertakings on the power to behave independently without taking into account their competitors while controlling production or distribution for significant part of products.

Continental Can Co v Commission (Case 6/72) 1973 ECR 215
Facts: A multinational, possessed 86 per cent share of a company enjoying a dominant position in Germany in the market for tins meat and fish products. When the multinational proposed to engage in a takeover of another leading company of the same market, it was challenged for breach under Article 102. The Commission held that it was in fact an abuse of dominant position because it resulted in an elimination of competition in this market reducing the choice for consumers. However, it did not identify the relevant product market.
Preliminary question before the Court: The question was to know if the elements of dominance and abuse of this position were sufficient or if it was necessary to identify the relevant market.
Preliminary Ruling: The Court disagreed with the Commission and held that it failed to establish a breach of Article 102 because it did not identify the relevant product market. More importantly, in this case, the Luxembourg Court delivered an early definition of dominance: "*Dominance results on the power to behave*

independently without taking into account their competitors, purchasers or suppliers because of their share of the market or ... availability of technical knowledge, raw materials or capital, they have power to control production or distribution for significant part of products".

Application: In **Continental Can** the Court of Justice delivers a first jurisprudential definition of the concept of dominance.

The Court of Justice reaffirmed and supplemented this definition in **United Brands v Commission** (Case 27/76) 1978 ECR 207. It stated, in its judgement that dominance was *"a position of economic strength ... which enables it to prevent competition being maintained on the relevant market by giving it the power to behave to an appreciable effect independently of its competitors, and ultimately its consumers"*. The Court later added that the calculation of the market share of the undertaking in question was crucial. For instance, in the case **Re flat Glass** (Decision 89/93) 1992 5 CMLR 120, it held that undertakings detaining between 79 and 95 per cent share detained a dominant position in a market for the production of "flat glass".

The relevant market

In order to establish an infringement to Article 102, it is crucial to identify the *"relevant market"* in which the undertaking in question is operating. It is an economic concept requiring the expertise of highly qualified economists. As the Commission explained in its notice on the definition of relevant market for the purposes of community competition Law (97/C 372/03) [1997] OJ C372/5: *"Market definition is a tool to identify and define the boundaries of competition between firms. It serves to establish the framework within which competition policy is applied by the Commission. The main purpose of market definition is to identify in a systematic way the competitive constraints that the undertakings involved face. The objective of defining a market in both its product and geographic dimension is to identify those actual competitors of the undertakings involved that are capable of constraining those undertakings' behaviour and of preventing them from behaving independently of effective competitive pressure*". Thus, in determining the relevant market, one should examine successively the product market and the geographic market.

(i)   The relevant product market

This part of the market definition focuses on the product at stake. It is usually a long and complicated process that involves both economists and lawyers. In these cases, the investigations of the Commission can last for long. The Court of justice, in the case **United Brands v Commission** (Case 27/76) 1978 ECR 207, clarified a couple of points on the relevant product market that should be reminded:

- The relevant product market is one where there is no interchangeability of goods so a relevant product is the product in question plus anything that can be reasonably substituted for it.

- As a matter of fact, bananas are relatively unaffected by the competition of other fresh fruit because they have unique characteristic and they are consumed by the young, the aged and the sick. Furthermore, there are not seasonal so there is no seasonal substitute for bananas. Therefore, bananas are a relative product market in their own right.

The Court of Justice made clear that the factor of "*interchangeability*" of the products is very important while determining the relevant product market. In **Hoffman La Roche v Commission** (Case 85/76) 1979 ECR 461 the Court stated that: "*sufficient interchangeability between all products forming part of same market insofar as specific use of products is concerned*".

Relevant product market then is said to depend on "*cross-elasticity of demand*" and "*cross-elasticity of supply*". The CJEU case law provided a range of examples of relevant product market:

- Cash register parts (see **Hugin Kassaregister AB v Commission** (Case 22/78) 1979 ECR 1869). This is considered as a specific relevant product market because of the particularity of cash register parts compared to spare parts generally.

- Separate cartons for pasteurised and UHT milk (see **Tetra Pak v Comission No.1** (Case T-51/89) 1990 ECR II-309).

(ii)   The relevant geographic market

The notion of geographical market refers to the territory within which goods can expect to be sold. According to Article 102 TFEU, the relevant market must be *"... within the common market or in a substantial part of it"*. The Court of Justice, in **United Brands v Commission**, described the relevant geographic market as *"a clearly defined geographic area in which [the product] is marketed and where the conditions of competition are sufficiently homogeneous for the effect of the economic power of the undertaking concerned to be able to be evaluated"*. In its notice mentioned above, the Commission provided Member States with further guidance: *"The relevant geographic market comprises the area in which the undertakings concerned are involved in the supply and demand of products or services, in which the conditions of competition are sufficiently homogeneous and which can be distinguished from neighbouring areas because the conditions of competition are appreciably different in those areas"*.

General principle: The territory of a single Member State can form the relevant geographic market.

Nederlandsche Banden-Industrie Michelin NV v Commission (Case 322/81) [1983] ECR 3461 (**'Michelin I'**)
Facts: The multinational Michelin abused a dominant position in the product market of heavy vehicles tyres. The Commission, while establishing the breach, considered that the relevant geographic market was the Netherlands. In response, Michelin

claimed that the Commission had taken into account irrelevant factors which concerned the Michelin Group as a whole in the wider market.

Preliminary question before the Court: Which territory can be taken as the relevant geographic market?

Preliminary Ruling: The Court of Justice held, despite the argument presented by Michelin, that the subject of the Commission's decision was the subsidiary in the Netherlands. This was because, in practice, dealers of tyres established in the Netherlands obtained their supplies only from suppliers operating in the Netherlands.

Application: In this case, the Court of Justice held that the territory of a Member State can be classed as the relevant geographic market while establishing the abuse of dominant position in the relevant market.

Finally, the temporal dimension can be crucial to determine the relevant market. Although it is usually embodied in the product or geographic dimensions of the relevant market (the Commission did not treat it as a separate requirement in its Notice), time can be significant according to the CJEU. Indeed, in the case **Benzine en Petroleum Handelsmaatschappij BV v Commission** ('ABG Oil') (Case 77/77) [1978] ECR 1513, the Court of Justice held that for some cases an additional relevant temporal market had to be identified.

Abusive behaviour

As stated above, Article 102 does not restrict the position of dominance in itself, but rather its abuses. Therefore, in order to establish a breach of Article 102, it is necessary to prove that the undertaking committed an abuse. Once again, there is no definition of the notion of abuse in primary legislation; hence the Court of Justice had to intervene. It has done so in **Hoffman La Roche v Commission** (Case 85/76) 1979 ECR 461 by holding that: *"The concept of abuse is an objective concept relating to the behaviour of an undertaking which is such as to influence the* *structure of the market where, as a result of the very presence of the undertaking in question, the competition is weakened, and which, through recourse to methods different from those which conditions normal competition in products or services on the basis of the transactions of commercial operators, has the effect of hindering the maintenance of the degree of competition still existing in the market or the growth of that competition".*

Abusive behaviours have anti-competitive goals. Undertakings adopting such conducts seek to either secure a reduction of competition or to create an unfair competition. Regarding to examples of abusive behaviours, Article 102 provides with a list of specific behaviours that may amount to abuse. These include unfair pricing, limiting production, contractual discrimination and imposing supplementary obligations. However, this list is non-exhaustive. The CJEU enlarged this list to a couple of other behaviours:

- Price reduction to kill competition. In **AZKO v Commission** (Case 62/86R)1986, the Court of Justice considered that the fact that a company cut its prices for a long period of time in order to put a small competitor out of business amounted to an abusive behaviour.

- Refusal to supply. In **Commercial Solvents Corporation (CSC) v Commission** (Cases 6 & 7/73) [1974] ECR 223, the Court considered that a refusal to supply a company simply because of its position of competitor breached Article 102. However, a refusal to supply will never breach Article 102 if it can be justified by an objective economic reason. For example, a company can refuse to supply another company which is not creditworthy.

- Discounts and rebates. This will amount to abuses where it prevents some competitors to enter the market because they cannot match the reductions offered by discounts to other competitors. In **Hoffman La Roche** the Court stated that: *"The fidelity rebate, unlike quantity rebates exclusively linked with the volume of purchases from the* *producer concerned, is designed through the grant of a financial advantage to prevent customers from obtaining their supplies from competing producers".*

- Limiting production or technical development to the prejudice of consumers. In **AEVE Farmakeftikon prioton** (Case C486/06), the Court qualified as an abuse the refusal to supply medicinal products to Member States for the purposes of research, in order to prevent parallel imports.

- Unfair terms. If for instance an undertaking takes advantage of a dominant position to impose unfair conditions on an agreement with other another undertaking, this may constitute an abusive behaviour. This was the case in **Belgische Radio en Televisie (BRT) v Société Belge des Auteurs, Compositeurs et Éditeurs (SABAM)** (Case 127/73) [1974] ECR 313.

The potential effect on inter-state trade

As with Article 101, the anti-competitive measures, in order to be declared in breach, have to affect trade between Member States. There must be an effective link of causality between the abuse and the effect on inter-state trade. The requirement is the same as for Article 101, the abuse must have the potential to affect trade, it does not need to actually have affected trade. The test is similar; the abuse must constitute a threat *"direct or indirect, actual or potential on the pattern of trade".*